Advanced Management
Accounting Problems

Also by Kenneth P. Gee

Management Planning and Control in Inflation
Management Control and Information
(with R. Beresford Dew)

ADVANCED MANAGEMENT ACCOUNTING PROBLEMS

Kenneth P. Gee
Professor of Accountancy
Department of Business and Administration
University of Salford

MACMILLAN

First published 1986

Published by
MACMILLAN EDUCATION LTD
Houndmills, Basingstoke, Hampshire RG21 2XS
and London
Companies and representatives
throughout the world

Printed in Hong Kong

British Library Cataloguing in Publication Data
Gee, Kenneth P.
Advanced management accounting problems.
1. Managerial accounting—Problems, exercises, etc.
I. Title
658.1' '511'076   HF5661
ISBN 0–333–36269–1
ISBN 0–333–36270–5 Pbk

Contents

17   Joint Product Decisions   190
Primary Reference: Amey (1984)

PART II: PROBLEMS FOR SELF-STUDY

Introduction

It is a fair generalisation to say that scholars in the field of management accounting may broadly be divided into two groups. These groups may be distinguished from each other by their implicit response to this question: from which disciplines should the study of management accounting draw most heavily? To this question, one group would reply 'psychology, sociology and general systems theory' while the other group would say 'statistics, operational research and microeconomics'. This book is firmly in the latter tradition; it could hardly be otherwise, since the former tradition is much more concerned with the description of contexts than it is with the analysis of problems. It would be foolish for either group of scholars to disparage the other – their roles are complementary. However, in recent years rather more of the academic work in management accounting has conformed to the positive, behavioural mould than has conformed to the normative, quantitative mould. This book represents a small movement in the direction of redressing this balance.

In making this movement, the book endeavours to fill what is currently a fairly substantial gap in the literature available to students and teachers of management accounting at second and third year undergraduate level. Once the first year background material in statistics and quantitative methods has been assimilated, it is a logical progression to apply this material to acceptably realistic management accounting problems. It is helpful if these problems are such as to provide practice in the use of the microcomputer, while at the same time they must illustrate the employment of techniques advanced in the research literature.

The desirability of a significant computing content implies that the problems should not be so small as to give inadequate 'hands-on' practice, while the need to illustrate selected aspects of the research literature implies a requirement for close cross-referencing. Matters are further complicated by the fact that teachers differ in their identification of the most crucial papers within the literature, so that an approach placing restrictions upon the order in which topics can be dealt with may compel excessive attention to be paid to topics which are not conceived as being of central importance.

All of the issues mentioned above, but especially the last one, give rise to a need for something other than a conventional textbook to underpin the teaching of second and third year management accounting. A textbook which is to be used from 'cover to cover' in this area has to be very lengthy (and thus expensive) to cater exhaustively for the divergent emphases present in teaching. Moreover, a general purpose textbook cannot devote sufficient space to the development of realistically sized problems without compromising the interests of teachers who prefer to work through an approach which is not problem based, or whose students do not have access to the computing facilities required to handle substantial problems.

The gap in the literature faced by teachers who employ a quantitative, computational approach to the study of advanced management accounting is that there is no readily available set of problems which can be used in a flexible way to identify and illuminate those research studies having relatively immediate implications for the improvement of practice. This set of problems is intended to fill this gap. In doing so, it may also provide insights which help students (and managers) to visualise the associations between real world phenomena in management accounting and that part of the literature which addresses these phenomena sufficiently directly to enable problems to be written. Indeed, the author's aspirations extend a little further than the simple recognition by readers of a correspondence between their interests and the content of the problems presented here. It is hoped that the techniques used to solve the problems may in some cases be transferable, with adaptation, to ongoing industrial situations. The discipline imposed by the requirement that the institutional details of each problem must be spelled out is quite a stringent one; many ideas within the literature, such as those of agency theory, have had to be omitted from this book simply because no plausible mechanism could be found whereby managers could have in their possession the necessary information to enable analysis using these ideas to take place. Those problems which could be clothed with institutional detail must by definition be at least partially realistic – the reader may judge whether the obtrusion of unrealistic, simplifying assumptions from that detail is such as to render a particular technique inapplicable to the everyday experience of industry and commerce.

The analysis of each of the problems here constitutes a self-contained guide to the contents of the paper or papers which make up the Primary Reference(s) to that problem. Put in another way, the problems have been tailor-made to fit the Primary Reference(s), and to bring out all of their central features. There is thus no need, when using this book, to refer to any other exposition of the material than that in the papers with which it deals. It is, however, necessary to have access to some of the usual computer software for operational research and statistics. In dealing with specific problems, computations are required involving operations on matrices, linear programming and the solution of moderately sized systems of simultaneous equations. The author's computational experience has been confined to work on the Commodore PET and DEC Rainbow 100 microcomputers, thus restricting the guidance that may be offered on software. However, taking the DEC machine as approximating the 'state of the art', the following packages have been found to perform satisfactorily in dealing with the problems associated with the topics enumerated below:

Software package	*Application*
OPTIMIZER (runs with MBASIC compiler on CP/M; requires 64K of memory)	Deals with linear programming problems, can thus carry out some of the computations required by Topics 5, 6, 7A, 7B, 15.
MINITAB (runs on CP/M 80/86 with 64K of memory)	Performs operations on matrices and can thus carry out some of the computations required by Topics 1, 2, 3, 4, 7A, 7B

	Also a valuable general purpose statistical package
TK!SOLVER 86 (runs on CP/M with 128K of memory)	Solves systems of simultaneous equations, and can thus carry out some of the computations required by Topic 17
	Also useful in performing iterative calculations for Topic 16, and arithmetic for Topic 8

Turning from technical to personal matters, I am delighted to record my gratitude to Mrs Jean Waring, who typed the manuscript of this book in its many drafts with unfailing patience and efficiency. The finished book I dedicate to my wife, Hilary, without whose constant encouragement and support it could never have been written.

Kenneth P. Gee

Part I
Fully-worked
Problems and Their
Analysis

Standard Costing and Matrix Algebra

1

1.1 Radium Dyestuffs Ltd

Radium Dystuffs Ltd manufactures a radioactive dye in powder form called arquenol. To do this, it requires three types of material and three grades of labour. There is scope for substitution between one type of material and another and between one grade of labour and another, but labour cannot be substituted for materials or vice versa. The standard composition of inputs for the production of a kilogram of arquenol is given below, together with the standard cost of each input.

Input	Standard amount per kg of arquenol	Standard cost
Material		£ per kg
A	1.80 kg	0.60
B	0.14 kg	1.20
C	0.26 kg	4.50
Labour grade		£ per hr
R	0.5 hr	2.50
S	0.7 hr	2.00
T	0.8 hr	1.75

In April 1989, 18 000 kilograms of arquenol were produced. The tabulation on p. 2 shows the volume of inputs consumed during April, and indicates the unit cost of each input.

Input	Total actual quantity used	Unit cost
Material		*£ per kg*
A	36 000 kg	0.57
B	2 460 kg	1.38
C	4 100 kg	5.10
Labour grade		*£ per hr*
R	8 250 hr	2.60
S	14 400 hr	2.30
T	16 100 hr	2.15

Using matrix algebra techniques, **you are required** to calculate:

1. Price, quantity and mixed ('price-quantity') variances for each of the materials at the time of their entry into production.
2. Quantity, rate of pay and mixed variances for each of the grades of labour.
3. Mix and yield variances for labour and for materials at the aggregate level, but not for individual inputs.

1.2   Analysis

Introduction

As a preliminary to the analysis, it is necessary to establish some terminology, as follows. Let:

P represent the standard price for an input

P_A represent the actual price for an input

ΔP represent the deviation of actual from standard price, that is of P_A from P

Similarly, let:

Q represent the standard quantity of an input required for the output actually produced

Q_A represent the actual quantity of an input consumed in producing the actual output

ΔQ represent the deviation of Q_A from Q

The total actual cost of any input is given by $(P + \Delta P)(Q + \Delta Q)$. This expression may be expanded as below:

$$(P + \Delta P)(Q + \Delta Q) = PQ + P\Delta Q + Q\Delta P + \Delta P\Delta Q$$

(1.1)

The terms on the right-hand side of equation (1.1) may be interpreted in the following manner:

PQ represents the input's standard cost for the actual volume of production

$P\Delta Q$ represents the quantity variance

$Q\Delta P$ represents the price variance

$\Delta P\Delta Q$ represents the mixed (or 'price-quantity') variance

There is no element of price change in the calculation of the quantity variance, as this is represented by the deviation of the actual quantity consumed from the standard quantity required for the actual output, valued at the *standard* price. Likewise, no element of actual usage enters into the calculation of the price variance, which is given by the deviation of actual from standard price multiplied by the *standard* quantity required for the actual output. However, this leaves a residual variance $\Delta P\Delta Q$, which has no clear interpretation in that it is the product of both price and quantity deviations, and is therefore the joint outcome of activities both in purchasing and in production.

This mixed (or 'price-quantity') variance is always present in the analysis of labour costs, but may be absent from the analysis of material costs. It is present only where material cost variances are isolated when materials enter into production. This is the case in the Radium Dyestuffs problem, but the modern tendency is instead to isolate price variances for materials at their date of purchase.

Digressing to illustrate this approach, let:

Q_{bt} represent the quantity of a material bought in period t

ΔQ_{ut} represent the difference between the quantity of that material consumed in period t and the standard quantity required for the output of period t

P_t represent the standard price per unit of the material in period t

ΔP_t represent the difference between the standard price per unit and the price per unit actually paid in period t

Then the mixed variance may be eliminated by defining price and quantity variances as follows:

$$\text{Price variance} = Q_{bt}\,\Delta P_t \qquad (1.2)$$
$$\text{Quantity variance} = \Delta Q_{ut} P_t \qquad (1.3)$$

However, since labour services are paid for as they are used, the quantity of them bought in period $t(Q_{bt})$ is always identical to the quantity used (Q_{ut}). Consequently, the time subscript t in equations (1.2) and (1.3) becomes redundant, and these equations revert to the definitions of price and quantity variances associated with equation (1.1), leaving a mixed variance $\Delta P \Delta Q$ as a residual.

Computation of price, quantity and mixed variances

The implementation of equation (1.1) through matrix algebra involves a matrix multiplication of the form:

$$\begin{bmatrix} P \\ \Delta P \end{bmatrix} [Q \ \ \Delta Q] = \begin{bmatrix} PQ & P\Delta Q \\ \Delta PQ & \Delta P\Delta Q \end{bmatrix} \qquad (1.4)$$

For the six inputs in the Radium Dyestuffs problem, this approach gives rise to a partitioned multiplication of a 2×6 matrix by a 6×2 matrix:

		Q	ΔQ
P	$\begin{bmatrix} 0.60 \mid 1.20 \mid 4.50 \mid 2.50 \mid 2.00 \mid 1.75 \end{bmatrix}$	32 400	3 600
ΔP	$\begin{bmatrix} -0.03 \mid 0.18 \mid 0.60 \mid 0.10 \mid 0.30 \mid 0.40 \end{bmatrix}$	2 520	−60
		4 680	−580
		9 000	−750
		12 600	1 800
		14 400	1 700

To illustrate the operation of equation (1.4), consider its application to Material A. Here, the partitioned matrix multiplication is:

$$\begin{bmatrix} 0.60 \\ -0.03 \end{bmatrix} \begin{bmatrix} 32\,400 & 3\,600 \end{bmatrix} = \begin{bmatrix} 19\,440 & 2\,160 \\ -972 & -108 \end{bmatrix}$$

Standard and actual cost for Material A may be reconciled as follows:

	£
Actual cost of Material A consumed in April 1989	20 520
Less unfavourable quantity variance	2 160
	18 360
Add favourable price variance	972
favourable mixed variance	108
standard cost of Material A	19 440

The remaining five partitioned matrix multiplications give rise to variances as tabulated overleaf, with *F* denoting a favourable variance and *U* an unfavourable one.

Computation of mix and yield variances

The sum of the quantity variances for the three materials forms the total quantity variance for materials, and the sum of the quantity variances for the three grades of labour forms the total quantity variance for labour. Each of these total quantity variances can be broken down into two components, called the mix variance and the yield variance. The mix variance is the deviation from standard cost arising because inputs were used in proportions differing from those specified in the budget, and the yield variance is the deviation from standard cost arising because the output obtained from a given quantity of the budgeted mix of inputs differed from that which the budget said should be obtained.

6

Material	Actual cost £		Quantity variance £		Price/Rate of pay variance £		Mixed variance £		Standard cost £
B	3 394.8	+	72F	−	453.6U	+	10.8F	=	3 024
C	20 910.0	+	2 610F	−	2 808.0U	+	348.0F	=	21 060
Labour grade									
R	21 450.0	+	1 875F	−	900.0U	+	75.0F	=	22 500
S	33 120.0	−	3 600U	−	3 780.0U	−	540.0U	=	25 200
T	34 615.0	−	2 975U	−	5 760.0U	−	680.0U	=	25 200

It is first necessary to number the inputs in the order in which they appear in the question, so that (for example) Material C is input 3 and Labour Grade T is input 6. Then let:

SQ_i represent the standard quantity of the ith input required to produce a kilogram of arquenol

SQ_M represent the total standard quantity of materials required to produce a kilogram of arquenol

SQ_L represent the total standard labour input required to produce a kilogram of arquenol

Then the standard mix proportion for material input i is given by SM_i where:

$$SM_i = SQ_i/SQ_M \tag{1.5}$$

Correspondingly, the standard mix proportion for labour input i is given by SM_i where:

$$SM_i = SQ_i/SQ_L \tag{1.6}$$

To give an example of the computation of SM_i, consider the standard mix proportion for Material C, given by SM_3. This is:

$$SM_3 = 0.26/(1.8 + 0.14 + 0.26) = 0.1182$$

In April 1989, a total of 42 560 kilograms of Materials A, B and C together were consumed. If, therefore, the budgeted mix of materials had been adhered to, some (42 560) (0.1182) = 5030 kilograms of Material C would have been used. This amount is referred to as the 'actual quantity recalculated in accordance with the standard mix'. This recalculation should be carried out for each of the six inputs. Then a 3×6 quantity matrix Q may be drawn up in which the first row shows for each input i the standard quantity required for the actual output in June 1989, and the third row shows the actual quantity of input i consumed in that month. The second row of Q shows the actual quantity of input i

recalculated in accordance with the standard mix, so that Q for this problem appears as follows:

$$Q = \begin{bmatrix} 32\,400 & 2\,520 & 4\,680 & 9\,000 & 12\,600 & 14\,400 \\ 34\,822 & 2\,708 & 5\,030 & 9\,687.5 & 13\,562.5 & 15\,500 \\ 36\,000 & 2\,460 & 4\,100 & 8\,250 & 14\,400 & 16\,100 \end{bmatrix}$$

The physical quantities within Q may be valued at standard cost by reference to a 6×2 matrix P, in which there is one row for each input and the first column relates to unit standard costs for materials, while the second relates to unit standard costs for labour. Since there are three material and three labour inputs, the first column of P contains zeros in the fourth to sixth rows and the second column contains zeros in the first to third rows. For this problem, the P matrix is:

$$P = \begin{bmatrix} 0.60 & 0 \\ 1.20 & 0 \\ 4.50 & 0 \\ 0 & 2.50 \\ 0 & 2.00 \\ 0 & 1.75 \end{bmatrix}$$

Postmultiplying Q by P gives rise to a new matrix:

$$R = QP \qquad (1.7)$$

The entries within R relate to the total physical quantities of materials and labour (respectively in the first and second columns) valued at standard cost. As in Q, the first row relates to the standard quantity for the actual output, the third row to the actual quantity consumed and the second row to the actual quantity recalculated in accordance with the standard mix. The computation associated with equation (1.7) gives rise to the following result:

$$R = \begin{bmatrix} R_{11} = 43\,524 & R_{12} = 72\,900 \\ R_{21} = 46\,777.8 & R_{22} = 78\,468.75 \\ R_{31} = 43\,002 & R_{32} = 77\,600 \end{bmatrix}$$

The mix variance is given by the difference between the actual mix and the standard mix for the actual quantity of inputs, all valued at standard cost. Consequently:

Materials mix variance $\quad = R_{31} - R_{21}$ $\qquad\qquad$ (1.8)

Labour mix variance $\quad = R_{32} - R_{22}$ $\qquad\qquad$ (1.9)

The yield variance is given by the difference between the standard mix for the actual quantity of inputs and the standard quantity of inputs, all valued at standard cost. Consequently:

Materials yield variance $\quad = R_{21} - R_{11}$ $\qquad\qquad$ (1.10)

Labour yield variance $\quad = R_{22} - R_{12}$ $\qquad\qquad$ (1.11)

Performing the computations for the matrix R above gives rise to the following results:

	Mix variance £	Yield variance £
Materials	3775.8F	3253.8U
Labour	868.75F	5568.75U

These results show that savings arising from the substitution of the relatively cheap Material A for the relatively expensive Material C were largely nullified by the diminution in yield which ensued. As regards labour, the substitution of Grades S and T for the relatively expensive Grade R did not result in a much cheaper mix of labour, but affected yield very adversely.

Stochastic Process Costing 2

2.1   Ottoline Electronics

One of the products of Ottoline Electronics is a Reserved Density Array (RDA), which is a device with applications in military electronics. The manufacture of RDA units involves four processes, forming a sequence from Process A through Processes B and C to the final Process D. Each of these processes takes the same amount of time to complete, namely an 8-hour shift, and partially-completed RDA units are transferred from one process to another as shifts change.

Because the manufacture of RDA units is technically very demanding, a great many RDA units fail the tests to which they are exposed as the last stage of each of Processes A–D. Such failures may be total, in which case the RDA units concerned are simply thrown away, or they may be partial, in which case either of two things can happen. If the partial failure is attributable to defective manufacture in the process ending in the tests locating that failure, then the RDA units concerned can be 'looped'. This word is part of the jargon of Ottoline Electronics, and refers to the practice of sending RDA units which have suffered a defect in a process through the same process again in the next shift. On the other hand, the partial failure may be attributable to defective manufacture in a process prior to the one which ended in the tests which located the failure. In this case, the RDA units concerned have to be 'reworked' by being sent back to the beginning of the process in which the defect arose, and then going through all the subsequent processes once again.

At the end of Process A, 90 per cent of the RDA units which have gone through this process pass all the tests and are transferred on to Process B. Of the remainder, 7 per cent fail the tests completely and are thrown away, while the other 3 per cent fail partially and are looped back to repeat Process A. When Process B is finished, 86 per cent of the RDA units produced are found to be satisfactory and go on to Process C. Looping back through Process B accounts for 5 per cent of the RDA units reaching this stage, while 4 per cent are sent back to the beginning of Process A for reworking and 5 per cent are thrown away. The corresponding figures for Process C are that 82 per cent of the RDA output from this process is satisfactory and goes on to Process D, 4 per cent of the output is looped again through Process C, 7 per cent is sent back to the start of Process B for reworking and 7 per cent is thrown away.

Finally, at the end of Process D, 88 per cent of the RDA units produced pass the tests completely to become finished products, while by contrast 3 per cent of the RDA units fail the tests entirely and are thrown away as being beyond repair. Of the remaining 9 per cent, 4 per cent are sent back to the beginning of Process C for reworking, 2 per cent are sent back to the beginning of Process B and 3 per cent are looped, thus undergoing Process D again.

The management of Ottoline Electronics are currently planning to supply 1 250 RDA unit assemblies to commence Process A at the beginning of each shift, and to operate each of Processes B, C and D at the levels of activity required to deal with the throughput derived from running Process A at the above rate. Given this data, **you are required** to answer the following questions:

1. In the steady state, what will be the mean and standard deviation for the number of RDA units undergoing each process at any given time?
2. What will be the expected output of finished RDA units per shift, and how many defective RDA units will on average be thrown away per shift?
3. What will be the expected variable cost per shift of operating each of the processes?
4. What will be the expected variable cost of producing a finished RDA unit?

5. In the steady state, what will be the standard deviations firstly of the output of finished RDA units per shift and secondly of the number of defective RDA units thrown away per shift?

6. If it were desired to produce an average of 1 000 finished RDA units per shift, by how much would the number of RDA unit assemblies commencing Process A per shift have to increase to attain this target?

7. A substantial simplification of the tests carried out at the culminations of Processes B, C and D could be achieved if these tests were not required to isolate out those RDA units which require to be sent back to previous processes for reworking. Whilst it is quite straightforward and inexpensive to find out by testing at the end of a process those units which need to be looped back into that process, it is much harder and costlier to isolate out those units which need to be returned to earlier processes; if these units were simply treated as being defective and thrown away, large savings in testing costs could be achieved. It is estimated, indeed, that these savings might amount to a total of £600 per shift at an output of 1 000 finished RDA units per shift. If this were to be the case, could the proposed simplification of the tests be justified economically?

8. An alternative to the proposal in question 7 above would be to modify the manufacturing system radically along lines suggested by the Japanese 'zero defects' system. Ottoline's management are acutely sceptical of the proposition that the manufacturing system could be so altered that no RDA units at all were ever thrown away as being beyond repair, but are sufficiently interested to want to cost out this proposition. Assuming that the average output were to be 1 000 finished RDA units per shift, what would be the cost savings per shift associated with moving to a 'zero defects' system?

2.2   Analysis

Development of a stochastic matrix

The Ottoline Electronics problem is one in which there is uncertainty about the outcome of each production process for the RDA units passing through that process. At its end, some units will be transferred to the next process, others will be 'looped' back to repeat the process again and still others will be sent back to the start of some earlier process for reworking. Because of this uncertainty, it is necessary to describe product flows within the RDA manufacturing system in a stochastic manner, and more specifically to represent these flows as a Markov process.

A Markov process is a process which can be characterised as always being in some state of a set of mutually exclusive states, and whose future behaviour depends probabilistically only on the current state and not on any past behaviour (such as which state the process previously occupied). For this problem, a partially-completed unit entering a stage in production has a probability of passing through that stage and out of it, a probability of looping back through that stage, and a probability of being sent back to one or other of the prior stages. The important point is that these probabilities are independent of what has happened to that RDA unit prior to reaching the stage in production it now occupies. Here, it is a discrete transition process that is being modelled, in that transitions of a unit from one state to another take place at evenly spaced intervals of time – that is, once per shift. Since the probabilistic dependence of transitions on the current state does not change from transition to transition, the Markov process in Ottoline Electronics is said to be stationary. The probability that a (RDA) unit will be in state $S = j$ in period $t + 1$ given that it is in state $S = i$ in period t is given by a fixed value p_{ij}, referred to as a one-step transition probability. This is represented formally by equation (2.1) below:

$$p_{ij} = p(S_{t+1} = j \mid S_t = i) \tag{2.1}$$

The matrix containing the p_{ij} values is referred to as the stochastic matrix, and will here be labelled P. For Ottoline Electronics, each element p_{ij} within the matrix P represents the probability of a (RDA) unit being transferred from state (or process) i in period t to state (or process) j in period $t + 1$. If, for a particular state i, the one-step transition probability is given by $p_{ii} = 1$, then that state is referred to as an absorbing state. Clearly, if a unit is either completed (at the end of Process D) or discarded at the end of one of the processes, then the state into which it has passed is an absorbing state. By contrast, the state of being in any one of

Processes A – D is one from which it is possible to move to another state, and is therefore referred to as a transient state. Where a Markov process must eventually enter an absorbing state, but can pass between transient states in the meantime, then it is referred to as making up an absorbing Markov chain. The problem in Ottoline Electronics can be modelled as such a chain.

In carrying out this modelling, the first step is to draw up the partitioned stochastic matrix P. This is made up in part of those elements p_{ij} whose values are derived from the proportions, for each process, of good production, defective production, reworked production and production subject to looping. The proportions relating to the transient states may be obtained directly from the problem; the remainder of the p_{ij} values are either one (where $i = j$, for absorbing states) or zero. In detail, the partitioned stochastic matrix P appears as follows:

| | Process | | | | Finished product | Discarded unit |
	A	*B*	*C*	*D*		
A	0.03	0.90	0	0	0	0.07
B	0.04	0.05	0.86	0	0	0.05
C	0	0.07	0.04	0.82	0	0.07
D	0	0.02	0.04	0.03	0.88	0.03
Finished	0	0	0	0	1	0
Discarded	0	0	0	0	0	1

In the general case, there are taken to be n production processes and m output states (so that the above matrix P may be taken to be a special case with $n = 4$ and $m = 2$). For this general case, the P matrix may be partitioned and relabelled as below:

$$P = \begin{bmatrix} Q & R \\ \phi & I \end{bmatrix} \begin{matrix} n \\ m \end{matrix}$$

with column labels n and m above.

In this schematisation, the four submatrices serve the following purposes:

1. The Q submatrix gives the transition probabilities among the n production processes.
2. In the R submatrix, the non-zero elements indicate the probabilities associated with movements from the production processes (transient states) to the absorbing states.
3. The symbol I is used to represent an identity submatrix; within the P matrix for Ottoline Electronics it shows that the states represented by 'finished product' and by 'discarded unit' are both absorbing states, and that it is not therefore possible to pass from one of these states to the other.
4. ϕ is a null submatrix, showing that it is not possible to move from any of the absorbing states to any of the transient states.

The fundamental matrix

The fundamental matrix F is defined by the equation:

$$F = (I - Q)^{-1} \qquad (2.2)$$

Entries in the first row of this matrix show, for Ottoline Electronics, the mean number of times a (RDA) unit entering Process A can be expected to pass through each of Processes A–D before leaving the manufacturing system, either as a finished product or having been discarded. The second, third and fourth rows show the equivalent mean number of passages through A–D for units entering Processes B, C and D respectively. The calculation of F proceeds as follows:

$$F = \left(\begin{bmatrix} 1 & 0 & 0 & 0 \\ 0 & 1 & 0 & 0 \\ 0 & 0 & 1 & 0 \\ 0 & 0 & 0 & 1 \end{bmatrix} - \begin{bmatrix} 0.03 & 0.90 & 0 & 0 \\ 0.04 & 0.05 & 0.86 & 0 \\ 0 & 0.07 & 0.04 & 0.82 \\ 0 & 0.02 & 0.04 & 0.03 \end{bmatrix} \right)^{-1}$$

$$F = \begin{bmatrix} 1.077 & 1.115 & 1.035 & 0.875 \\ 0.05 & 1.202 & 1.116 & 0.943 \\ 0.005 & 0.113 & 1.184 & 1.001 \\ 0.001 & 0.029 & 0.072 & 1.092 \end{bmatrix}$$

The interpretation of the first row of this matrix is that a (RDA) unit starting in Process A will on average pass through Process A 1.077 times (with looping), Process B 1.115 times, Process C 1.035 times and Process D 0.875 times. Here, the relatively small number for Process D is attributable to the discarding of defective units at the ends of Processes A–C. A similar explanation may be advanced for the remaining three rows of the matrix, where (for example) the small number in the first column of the second row arises from the fact that a unit starting in Process B can pass through Process A only in the relatively rare event of the reworking of that process being required.

Steady-state in-process inventories

To establish the volume of RDA units undergoing each process at any given time, it is necessary to define a row vector k, which for the general case of n processes will be of dimension $1 \times n$. This vector contains the new elements started into production at the beginning of each transfer period (which is here each shift). In the problem, the information is given that 1 250 RDA unit assemblies are introduced into Process A at the beginning of each shift. By implication, it is understood that partially-completed RDA units can enter Processes B, C and D only by transfer from prior processes, and not from outside the manufacturing system by purchase. The vector k is thus given by:

	k_1	k_2	k_3	k_4
$k =$	[1 250	0	0	0]

Here, k_1 refers to the input of RDA unit assemblies from outside to Process A, k_2 to their input to Process B, and so on. The average steady-state in-process inventories are given by postmultiplying the k vector by the fundamental matrix, so that if these inventories are given by v, then:

$$v = kF \tag{2.3}$$

By computation:

$$v = [1\,346.25 \quad 1\,393.75 \quad 1\,293.75 \quad 1\,093.75]$$

The row vector v states that on average there will be $1\,346.25$ RDA units undergoing Process A, $1\,393.75$ undergoing Process B, $1\,293.75$ undergoing Process C, and $1\,093.75$ undergoing Process D.

Turning from the means to the standard deviations of the in-process inventories, the first step in their computation is to define a new $1 \times n$ row vector g, such that:

$$g = k / \sum_{i=1}^{n} k_i \tag{2.4}$$

In this case, where RDA unit assemblies enter the manufacturing system only at the beginning of Process A, g is given by:

$$g = [1 \quad 0 \quad 0 \quad 0]$$

Let a represent an n-element sum (column) vector, i.e. a column vector in which each component is 1. Then it can be shown that the upper bound of the variances for the steady-state inventory of RDA units undergoing each process is given by:

$$\text{Var. } (v) \leq ka \, [gF - g_{sq}(I - Q_{sq})^{-1}] \tag{2.5}$$

In equation (2.5), the subscript sq indicates that each element in the matrix to which that subscript is assigned is squared. The computation of Var. (v) proceeds as follows:

$$I - Q_{sq} = \begin{bmatrix} 0.9991 & -0.81 & 0 & 0 \\ -0.0016 & 0.9975 & -0.7396 & 0 \\ 0 & -0.0049 & 0.9984 & -0.6724 \\ 0 & -0.0004 & -0.0016 & 0.9991 \end{bmatrix}$$

$$(I - Q_{sq})^{-1} = \begin{bmatrix} 1.002 & 0.817 & 0.606 & 0.408 \\ 0.002 & 1.008 & 0.747 & 0.503 \\ 0 & 0.005 & 1.007 & 0.677 \\ 0 & 0 & 0.002 & 1.002 \end{bmatrix}$$

$$g_{sq}(I - Q_{sq})^{-1} = [1.002 \quad 0.817 \quad 0.606 \quad 0.408]$$

$$gF = [1.077 \quad 1.115 \quad 1.035 \quad 0.875]$$

$$ka[gF - g_{sq}(I - Q_{sq})^{-1}] = 1\,250\,[0.075 \quad 0.298 \quad 0.429 \quad 0.467]$$

$$\text{Var.}\ (v) \leqq [93.75 \quad 372.5 \quad 536.25 \quad 583.75]$$

Taking square roots gives:

$$\text{Sd.}\ (v) \leqq [9.68 \quad 19.30 \quad 23.16 \quad 24.16]$$

The upper limits on the standard deviations of the steady-state in-process inventories for Processes A–D are thus respectively 9.68, 19.30, 23.16 and 24.16 RDA units. It is interesting to note that the standard deviations expressed as a percentage of the mean number of RDA units undergoing each process rise from 0.7 per cent of the mean for Process A to 2.2 per cent of the mean for Process D. This increase reflects the wider variation in inventories arising from the larger number of 'routes' (involving loopings and reworkings) by which RDA units could reach later processes, relative to the smaller number of routes for units entering earlier processes. A final point to note is that more detailed computations suggest that the upper limit figures for standard deviations may be no more than 2–3 per cent in excess of the true figures for standard deviations.

Expected outputs of good and defective production

Having now dealt with part 1. of the Ottoline Electronics problem, part 2. can be despatched with relative brevity. The expected outputs of good and defective RDA units per shift are given by the 1×2 row vector y, where:

$$y = kFR \qquad (2.6)$$

By computation, and rounding to the nearest whole number:

$$y = [963 \quad 287]$$

The average output will thus be 963 finished RDA units per shift, which together with the average of 287 defective units produced per shift gives a total of 1 250 units. This corresponds to the input per shift of RDA unit assemblies into Process A, as would be expected in the steady state.

Expected variable cost per shift

To find the expected variable cost per shift associated with each of the processes, it is necessary to look at the first row of the F matrix. This indicates the expected number of times that a (RDA) unit starting Process A will pass through each of Processes A–D. If these figures are multiplied by the number of RDA units per shift entering Process A, the resulting products will represent the number of expected units of activity undertaken in each of Processes A–D. These expected activity levels may then in turn be multiplied by the variable cost per unit of activity in each process, to give rise to the expected variable cost per shift for each process. The computation proceeds as follows:

Process	Expected no. of units of activity	Variable cost per unit	Expected variable cost per shift
		£	£
A	1 346.25	3.50	4 711.87
B	1 393.75	2.25	3 135.94
C	1 293.75	4.40	5 692.50
D	1 093.75	3.95	4 320.31
			17 860.62

The expected units of activity for a process must be identical to its steady-state in-process inventories, since each RDA unit that undergoes a process must give rise to a unit of activity of that process. It would thus have amounted to exactly the same thing if the elements in the row vector v had each been multiplied by the variable cost per unit for the process concerned.

Expected variable cost per assembly

If the fundamental matrix F is postmultiplied by the submatrix R, then a 4×2 matrix B is obtained. This matrix gives in each of its rows the probability that a (RDA) unit started in each of Processes A–D respectively will turn out to be good or defective. In formal terms:

$$B = FR \tag{2.7}$$

Performing the computation for the Ottoline Electronics problem:

$$B = \begin{bmatrix} 0.770 & 0.230 \\ 0.830 & 0.170 \\ 0.881 & 0.119 \\ 0.961 & 0.039 \end{bmatrix}$$

From the first row of the B matrix, it may be seen that in order to obtain a finished RDA unit from the Ottoline manufacturing system, it is necessary on average to start $1/0.77 = 1.299$ unit assemblies in Process A. The first row of the F matrix shows the number of expected units of activity to which a unit assembly started in Process A would give rise, and the product of this and the number of units started, when costed out, gives the expected variable cost of producing a finished unit. In detail, the calculation is as follows:

Process	Units started (1)	Activity level per unit (2)	Variable cost (3)	Total expected cost (1)×(2)×(3)
			£	£
A	1.299	1.077	3.50	4.90
B	1.299	1.115	2.25	3.26
C	1.299	1.035	4.40	5.92
D	1.299	0.875	3.95	4.49
				18.57

Standard deviations of good and defective output levels

Denoting the variance of output by Var. (y), the formula for deriving this variance is:

$$\text{Var. } y \leq ka\,[gB - g_{sq}(I - Q_{sq})^{-1} R_{sq}] \tag{2.8}$$

By computation:

$$g_{sq}(I - Q_{sq})^{-1} R_{sq} = [0.316 \quad 0.0103]$$
$$gB = [0.77 \quad 0.23]$$

From a previous calculation, $ka = 1\,250$. Putting these three component together gives:

$$\text{Var. } (y) \leq [567.5 \quad 274.6]$$

Taking square roots to obtain the standard deviations:

$$\text{Sd. } (y) \leq [23.82 \quad 16.57]$$

The standard deviation of the output of finished RDA units per shift is not more than 23.82, and the standard deviation of the number of defective units discarded is not more than 16.57. As with the analysis of part 1 of the problem, more detailed computations suggest that these upper limit figures for standard deviations may be no more than 2–3 per cent in excess of the true figures.

The above calculations show that an output level of 1 000 finished RDA units per shift lies more than 1 standard deviation above the expected output level. To achieve an average output level of 1 000 finished RDA units per shift, it would be necessary to start $1\,000 \times 1.299 = 1\,299$ RDA unit assemblies in Process A per shift, an increase of 49 assemblies per shift on the present input level.

Economics of test simplification

It is possible to phrase the issue raised by part 7. of the problem in the following manner. Suppose the practice of reworking by sending defective RDA units back to previous processes were to be abandoned, and the defective units concerned were instead to be thrown away. Would the extra costs associated with the need to introduce more RDA unit assemblies in order to obtain an output of 1 000 finished units per shift exceed the cost savings of £600 per shift arising from test simplification?

To examine this issue, it is necessary first to draw up the partitioned stochastic matrix as it would appear without reworking. Labelling this P', it appears as below:

$$P' = \left[\begin{array}{cccc:cc} 0.03 & 0.90 & 0 & 0 & 0 & 0.07 \\ 0 & 0.05 & 0.86 & 0 & 0 & 0.09 \\ 0 & 0 & 0.04 & 0.82 & 0 & 0.14 \\ 0 & 0 & 0 & 0.03 & 0.88 & 0.09 \\ \hdashline 0 & 0 & 0 & 0 & 1 & 0 \\ 0 & 0 & 0 & 0 & 0 & 1 \end{array} \right]$$

Inserting into equation (2.2) the Q submatrix values (from the upper left-hand area of P') gives rise to a new fundamental matrix F', as below:

$$F' = \left[\begin{array}{cccc} 1.031 & 0.977 & 0.875 & 0.740 \\ 0 & 1.053 & 0.943 & 0.797 \\ 0 & 0 & 1.042 & 0.881 \\ 0 & 0 & 0 & 1.031 \end{array} \right]$$

Then, applying equation (2.7) gives rise to:

$$B = F' \, R = \begin{bmatrix} 0.651 & 0.349 \\ 0.701 & 0.299 \\ 0.775 & 0.225 \\ 0.907 & 0.093 \end{bmatrix}$$

To obtain a finished RDA unit from the Ottoline manufacturing system without reworking, it would be necessary to start $1/0.651 = 1.536$ RDA unit assemblies into the system. The expected variable cost of producing a finished unit would be given as follows:

Process	Units started (1)	Activity level per unit (2)	Variable cost (3)	Total expected cost $(1) \times (2) \times (3)$
			£	£
A	1.536	1.031	3.50	5.54
B	1.536	0.977	2.25	3.38
C	1.536	0.875	4.40	5.91
D	1.536	0.740	3.95	4.49
				19.32

The cost saving per shift from simplifying the tests and throwing away RDA units with defects in them deriving from previous processes must exceed $1\,000 \; £(19.32 - 18.57) = £750$ for this simplification to be economically justifiable. In fact the cost saving available (of £600 per shift) falls well below this, so that the test simplification should not be undertaken.

Economics of the 'zero defects' approach

Suppose that, by extensive expenditure of time and money on quality control, a 'zero defects' regime were to be established, in which all the RDA unit assemblies which entered Process A ultimately emerged from Process D as finished RDA units, and none were ever withdrawn from the manufacturing system as being beyond repair. It would then be possible to draw up a new version of the existing matrix Q, being conditional upon all of the units of output being good. This new matrix will be labelled $\hat{Q}$. It is obtained from equation (2.9) below. In this equation, H is a diagonal matrix, that is a square matrix in which all the elements are zero except those on the principal diagonal. The principal diagonal elements correspond to the probabilities of RDA units entering Processes A–D emerging as good production if they may be sent back to previous processes for reworking. Formally, the elements on the principal diagonal correspond to the elements b_{j1} in the B matrix immediately below equation (2.7). Thus:

$$H = \begin{bmatrix} 0.770 & 0 & 0 & 0 \\ 0 & 0.830 & 0 & 0 \\ 0 & 0 & 0.881 & 0 \\ 0 & 0 & 0 & 0.961 \end{bmatrix}$$

Equation (2.9) may be written as follows:

$$\hat{Q} = H^{-1} QH \tag{2.9}$$

Computation then yields:

$$\hat{Q} = \begin{bmatrix} 0.03 & 0.97 & 0 & 0 \\ 0.037 & 0.05 & 0.913 & 0 \\ 0 & 0.066 & 0.04 & 0.894 \\ 0 & 0.017 & 0.037 & 0.03 \end{bmatrix}$$

To interpret $\hat{Q}$, it is necessary to place it in context within a new conditional stochastic matrix $\hat{P}$. This matrix resembles the original stochastic matrix P in its partitioning, but it is conditional upon no RDA units being discarded as defective. Consequently, it has no 'discarded unit' row or column, and consists only of $\hat{Q}$ together with a row and a column for 'finished product':

		Process				Finished product
		A	B	C	D	
$\hat{P} =$	A	0.03	0.97	0	0	0
	B	0.037	0.05	0.913	0	0
	C	0	0.066	0.04	0.894	0
	D	0	0.017	0.037	0.03	0.916
Finished product		0	0	0	0	1

From $\hat{P}$, it is possible to construct a conditional fundamental matrix by the same procedure as was used with the original stochastic matrix P. That is, the conditional fundamental matrix $\hat{F}$ is given by:

$$\hat{F} = (I - \hat{Q})^{-1} \tag{2.10}$$

By computation, the matrix below is obtained:

$$\hat{F} = \begin{bmatrix} 1.077 & 1.201 & 1.185 & 1.092 \\ 0.046 & 1.201 & 1.185 & 1.092 \\ 0.004 & 0.106 & 1.185 & 1.092 \\ 0.001 & 0.025 & 0.066 & 1.092 \end{bmatrix}$$

A characteristic feature of the $\hat{F}$ matrix is that, in each column, the elements above the principal diagonal and those on the principal diagonal are all equal. This reflects the fact that whichever process a (RDA) unit starts off in, and thus whichever row it initially occupies, the number of times it will pass through the remaining processes will on average be equal. Thus a unit starting off in Process A will on average pass through Process B 1.201 times, and so will a unit starting off in Process B. This follows from the fact that no RDA units are now discarded at the end of Process A. A similar effect holds for the processes prior to and including Processes C and D, and arises from the same cause.

It is also worth noting that, compared with the F matrix, a (RDA) unit started in Process A will now pass through Processes B, C and D more often with the $\hat{F}$ matrix. For example, such a unit will on average pass through Process D 1.092 times with the $\hat{F}$ matrix, as compared with 0.875 times with the F matrix. This is a consequence of the fact that under the $\hat{F}$ matrix all the units started in Process A reach Process D, and none are discarded at the ends of Processes A–C.

By reference to the analysis of part 6. of the problem, it may be seen that in the absence of a zero defects system it would be necessary to start 1 299 unit assemblies in Process A per shift in order to obtain an average output of 1 000 finished units per shift. By definition, with a zero defects system it would be necessary to start only 1 000 unit assemblies per shift in Process A.

The difference between the number of units of activity required with and without a zero defects system may be expressed by postmultiplying a row vector relating to the number of unit assemblies started in Process A by the matrices F and $\hat{F}$ respectively. In detail, the calculations are:

Units of activity without zero defects

$$[1\,299 \quad 0 \quad 0 \quad 0]F$$
$$= [1\,399 \quad 1\,448 \quad 1\,344 \quad 1\,137]$$

Units of activity with zero defects

$$[1\,000 \quad 0 \quad 0 \quad 0]\hat{F}$$
$$= [1\,077 \quad 1\,201 \quad 1\,185 \quad 1\,092]$$

The cost savings per shift associated with moving to a zero defects system may be obtained by costing out the differences between the number of units of activity for a given output with and without such a system, as follows:

Process	Units of activity saved by zero defects	Variable cost per unit	Cost saving per shift
		£	£
A	322	3.50	1 127
B	247	2.25	555.75
C	159	4.40	699.60
D	45	3.95	177.75
			2 560.10

This saving from the institution of zero defects represents over 14 per cent of the expected variable cost per shift for the production of 1 000 finished RDA units by existing technology. Though a zero defects system may be very difficult to introduce, its effect on costs would clearly be profound.

Credit Management and Markov Chains: Partial Balance Aging Method

3

3.1 Stryford Ltd

Stryford Ltd is a dealer in agricultural machinery, and in the Spring of 1989 is facing the usual surge in demand from farmers, associated with the improving weather. While this Spring selling period is vital to Stryford, it brings with it problems in the management of working capital. These problems are especially acute in 1989 since Stryford is operating near to its overdraft limit. At the end of March, Stryford's management have been asked by their bankers to provide a forecast of cash receipts for April, and it is important that this forecast should be as accurate as possible. As a basis for the forecast, Stryford's management have available data on debts owed by their customers. Debts are classified on a partial balance aging basis – that is by reference to the length of time that has elapsed since a sales transaction created the debt. This data, for the first three months of 1989, is shown on p. 28.

In making a forecast from this data, three additional pieces of information will prove to be of value. They are as follows:

1. By trial and error procedures performed on a computer, Stryford's management have found that the best forecasts are obtained if a smoothing constant of 0.9 is applied to the most recent stochastic matrix for debts.
2. The Credit Control Manager of Stryford Ltd says that, in her experience, about 50 per cent of the debts falling into the '3–4

months old' category in any given month are paid off in the
following month.
3. Stryford Ltd wrote off bad debts of £6 649 in February 1989 and
of £8 211 in March 1989.

Partial balance aging data for 1989
Balances owing at dates below:

Period over which debt owed	End of **January** £	End of **February** £	End of **March** £
Less than 1 month (state 0)	656 369	1 018 682	1 229 197
1–2 months (state 1)	143 984	76 416	170 510
2–3 months (state 2)	70 316	81 580	43 193
3–4 months (state 3)	30 605	38 894	47 947
Over 4 months (state 4)	93 884	87 641	89 191
Total owed	9 951 158	1 303 213	1 580 038

You are required to use Markov chain analysis to forecast cash
receipts from debtors for April 1989.

3.2 Analysis

Development of a stochastic matrix

Within this problem, a unit of 1 pound owed may fall into any one
of five transient states (numbered 0–4), corresponding to differing
periods of time since the debt concerned was created. There are
also two absorbing states, represented by debt paid (state P) or
debt written off as bad (state B). Thus a 7×7 stochastic matrix
may be drawn up, which to be consistent with the literature on this
topic will be partitioned in the following manner:

$$\left[\begin{array}{c|c} I & \phi \\ \hline R & Q \end{array}\right]$$

In this schematisation, the definitions of the submatrices are identical to those advanced previously in the analysis of the Ottoline Electronics problem. However, the elements within each of the submatrices are derived in a rather different manner, which will now be explained. For the purposes of this explanation, January, February and March will be referred to respectively as months 1, 2 and 3. The vector showing the actual partial balance age structure of debts at the end of month j will be referred to as I_j, and within I_j the kth element will be referred to as $i_{j,k}$, with $k = P$, B, 3, 4, 5, 6, 7 corresponding respectively to states P, B, 0, 1, 2, 3 and 4. To give an example of this notation, I_1 appears as:

$$I_1 = [0 \quad 0 \quad 656\,369 \quad 143\,984 \quad 70\,316 \quad 30\,605 \quad 93\,884]$$

To obtain the transition probabilities for insertion in the stochastic matrix, it is necessary to note how many pounds go from state k in month j to state $k + 1$ in month $j + 1$. The amount remaining, that was in state k in month j but did not pass to state $k + 1$ in month $j + 1$, is considered to be paid in month j. For $k = 3\ldots6$, the transition probability of payment t_{kP} is given by:

$$t_{kP} = (i_{j,k} - i_{j+1,k+1})/i_{j,k} \tag{3.1}$$

Comparing the January and February aging data gives transition probabilities for payment as follows for $k = 3\ldots5$:

k	$i_{1,k}$	$i_{2,k+1}$	Paid	Probability of payment t_{kP}
			£	
3	656 369	$-$ 76 416	= 579 953	$\dfrac{579\,953}{656\,369} = 0.884$
4	143 984	$-$ 81 580	= 62 404	$\dfrac{62\,404}{143\,984} = 0.433$
5	70 316	$-$ 38 894	= 31 422	$\dfrac{31\,422}{70\,316} = 0.447$

The transition probabilities from states 0, 1 and 2 to payment are respectively thus $t_{3P} = 0.884$, $t_{4P} = 0.433$ and $t_{5P} = 0.447$. In words, the probability that a given pound of debt in state 0 in January 1989 would be paid during February 1989 was 0.884, and so on. But since state 0 is a transient state, a pound in that state can only be paid or pass from state 0 to state 1. For a given pound, the transition probability associated with moving from state 0 to state 1 as between January and February 1989 is thus given by:

$$t_{34} = 1-0.884 = 0.116$$

In general, the transition probabilities for movements from one state to another for $k = 3 \ldots 5$ are given by:

$$t_{k,k+1} = 1 - t_{kP} \tag{3.2}$$

For $k = 6$, the information given by the credit control manager indicates a transition probability of payment $t_{6P} = 0.5$. Since a pound in state 3 can only either move from there to state 4 or be paid, it must follow that $t_{6P} + t_{67} = 1$, and hence that $t_{67} = 0.5$.

It is next necessary to compute the transition probabilities from state 4 (that is, from $k = 7$). This is trickier, because of the existence of three, rather than two, possibilities. They are as follows:

1. There may be a transition from state 4 to payment, with a transition probability of t_{7P}.
2. There may be a transition from state 4 to bad debt, with a transition probability of t_{7B}.
3. There may be a transition from state 4 to itself, in the sense that a pound of debt may remain in state 4 from one month to the next.

   This is because state 4 is a limiting state, covering all debt more than 4 months old, which also serves to explain why the amounts in state 4 in month j are always in excess of the amounts in state 3 in month $j - 1$.

   While state 4 is limiting, it is not absorbing – all pounds must ultimately pass from it either to be paid or to enter into bad debt.

Hence only P and B are absorbing states.

The approach to computing t_{7P} may be expressed in words as follows:

> Amount paid from state 4 = (Opening balance in state 4 + amount assumed to enter state 4) − (Closing balance in state 4 + amount leaving state 4 as bad debt)

The transition probability of payment is given by the amount paid from state 4 divided by the opening balance in that state. Consequently, it may be expressed symbolically in these terms:

$$t_{7P} = (i_{j,7} + t_{67}\, i_{j,6} - i_{j+1,7} - i_{j+1,B})/i_{j,7} \qquad (3.3)$$

A numerical example for equation (3.3), using the data for January and February 1989, is given below:

$$t_{7P} = [93\,884 + (0.5)\,(30\,605) - 87\,641 - 6\,649]/93\,884 = 0.1587$$

Using a similar line of argument, the transition probability t_{7B} is given by:

$$t_{7B} = i_{j+1,B}/i_{j,7} \qquad (3.4)$$

In numerical terms, for the January and February data $t_{7B} = 0.0708$. Since a pound in state 4 has only three possibilities of movement, and the probabilities for two of them have been calculated, the remaining transition probability can be obtained by elimination as follows:

$$t_{77} = 1 - (t_{7P} + t_{7B}) \qquad (3.5)$$

For the January and February data, $t_{77} = 0.7705$. Given that each row of a stochastic matrix must sum to 1, then the computations performed so far are sufficient to construct the matrix for the January and February data, which will be labelled T_2. The matrix

T_2 appears as follows, with its rows and columns labelled by reference to the states they represent:

	P	B	0	1	2	3	4
P	1	0	0	0	0	0	0
B	0	1	0	0	0	0	0
0	0.884	0	0	0.116	0	0	0
1	0.433	0	0	0	0.567	0	0
2	0.447	0	0	0	0	0.553	0
3	0.5	0	0	0	0	0	0.5
4	0.1587	0.0708	0	0	0	0	0.7705

An identical series of calculations to the one carried out above may be applied to the data for February and March, to obtain a further stochastic matrix T_3, as below:

	P	B	0	1	2	3	4
P	1	0	0	0	0	0	0
B	0	1	0	0	0	0	0
0	0.833	0	0	0.167	0	0	0
1	0.435	0	0	0	0.565	0	0
2	0.412	0	0	0	0	0.588	0
3	0.5	0	0	0	0	0	0.5
4	0.111	0.094	0	0	0	0	0.795

Having obtained two stochastic matrices representing the transition probabilities for the January–March period, the question which then arises is one of how to combine their information in deriving an estimate of the stochastic matrix for March–April. This may be done in a variety of ways, but the approach which has been specifically advocated is one involving exponential weighting.

Combining matrices by exponential weighting

To explain this approach, it is necessary to define two new terms as follows. Let:

α   represent the smoothing constant to be applied to the stochastic matrices. From note 1 within the problem, α = 0.9 in this case

$\bar{A}_j$ represent the 'average' (exponentially smoothed) matrix for month j

When a month ends (which call month j), then the average matrix for the preceding month, $\bar{A}_{j-1}$, may be updated by reference to the following formula:

$$\bar{A}_j = \alpha T_j + (1 - \alpha)\bar{A}_{j-1} \tag{3.6}$$

From this approach, it would appear that obtaining the March–April average matrix $\bar{A}_3$ must involve updating $\bar{A}_2$ by reference to T_3. But there is not sufficient data in the problem from which to compute A_2, so that T_2 must serve as a surrogate for A_2, hence in this case:

$$\bar{A}_3 = 0.9T_3 + 0.1T_2$$

Performing this computation gives rise to a matrix $\bar{A}_3$, as follows:

	P	B	0	1	2	3	4
P	1	0	0	0	0	0	0
B	0	1	0	0	0	0	0
0	0.838	0	0	0.162	0	0	0
1	0.435	0	0	0	0.565	0	0
2	0.415	0	0	0	0	0.585	0
3	0.5	0	0	0	0	0	0.5
4	0.1158	0.0917	0	0	0	0	0.7926

From its third row downwards, the P column of $\bar{A}_3$ represents the transition probabilities for a pound from each of states 0–4 to payment. If the transition probabilities are premultiplied by the vector I_3 showing the partial balance age structure of debts at the end of March, then a vector E_4 is obtained showing the estimated aging of debtor balances including payments and bad debts. This appears as below:

$$E_4 = I_3 \bar{A}_3$$
$$= [1\,156\,466 \quad 8\,179 \quad 0 \quad 199\,130 \quad 96\,338 \quad 25\,268 \quad 94\,666]$$

The E_4 vector may be interpreted as supplying a forecast that £1 156 466 will be received from debtors in April, while £8 179

worth of debts will be declared bad. Next in E_4 there is a zero, to
indicate that this forecasting system makes no prediction about the
volume of debts in state 0 at the end of April. The remaining
figures in E_4 relate respectively to the forecast debtor balances in
states 1, 2, 3 and 4. In summary, what the E_4 vector represents is a
forecast of the disposition of the balances in the debtor accounts at
the end of March as they will appear at the end of April. Subject to
rounding error, the total of the amounts in E_4 is thus equal to the
total of the amounts in I_3.

A final point to note is that the method outlined here can be
used to create forecasts for longer than a month ahead. For
example, letting the amount of credit sales budgeted for April be
x, then a vector I_4 can be formed from E_4, as follows:

$$I_4 = [0 \quad 0 \quad x \quad 199\,130 \quad 96\,338 \quad 25\,268 \quad 94\,666]$$

Then taking $\bar{A}_3$ as representing the best available estimate of
transition probabilities for the April–May period, a forecast of
May's cash receipts can be read out from the vector $I_4\,\bar{A}_3$. This
process can be continued as far into the future as is desired.

Credit Management and Markov Chains: Modified Total Balance Aging Method

4

4.1 Michelsky Ltd

Michelsky Ltd is a wholesale jewellers which permits retail jewellers to purchase from it on credit. At the end of March 1989 it had twelve credit customers, whose accounts stood as follows, with all figures in thousands of pounds:

Customer account no.	Owed from March invoices	Owed from February invoices	Owed from invoices in or before January
1	9	14	–
2	–	–	8
3	26	–	12
4	–	22	–
5	18	–	–
6	–	31	5
7	–	11	–
8	9	22	–
9	–	16	–
10	14	4	–
11	5	21	–
12	9	–	–

The same accounts stood as follows at the end of April 1989:

Customer account no.	Owed from April invoices	Owed from March invoices	Owed from invoices in or before February
1	12	9	–
2	–	–	8
3	17	26	–
4	11	–	5
5	21	–	–
6	9	–	22
7	–	–	–
8	14	9	–
9	12	–	–
10	8	14	4
11	17	5	9
12	4	9	–

The managers of Michelsky believe that all of the amounts owed at the end of April 1989 will ultimately be paid, with the exception of £8000 owed on Account 2. It was decided during April that this amount represented a bad debt. Excluding this bad debt, the total amounts owed at the end of April were as follows:

Owed from	£
April invoices	125 000
March invoices	72 000
Invoices in or before February	40 000
	237 000

Using this data, **you are required**:

1. To compute the expected value of receipts from the £237 000 owed at the end of April.
2. To calculate the provision for bad debts that should be made in respect of the £237 000 owed, upon the assumption that this amount should be equal to the expected value of bad debts

within this £237 000 plus a safety margin of two standard deviations from this expected value.
3. To work out the present value of receipts from the £237 000 given a rate of discount of 2 per cent per month.
4. To estimate the size of the investment in debtors that Michelsky Ltd will have in the steady state if it acquires new debts at a constant rate of £150 000 per month.

4.2 Analysis

Modified total balance aging

In total balance aging, the age of a customer account is defined to be the age of its oldest unpaid invoice. To illustrate this concept in a concise manner, some terminology must first be defined. Call the end of March 1989 time t, and call the end of April 1989 time $t + 1$. In each case, refer to the month just completed as age category 1, so that for time t March 1989 is age category 1 and for time $t + 1$ April 1989 is age category 1.

Applying this terminology to Customer Account 1 at time t, this account is then said to be of age 2, because its oldest unpaid invoice relates to £14 000 of transactions in February, which at time t constitutes age category 2. In the same way, Customer Account 4 at time $t + 1$ is said to be of age 3, since its oldest unpaid invoice relates to £5 000 of transactions in or before February, which at $t + 1$ is age category 3.

Summing the amounts in each age category at time t gives rise to the following results. There is a total of £27 000 in age category 1, being the sum of the balances in Accounts 5 and 12. The accounts which fall into age category 2 are 1, 4, 7, 8, 9, 10 and 11, with a total of £147 000 in all of them together. Finally, in age category 3 are Accounts 2, 3 and 6, with a total balance of £82 000.

Two extra categories must now be defined. Category 0 is taken to represent 'amount paid' and category 4 to represent 'amount declared bad debt'. Then account movements may be described as follows. Let:

B_{jk} represent the amount of the balance at time t that comes from category j at time t and goes to category k at time $t + 1$.

To illustrate this variable, consider Customer Account 1. Of the £23 000 owed in respect of this account at time t, £14 000 is paid by $t + 1$ (and so passes into age category 0) and £9 000 remains outstanding for a further month (and so passes into age category 2). Expressing amounts in thousands of pounds, $B_{20} = 14$ and $B_{22} = 9$.

By way of comparison, consider Customer Account 10. Like Account 1, this is in age category 2 at period t, so that $j = 2$. There are no payments at all in respect of this account during April, so that the account as a whole moves into age category 3 by the end of April. Since the amount owed in respect of this account at time t was £18 000, for this account $B_{23} = 18$.

The contrast between Accounts 1 and 10 exposes a fundamental point. If there is no payment of amounts outstanding on an account between time t and time $t + 1$, the (single) B value for that account has subscripts showing the total balance age category it occupied at time t and then at time $t + 1$. But if there is a payment of part of the balance on the account (as with Customer Account 1) then that payment gives rise to a separate B value, which in this case is $B_{20} = 14$. The operation of this modification of strict total balance aging is illustrated below for each of the twelve accounts:

From age category	*Account no.*	*To category*					*B values*
		0	4	1	2	3	
1	5	18	–	–	–	–	$B_{10} = 18$
	12	–	–	–	9	–	$B_{12} = 9$
	1	14	–	–	9	–	$B_{20} = 14;\ B_{22} = 9$
	4	17	–	–	–	5	$B_{20} = 17;\ B_{23} = 5$
	7	11	–	–	–	–	$B_{20} = 11$
2	8	22	–	–	9	–	$B_{20} = 22;\ B_{22} = 9$
	9	16	–	–	–	–	$B_{20} = 16$
	10	–	–	–	–	18	$B_{23} = 18$
	11	12	–	–	–	14	$B_{20} = 12;\ B_{23} = 14$
	2	–	8	–	–	–	$B_{34} = 8$
3	3	12	–	–	26	–	$B_{30} = 12;\ B_{32} = 26$
	6	14	–	–	–	22	$B_{30} = 14;\ B_{33} = 22$

Let p_{jk} represent the transition probability that a pound in category j at time t will pass to category k at time $t + 1$. Then:

$$p_{jk} = B_{jk} \bigg/ \sum_{s=0}^{4} B_{js} \tag{4.1}$$

These transition probabilities make up the Q and R submatrices of a partitioned stochastic matrix P. The form of the partitioning is exactly as shown in the analysis of the Stryford Ltd problem, and the complete stochastic matrix, with its rows and columns labelled with the categories to which they refer, appears as below:

$$
P = \begin{array}{c c}
 & \begin{array}{c c c c c} 0 & 4 & 1 & 2 & 3 \end{array} \\
\begin{array}{c} 0 \\ 4 \\ 1 \\ 2 \\ 3 \end{array} &
\left[\begin{array}{c c | c c c}
1 & 0 & 0 & 0 & 0 \\
0 & 1 & 0 & 0 & 0 \\
\hline
0.667 & 0 & 0 & 0.333 & 0 \\
0.626 & 0 & 0 & 0.122 & 0.252 \\
0.317 & 0.098 & 0 & 0.317 & 0.268
\end{array} \right]
\end{array}
$$

Expected value of receipts

The first step in computing the expected value of receipts is to evaluate the fundamental matrix F, which is given by:

$$F = (I - Q)^{-1} \tag{4.2}$$

In equation (4.2), Q refers to the submatrix in the bottom right-hand section of P, and I is a 3×3 identity matrix. Computation yields:

$$
F = \begin{bmatrix}
1 & 0.4332 & 0.1491 \\
0 & 1.3006 & 0.4478 \\
0 & 0.5633 & 1.5601
\end{bmatrix}
$$

The bottom left-hand section of P constitutes the submatrix R. If F is postmultiplied by R, the 3×2 matrix which results contains within it the probabilities that a pound of debt initially in each of age categories 1, 2 and 3 will ultimately reach each of the absorbing states (that is, will ultimately be paid or be declared bad). Postmultiplication gives rise to:

$$FR = \begin{bmatrix} 0.985 & 0.015 \\ 0.956 & 0.044 \\ 0.847 & 0.153 \end{bmatrix}$$

The first row of this matrix indicates that a pound of debt in age category 1 (being part of a debt less than 1 month old) has a 0.985 probability of eventually being paid and a 0.015 probability of eventually being declared a bad debt. Similar interpretations hold for a pound within a debt one 1–2 months old and a pound within a debt more than 2 months old, in the second and third rows respectively of the *FR* matrix. This probabilistic data can be used to predict the amounts ultimately received and lost from a given debt structure, with the definition of an additional term as follows. Let:

k represent a vector of the debts outstanding, classified by age category

For the data in this problem:

$$k = [125\,000 \quad 72\,000 \quad 40\,000]$$

By postmultiplying k by *FR*, it is possible to estimate how much of this £237 000 of debt will ultimately be collected and how much will be lost in the form of bad debt. The computation is:

$$kFR = [225\,837 \quad 11\,163]$$

From these figures, the expected value of receipts is £225 837, and the remaining £11 163 constitutes the expected value of bad debts. However, to set the provision for bad debts equal to their expected value might well be regarded as insufficiently prudent, hence the need to calculate their standard deviation, which is done below.

Standard deviation of bad debts

As a preliminary to this calculation, two new terms need to be defined, as follows. Let:

  g represent a column unit vector with as many elements as are contained in k, so that here g is a 3×1 vector

  c represent a row vector indicating the probability that a given pound of debt falls into a particular age category

For this problem, an element c_i within this latter vector is defined by equation (4.3) below:

$$c_i = k_i \left/ \sum_{i=1}^{3} k_i \right. \tag{4.3}$$

The variance of expected value for receipts and bad debts is given by V, where:

$$V = kg \left[cFR - (cFR)_{sq} \right] \tag{4.4}$$

The subscript sq indicates that each element in the matrix to which that subscript is assigned is squared. By computation:

$$
\begin{aligned}
c &= [0.5274 \quad 0.3038 \quad 0.1688] \\
cFR &= [0.9529 \quad 0.0471] \\
V &= 237\,000\,[0.0449 \quad 0.0449] \\
&= [10\,641 \quad 10\,641]
\end{aligned}
$$

These figures represent respectively the variances of receipts and of bad debts, so that the standard deviation of bad debts is £103.15. If the provision for bad debts is to have a safety margin of two standard deviations, then it should be set at (just under) £11 370.

Present value of receipts

Let the discount rate per month be v, so that in this problem $v = 0.02$. Then define d such that:

$$d = 1/(1 + v) \qquad (4.5)$$

Here, $d = 0.9804$. If the present value vector for receipts and bad debts is represented by y_{pv}, then:

$$y_{pv} = k(I - dQ)^{-1} R \qquad (4.6)$$

Since all the terms on the right-hand side of equation (4.6) have already been defined, this involves only a simple matter of computation, yielding:

$$y_{pv} = [222\,902 \qquad 10\,805]$$

The present value of the expected receipts of £225 837, given a discount rate of 2 per cent per month, is £222 902. This computation supplies, in addition, the present value of expected bad debts, which is £10 805.

Steady-state investment in debtors

Let the vector p represent the amount of new debt entering each age category per month, so that:

$$p = [150\,000 \quad 0 \quad 0]$$

Then the vector representing debtor balances in the steady state is given by k_{ss}, where:

$$k_{ss} = pF \qquad (4.7)$$

This calculation, for Michelsky, produces:

$$k_{ss} = [150\,000 \quad 64\,980 \quad 22\,365]$$

The sum of the elements in the k_{ss} vector is £237 345. This figure therefore represents an estimate of Michelsky's investment in debtors in the steady state, with an acquisition rate for new debts of £150 000 per month. Within the overall £237 345 figure, amounts are estimated to fall into age categories corresponding to elements within k_{ss} above, so that for example £64 980 worth of debt would be 1–2 months old.

It is worth noting, however, that steady-state estimates are very dependent upon the assumption that the transition probabilities (the values in the R and Q submatrices) remain constant over time. An empirical study carried out by Barkman (listed in Appendix 2) has cast considerable doubt upon the validity of this assumption.

Linear Programming and Decisions on Internal v. External Purchases of Services

5

5.1 Knockshinnock Mines Ltd

Knockshinnock Mines Ltd is concerned with the open-cast mining of barytes in a remote area of the Cairngorm Mountains in Scotland. Because of its remoteness, the Knockshinnock site currently has to provide all of its own services. Of particular importance in this context are the pumping of water, the generation of electricity and the production of steam and of compressed air. These activities are carried out in four service departments numbered S_1 (water), S_2 (steam), S_3 (electricity) and S_4 (compressed air). The amounts and proportions of services consumed in the different departments may be tabulated as follows, with all figures in thousands of units:

From \ To	S_1	S_2	S_3	S_4	Mine	Total
S_1	0	2 115	470	0	2 115	4 700
	–	45%	10%	–	45%	(l)
S_2	160	0	1 920	640	480	3 200
	5%	–	60%	20%	15%	(m³)
S_3	3 710	1 060	0	2 650	3 180	10 600
	35%	10%	–	25%	30%	(KWH)
S_4	765	255	510	0	3 570	5 100
	15%	5%	10%	–	70%	(m³)

During 1988, the variable operating costs incurred in the service departments were as follows:

	£
Water	112 800
Steam	1 280 000
Electricity	1 590 000
Compressed air	510 000

1. At the end of 1988, the North of Scotland Electricity Board approached Knockshinnock Mines with a proposal to supply electricity at £0.25 per kilowatt hour. The machinery which Knockshinnock uses to produce electricity is leased, and the lease is just about to come up for renewal, so that a decision by Knockshinnock to cease to produce its own electricity can be evaluated solely in terms of its impact on variable operating costs. **You are required** to advise Knockshinnock as to whether it should accept the Electricity Board's offer.

2. Since the North of Scotland Electricity Board uses hydro-electric generating plant, it could offer water supplies as well as electricity to Knockshinnock Mines. Suppose, then, that at the end of 1988 it were to offer to supply electricity at £0.25 per kilowatt hour as before, or water at £0.03 per litre, or both these services together. Still carrying out the evaluation solely in terms of the impact on variable operating costs, **you are required** to advise Knockshinnock on the appropriate response to this further offer.

5.2   Analysis

Offer to supply electricity

This problem is concerned with the make-or-buy decision for a service, where services are provided by one service department to another as well as by service departments to the one operating department, which is the mine. The 1988 variable operating costs per unit of service provided for each of departments $S_1 - S_4$ work out as follows:

> Water (S_1) costs £0.024 per litre (l)
> Steam (S_2) costs £0.40 per cubic metre (m^3).
> Electricity (S_3) costs £0.15 per kilowatt hour (KWH)
> Compressed air (S_4) costs £0.10 per cubic metre (m^3).

By comparison with the £0.15 per kilowatt hour figure above, the offer by the North of Scotland Electricity Board to supply electricity at £0.25 per kilowatt hour appears a poor one. However, this simple comparison is grossly misleading. An obvious point is that electricity generation involves the consumption of water, of compressed air and especially of steam. If electricity generation were to be discontinued, then total variable costs of production for water, compressed air and steam would all decline. These are direct effects, but there are also indirect effects to be taken into account. S_2 (steam) supplies 60 per cent of its services to S_3 (electricity), but S_1 (water) in turn supplies 45 per cent of its services to S_2 (steam). Discontinuing electricity generation would thus not only reduce the demand for water directly by 470 000 litres per annum (10 per cent of water production), but would further reduce the demand for water indirectly as a result of the smaller requirement for water to be used in steam generation.

  The other factor which complicates the issue is that in order to provide services to electricity generation, the other service departments themselves require to consume electricity. If the services of S_1, S_2 and S_4 were to be required in smaller volume, their consumption of electricity would decline correspondingly. Hence Knockshinnock would not require to purchase from the Electricity Board the whole of the 10 600 000 kilowatt hours per annum that they currently consume, but some smaller figure reflecting the lower consumption of electricity by S_1, S_2 and S_4 arising because they no longer need to provide services to S_3 for electricity generation.

In this problem, the objective is to minimise the total amount per annum spent on the four service centres and on the electricity (if any) bought from the Board. The amount spent is the product of the cost per unit of service and the number of service units produced (or purchased) per annum. Denoting the output per annum of each of the four service centres $S_1 - S_4$ respectively by $X_1 - X_4$, and denoting the number of kilowatt hours per annum bought from the Board as X_5, an objective function C may be drawn up using the unit costs calculated above. This function appears as follows:

$$C = 0.024X_1 + 0.4X_2 + 0.15X_3 + 0.1X_4 + 0.25X_5$$

The minimisation of C is subject to constraints specifying the amount of each of the services which must be provided to the mine, and the resulting minimisation problem can be dealt with by linear programming. To derive the constraints, it is necessary first to work out the physical quantities of water, steam, electricity and compressed air required to produce a unit of output for each of the service centres S_1, S_2, S_3 and S_4 in turn. These quantities are referred to as 'technological coefficients' and may be tabulated as follows:

To produce		Requires	
1 l of water in S_1	$0.034m^3$ of steam from S_2	0.789 KWH of electricity from S_3	$0.163m^3$ of compressed air from S_4
$1m^3$ of steam in S_2	0.661 l of water from S_1	0.331 KWH of electricity from S_3	$0.080m^3$ of compressed air from S_4
1 KWH of electricity in S_3	0.044 l of water from S_1	$0.181m^3$ of steam from S_2	$0.048m^3$ of compressed air from S_4
$1m^3$ of compressed air in S_4	$0.125m^3$ of steam from S_2	0.520 KWH of electricity from S_3	

The above figures are obtained by dividing the inputs to service centres by their outputs. S_1 thus consumes $160\,000\text{m}^3$ of steam to produce $4\,700\,000$ litres of water, so that each litre of water produced must involve the consumption of 0.034m^3 of steam.

Each service centre provides an input to the mine, so that there must be as many constraints describing the volume of services provided to the mine as there are service centres. Since the requirements of the mine are absolute values (not maxima or minima), each constraint must take the form of an equality. If, for example, water were not required by any other service centre, then the constraint on water supply to the mine would simply take the form $X_1 = 2\,115\,000$. But reference to the technological coefficients shows that every cubic metre of steam produced (every X_2) requires $0.661X_1$ and every kilowatt hour of electricity (every X_3) requires $0.044X_1$. The amount of water that has to be produced thus depends on the values that X_2 and X_3 take in the optimal solution, so that the constraint on water supply must take the form:

$$X_1 - 0.661X_2 - 0.044X_3 + 0X_4 + 0X_5 = 2\,115\,000 \quad (5.1)$$

The other constraints are derived in exactly the same way, except for the constraint relating to electricity supply. The mine needs $3\,180\,000$ kilowatt hours, which it may obtain either from Knockshinnock's own generator or from the Electricity Board. If none of the service centres required electricity, the constraint would take the form that the sum of the internally-generated kilowatt hours and those supplied by the Board must equal the mine's requirements, so that the constraint would appear as $X_3 + X_5 = 3\,180\,000$. Putting into this constraint the requirements of the other service centres gives rise to constraint (5.3) in the listing of the remaining constraints shown below:

$$-0.034X_1 + X_2 - 0.181X_3 - 0.125X_4 + 0X_5 = 480\,000 \quad (5.2)$$
$$-0.789X_1 - 0.331X_2 + X_3 - 0.520X_4 + X_5 = 3\,180\,000 \quad (5.3)$$
$$-0.163X_1 - 0.080X_2 - 0.048X_3 + X_4 + 0X_5 = 3\,570\,000 \quad (5.4)$$

The solution to the problem of minimising C subject to constraints (5.1) – (5.4) above is as follows:

$X_1 = 2\,836\,411$; $X_2 = 1\,091\,394$; $X_3 = 0$; $X_4 = 4\,119\,647$; $X_5 = 7\,921\,396$

This solution involves a cost per annum of £2 896 946, which is a saving of £595 854 per annum over the cost of providing all services (including electricity) internally. Although purchasing 7 921 396 kilowatt hours of electricity from the Board is more expensive than producing 10 600 000 kilowatt hours of electricity internally, the purchase of electricity externally so far reduces Knockshinnock's requirements for water, steam and compressed air as to make it an economic proposition.

Offer to supply electricity and water

It is a relatively simple matter to incorporate within the linear programming formulation above the offer by the Board to supply water as well as electricity. A new variable (X_6) is required, representing the number of litres of water bought from the Board. This enters the objective function C with a coefficient representing the £0.03 cost per litre, and enters constraint (5.1) on water supply just as X_5 entered constraint (5.3) on electricity supply. The reformulated problem appears as below:

$$\text{Minimise } C = 0.024X_1 + 0.4X_2 + 0.15X_3 + 0.1X_4 + 0.25X_5 + 0.03X_6$$

subject to:

$$X - 0.661X_2 - 0.044X_3 + 0X_4 + 0X_5 + X_6 = 2\,115\,000 \tag{5.1}$$

$$-0.034X_1 + X_2 - 0.181X_3 - 0.125X_4 + 0X_5 + 0X_6 = 480\,000 \tag{5.2}$$

$$-0.789X_1 - 0.331X_2 + X_3 - 0.520X_4 + X_5 + 0X_6 = 3\,180\,000 \tag{5.3}$$

$$-0.163X_1 - 0.080X_2 - 0.048X_3 + X_4 + 0X_5 + 0X_6 = 3\,570\,000 \tag{5.4}$$

The solution to this problem involves a cost per annum of £2 166 979, with values of the variables as follows:

$$X_1 = 0; \ X_2 = 935\,606; \ X_3 = 0; \ X_4 = 3\,644\,848;$$
$$X_5 = 5\,385\,007; \ X_6 = 2\,733\,435$$

Although buying 2 733 435 litres per annum of water from the Board increases the total water bill from £68 074 (with internal production) to £82 003, the overall effect of purchasing water from the Board is to diminish cost by almost £730 000 per annum. This very large saving arises predominantly because 35 per cent of the electricity consumed on site is used in pumping water, and electricity is the most expensive of the services. It is interesting to note that it is in fact against the Board's interests to supply water to the Knockshinnock site, in that it loses far more revenue from diminished electricity consumption that it gains from sales of water. However, unless the Board could gain access to information about the pattern of electricity consumption on the Knockshinnock site prior to entering into a commitment to supply water to that site, it would be unable to avoid acting contrary to its own interests.

Linear Programming, Opportunity Losses and *ex post* Budgeting

6

6.1 Araque Perfumes Ltd

Araque Perfumes Ltd produces two perfumes, called Fleur and Jasmin. Each of these products requires four raw materials (P, Q, R and S), and passes through two processes (A and B). Denote the production (in litres) of Fleur as X_1 and of Jasmin as X_2. The following data then indicates the requirement for process time and for raw material input per litre of each product produced. It also indicates planned variable costs, together with the amount of process time and the volume of each raw material planned to be available during March 1989:

	Planned requirements per litre of product	
Process	Fleur	Jasmin
	hr	hr
A	1.6	1.1
B	0.8	1.8
Material		
	l	l
P	3.2	2.2
Q	7.2	8.7
R	3.2	4.7
S	2.4	2.9

Planned resource cost and availability
(March 1989)

Process	Resource availability hr	Variable cost £ per hr
A	8 800	5
B	10 000	10
Material	l	£ per l
P	25 000	1
Q	50 000	2
R	30 000	3
S	20 000	1.50

Fleur sells for £50.80 per litre and Jasmin sells for £63.55. During March 1989, 4 250 litres of Fleur were produced but no Jasmin was produced at all, and a contribution of £44 200 was earned. Actual variable costs during March 1989, and the actual availability of process time and of raw materials, may be tabulated as follows:

Actual resource cost and availability
(March 1989)

Process	Resource availability hr	Variable cost £ per hr
A	6 800	5
B	6 000	10
Material	l	£ per l
P	17 500	1
Q	40 000	2
R	18 000	1
S	14 000	1.50

All of the differences between planned and actual resource cost and availability during March 1989 arose for reasons outside the control of Araque's management:

You are required:

1. To use traditional cost variance analysis in computing:
   (a) The variance attributable to sales volume and sales mix together

    (b) The variance jointly attributable to sales prices, to the prices of variable inputs and to efficiency in the usage of these inputs.

2. To use *ex post* budgeting in computing the forecast variance and the opportunity cost variance, breaking each of these down into:
    (a) The portion of the variance attributable to volume and mix changes
    (b) The portion of the variance attributable to price and efficiency changes.
3. The *ex post* optimising model for March 1989 may be used as the *ex ante* optimising model for April. Conditions in April proved to be the same as those actually prevailing in March, with three exceptions. First, for reasons over which Araque's management exercised no influence, they could only purchase Material R at £1 per litre during the first half of April; in the second half it cost £3 per litre. Second, throughout April there was a technical problem in applying Process B to the production of Fleur, resulting in each litre of Fleur requiring 0.9 hours to go through Process B instead of 0.8 hours. This technical problem arose from a design flaw for which Araque's management could not be blamed. However, the third deviation from plan in April was caused by an avoidable error in product specification, which caused the consumption of Material P to rise from 3.2 litres to 3.8 litres per litre of Fleur produced.

    During April, Araque carried out production at a constant rate and produced 3 400 litres of Fleur and 800 litres of Jasmin, earning a contribution of £24 400. **You are required** to perform the same analysis as under 2(a) and 2(b) above for April 1989.

6.2 Analysis

Introduction

Before addressing the facts relating to Araque Perfumes, some preliminaries are required to establish fundamental concepts and terminology. Consider a very simple linear programming problem, in which the objective is to find the optimal mix of products X_1 and X_2 to be produced in a budget period, with no opening or closing inventories of either product. The contribution margins per unit for X_1 and X_2 are respectively c_1 and c_2, and both products are manufactured in a single department, which has b hours of manufacturing time available within the budget period. Product X_1 uses up a_{11} hours of manufacturing time per unit produced, and product X_2 uses up a_{12} hours. With the addition of a slack variable X_3 to convert the inequality constraint on manufacturing time to an equality, this problem may be formulated as follows:

$$\text{Maximise } c_1 X_1 + c_2 X_2 + 0 X_3$$
$$\text{Subject to: } a_{11} X_1 + a_{12} X_2 + X_3 = b$$

To compress the notation let:

$$C = [c_1 \quad c_2 \quad 0]$$
$$X^T = [X_1 \quad X_2 \quad X_3]$$
$$\text{and } A = [a_{11} \quad a_{12} \quad 1]$$

Then the problem appears as:

$$\text{Maximise } CX \text{ subject to } AX = b$$

Expressing the problem in this form focuses attention on the three data inputs A, b and C. It is possible to set out to solve this problem at two different times, as below.

1. Before the budget period commences, the optimal solution can be worked out based upon preperiod knowledge. The data inputs for this *ex ante* problem will be distinguished by a superscripts, so that they will appear as A^a, b^a and C^a, and the

outputs of products in the optimum *ex ante* plan will appear correspondingly as X^a.

2. After the budget period is over, the revised knowledge of A, b and C gained during it can be used to work out what it would have been optimal to do within the period if perfect knowledge had been available of the conditions that were going to prevail during it. The data inputs for this *ex post* problem will be represented as A^p, b^p and C^p, and the outputs of this *ex post* problem will be represented as X^p.

The inputs to the problem actually observed during the period will be represented as A^o, b^o and C^o. If, for example, $C^o = C^p$, this signifies that the contribution margins actually obtained were the best that could have been obtained, so that any deviations of actual margins C^o from margins in the *ex ante* plan C^a must be regarded as having arisen for reasons outside the management's control. Conversely, $C^o < C^p$ implies some controllable shortfall of contribution margins actually obtained below those which could have been obtained had the firm acted optimally with perfect hindsight. To complete the terminology, the amounts of products X_1 and X_2 actually produced during the budget period will be denoted as X^o.

Traditional variance analysis

In traditional variance analysis, the *ex ante* plan is compared against the actual outcome, without considering the *ex post* optimum plan at all. The only adjustment made to the *ex ante* plan in traditional variance analysis is to adjust the level of budgeted expenditure to the level of production actually achieved, in the process known as flexible budgeting. Representing the budgeted contribution with flexible budgeting as $C^a X^o$, an overview of traditional variance analysis can be given as follows:

$$C^a X^a - C^o X^o = (C^a X^a - C^a X^o) + (C^a X^o - C^o X^o)$$

Here, $C^a X^a$ and $C^o X^o$ represent respectively contribution in the *ex ante* plan and contribution actually achieved. The first term on the right, $C^a X^a - C^a X^o$, represents the sum of the sales volume and sales mix variances, shortened hereafter to the 'volume and mix variance'. The second term on the right, $C^a X^o - C^o X^o$, represents the sum of the sales price variances and the variances relating to the price and efficiency of usage of variable inputs. This will be labelled hereafter the 'price and efficiency variance'.

The computation of these variances may now be illustrated by reference to the Araque Perfumes problem. Working out contribution per litre figures for Fleur and Jasmin in March on an *ex ante* basis (using expected costs) gives rise to an objective function as follows:

Maximise $4X_1 + 2X_2$

This maximisation is subject to six constraints relating to the availability of process time and of raw materials:

$$1.6X_1 + 1.1X_2 \leq 8\,800 \tag{1.1}$$
$$0.8X_1 + 1.8X_2 \leq 10\,000 \tag{1.2}$$
$$3.2X_1 + 2.2X_2 \leq 25\,000 \tag{1.3}$$
$$7.2X_1 + 8.7X_2 \leq 50\,000 \tag{1.4}$$
$$3.2X_1 + 4.7X_2 \leq 30\,000 \tag{1.5}$$
$$2.4X_1 + 2.9X_2 \leq 20\,000 \tag{1.6}$$

Solving this problem yields an *ex ante* optimum of $X_1^a = 5\,500$, $X_2^a = 0$. However, in March 1989, Material R turned out to cost only £1 per litre, thus increasing the available contribution margin to £10.40 per litre of Fleur (X_1) and £11.40 per litre of Jasmin (X_2). Araque produced in March an amount $X_1^o = 4\,250$, $X_2^o = 0$, to earn a contribution of $4\,250$ (£10.40) = £44\,200, as compared with the *ex ante* planned contribution of $5\,500$ (£4) = £22\,000. Carrying out traditional variance analysis gives rise to the following tabulation, represented in a columnar format in which the symbols making up each expression are shown on the left-hand side and the figures corresponding to each expression for this problem are shown on the right-hand side:

$$
\begin{aligned}
&C^a\,X^a - C^o\,X^o = &&\text{£} \\
&(C^a\,X^a - C^a\,X^o) + &&22\,000 - 44\,200 = \\
&(C^a X^o - C^o\,X^o) &&[22\,000 - (4)\,(4\,250)] + \\
& &&[(4)\,(4\,250) - 44\,200]
\end{aligned}
$$

Computation then yields the following result:

	£	
Volume and mix variance	5 000*U*	(unfavourable)
Price and efficiency variance	27 200*F*	(favourable)
Total variance	22 200*F*	(favourable)

Ex post *variance analysis*

A very much more sophisticated analysis of the difference between the *ex ante* optimum plan and the actual outcome can be obtained if the *ex post* optimum plan is also considered, to give a breakdown as follows:

$$C^a X^a - C^o X^o = (C^a X^a - C^p X^p) + (C^p X^p - C^o X^o)$$

The first of the variances on the right-hand side, $C^a X^a - C^p X^p$, represents the difference between planned and *ex post* contribution, and in doing so indicates roughly the accuracy of the forecasting process contained in the budget. It may thus be referred to as the 'forecast variance'. The second variance, $C^p X^p - C^o X^o$, represents the difference between what, with hindsight, would have been the optimum contribution, and the contribution actually achieved. As such, it measures the opportunity cost of failing to use the firm's resources in the way which would have turned out to maximise contribution, and it may therefore be referred to as the 'opportunity cost variance'.

The distinction between the 'volume and mix variance' and the 'price and efficiency variance' noted above may be applied to *ex post* variance analysis to yield the further subdivision of variances tabulated below:

$C^a X^a - C^o X^o =$	Total variance =
$[C^p(X^a - X^p) +$	Volume and mix forecast
	variance +

$(C^a - C^p) X^a] +$	Price and efficiency forecast variance +
$[C^p (X^p - X^o) +$	Volume and mix opportunity cost variance +
$(C^p - C^o) X^o]$	Price and efficiency opportunity cost variance

The computation and interpretation of these variances may best be illustrated by a numerical example. Given the resource availabilities and variable costs that actually prevailed during March 1989, the best performance attainable by Araque Perfumes (the one yielding the largest contribution) is given by the solution to the following problem:

Maximise $10.4X_1 + 11.4X_2$

Subject to:

$$1.6X_1 + 1.1X_2 \leqq 6\,800 \tag{2.1}$$
$$0.8X_1 + 1.8X_2 \leqq 6\,000 \tag{2.2}$$
$$3.2X_1 + 2.2X_2 \leqq 17\,500 \tag{2.3}$$
$$7.2X_1 + 8.7X_2 \leqq 40\,000 \tag{2.4}$$
$$3.2X_1 + 4.7X_2 \leqq 18\,000 \tag{2.5}$$
$$2.4X_1 + 2.9X_2 \leqq 14\,000 \tag{2.6}$$

Solving this problem yields $X_1^p = 3\,040$, $X_2^p = 1\,760$, for a contribution of £51 680. Calculations for the *ex post* variance analysis may be tabulated in the same format as was employed for traditional variance analysis, to give:

$C^a X^a - C^o X^o =$	$22\,000 - 44\,200 =$
$[C^p(X^a - X^p) +$	$[\{(10.4)(5\,500-3\,040) + 11.4)(0 - 1\,760)\} +$
$(C^a - C^p) X^a] +$	$(4 - 10.4)(5\,500)] +$
$[C^p(X^p - X^o) +$	$[\{(10.4)(3\,040-4\,250) + 11.4)(1\,760 - 0)\} +$
$(C^p - C^o)X^o]$	$(10.4 - 10.4)(4\,250)]$

By computation, the variances are as follows:

	£
Volume and mix forecast variance	5 520U
Price and efficiency forecast variance	35 200F
Volume and mix opportunity cost variance	7 480U
Price and efficiency opportunity cost variance	0
Total variance	22 200F

Attention may first be focused on the unfavourable volume and mix opportunity cost variance, which indicates the amount that has been lost by pressing on with the *ex ante* optimum plan and producing exclusively Fleur (X_1), thus ignoring the need to adapt mix and volume to the new opportunities for the profitable production of Jasmin (X_2) arising from the fact that Material R turned out to be much cheaper than was budgeted. This variance may be contrasted with the volume and mix variance in traditional variance analysis, which indicates the loss occasioned by producing less Fleur than was budgeted ($X_1^o = 4\,250$ instead of $X_1^a = 5\,500$), without giving any indication whatever that producing entirely Fleur and no Jasmin was in any case inappropriate. Since $X_2^a = X_2^o = 0$, the fact that some Jasmin should have been produced during March 1989 is not revealed by traditional variance analysis, into which the figure for X_2^p does not enter.

The volume and mix forecast variance shows by how much the contribution available in the *ex post* optimal plan diverges from the contribution that would have been available had the *ex ante* optimal volume and mix of production been sold with the *ex post* optimal contribution margins. Similarly, the price and efficiency forecast variance shows by how much the contribution that could have been earned *ex post* on the *ex ante* optimal volume and mix diverges from the contribution that could have been earned *ex ante* on that volume and mix. The description of either forecasting variance as 'favourable' or 'unfavourable' is arithmetically neces-sary but managerially meaningless; these labels simply indicate the direction of the divergence between *ex ante* and *ex post*, and there is no reason to assume that a forecasting error in one direction is to be preferred to an equally-sized error in the opposite direction.

Finally, the price and efficiency opportunity cost variance indicates the loss (if any) incurred as a result of actual contribution margins falling below those which could have been achieved on the actual production. This variance will be illustrated in the next section, which is concerned with variations in conditions within a budget period.

Intra-period relationships

In proceeding to deal with part 3. of the Araque Perfumes problem, the first point to make is that the formulation of the *ex post* model for March serves the dual purpose of assisting with control in March and assisting with planning in April. For this problem, the expectation held at the end of March is that April will have the same conditions as prevailed in March. Consequently, the *ex ante* model for April has the same form and the same optimal solution as the *ex post* model for March, so that for April $X_1^a = 3\,040$, $X_2^a = 1\,760$ for a contribution of £51 680. In general, even if the conditions are expected to change as between the budget period that has just passed and the budget period that is about to commence, it may well still be useful to draw up the *ex post* model for the past budget period as a 'base case' to which revisions can be applied for the period to come.

The first complication in deriving the *ex post* model for April arises because the price of Material R changed halfway through the month, affecting the contribution margins for Fleur and Jasmin. For the first half of April, the margins were £10.40 per litre for Fleur and £11.40 per litre for Jasmin, but for the second half the Material R price increase caused them to fall to £4 per litre for Fleur and £2 per litre for Jasmin. This change can be dealt with by treating each product before and after the price increase as two separate products. Taking this approach involves the definition of four new variables. Let:

X_1 represent the production of Fleur (in litres) during the first half of April

X_2 represent the production of Jasmin (in litres) during the first half of April

X_3 represent the production of Fleur (in litres) during the second half of April

X_4 represent the production of Jasmin (in litres) during the second half of April

Allowing only for the Material R price increase would give rise to an objective function having coefficients of 10.4 associated with X_1, 11.4 with X_2, 4 with X_3 and 2 with X_4. However, this would fail to allow for the increase in the time required to process a litre of Fleur through Process B. This increase, from 0.8 hours to 0.9 hours, persisted throughout April and arose for reasons outside the control of Araque's management. Since even with perfect hindsight this increase could not have been avoided, the *ex post* optimal model must allow for its consequences. These involve a reduction in the contribution available on Fleur by £1 per litre, to give rise to a final objective function for April as follows:

$$\text{Maximise } 9.4X_1 + 11.4X_2 + 3X_3 + 2X_4$$

Since the objective function is now in four variables, each of the constraints must also be placed in this form. On the assumption that the availability of raw materials and of process time did not vary from week to week during April, the right-hand side values of constraints (2.1) – (2.6) above require to be halved, and two constraints inserted for every one that was present before. Consider, for example, constraint (2.1), which relates to Process A. Conditions for this process in April were identical to those prevailing in March, so that the March constraint of $1.6X_1 + 1.1X_2 \leqq 6\,800$ may be broken down into a constraint for the first half of April of $1.6X_1 + 1.1X_2 \leqq 3\,400$ and a constraint for the second half of April of $1.6X_3 + 1.1X_4 \leqq 3\,400$. These two new constraints are represented as constraints (3.1) and (3.2) below, and constraints (3.7) – (3.12) below are derived in an exactly identical manner. A discussion of the remaining constraints (3.3) – (3.6) is given after the full listing of the *ex post* model for April, which is as follows:

$$\text{Maximise } 9.4X_1 + 11.4X_2 + 3X_3 + 2X_4$$

Subject to:

$$1.6X_1 + 1.1X_2 + 0X_3 + 0X_4 \leqq 3\,400 \tag{3.1}$$
$$0X_1 + 0X_2 + 1.6X_3 + 1.1X_4 \leqq 3\,400 \tag{3.2}$$
$$0.9X_1 + 1.8X_2 + 0X_3 + 0X_4 \leqq 3\,000 \tag{3.3}$$
$$0X_1 + 0X_2 + 0.9X_3 + 1.8X_4 \leqq 3\,000 \tag{3.4}$$
$$3.2X_1 + 2.2X_2 + 0X_3 + 0X_4 \leqq 8\,750 \tag{3.5}$$
$$0X_1 + 0X_2 + 3.2X_3 + 2.2X_4 \leqq 8\,750 \tag{3.6}$$
$$7.2X_1 + 8.7X_2 + 0X_3 + 0X_4 \leqq 20\,000 \tag{3.7}$$
$$0X_1 + 0X_2 + 7.2X_3 + 8.7X_4 \leqq 20\,000 \tag{3.8}$$
$$3.2X_1 + 4.7X_2 + 0X_3 + 0X_4 \leqq 9\,000 \tag{3.9}$$
$$0X_1 + 0X_2 + 3.2X_3 + 4.7X_4 \leqq 9\,000 \tag{3.10}$$
$$2.4X_1 + 2.9X_2 + 0X_3 + 0X_4 \leqq 7\,000 \tag{3.11}$$
$$0X_1 + 0X_2 + 2.4X_3 + 2.9X_4 \leqq 7\,000 \tag{3.12}$$

Constraints (3.3) – (3.6) do not present any difficult issues. As regards constraints (3.3) and (3.4), the only respect in which they do not represent a simple 'halving' of constraint (2.2) in the *ex post* model for March lies in the substitution of 0.9 for 0.8 as the coefficient for X_1 and X_3. This arises because of the increase of 0.1 hour in the time taken to pass a litre of Fleur through Process B. By contrast, no modification is made to the X_1 and X_3 coefficients in constraints (3.5) and (3.6) to allow for the increase in the consumption of Material P from 3.2 to 3.8 litres per litre of Fleur produced. The point here is that this relatively heavy use of Material P arose from an *avoidable* error, so that the *ex post* optimum plan, applying perfect hindsight to the elimination of all deviations from optimality which could have been avoided, must take no notice of it.

The *ex post* model for April may be solved either as a single linear programming problem in four variables, or as two linear programming problems, one in X_1 and X_2 and the other in X_3 and X_4. The latter approach is quicker computationally, as it removes the need to insert the zeros in the left-hand sides of constraints (3.1) – (3.12) above. Whichever approach is taken, the optimum solution is $X_1^p = 1\,520$, $X_2^p = 880$, $X_3^p = 2\,125$, $X_4^p = 0$ for a contribution of £30 695. The *ex ante* optimal solution turns out to have been optimal only for the first half of April; in the second half it would have been optimal to concentrate entirely on Fleur and produce no Jasmin at all.

In fact, Araque's management did not respond in any way to this change of conditions as between the first and second halves of April; in both halves of the month they followed identical production plans, giving rise to an actual output of $X_1^o = 1\,700$, $X_2^o = 400$, $X_3^o = 1\,700$, $X_4^o = 400$. Using the techniques already outlined, an *ex post* variance analysis for April can be drawn up as follows:

	First half	*Second half*
$C^p X^a$	$9.4(3\,040/2)+11.4(1\,760/2)$	$3(3\,040/2)+2(1\,760/2)$
	$= 24\,320$	$= 6\,320$
$C^p X^p$	$9.4(1\,520)+11.4(880)$	$3(2\,125)+2(0)$
	$= 24\,320$	$= 6\,375$
$C^a X^a$	$10.4(3\,040/2)+11.4(1\,760/2)$	$10.4(3\,040/2)+11.4(1\,760/2)$
	$= 25\,840$	$= 25\,840$
$C^p X^o$	$9.4(3\,400/2)+11.4(800/2)$	$3(3\,400/2)+2(800/2)$
	$= 20\,540$	$= 5\,900$
$C^o X^o$	$(9.4 - 0.6)(3\,400/2) + 11.4(800/2)$	$(3 - 0.6)(3\,400/2)+2(800/2)$
	$= 19\,520$	$= 4\,880$

First half of April:	£	£
Volume and mix forecast variance	0	
Price and efficiency forecast variance	1 520U	
Volume and mix opportunity cost variance	3 780U	
Price and efficiency opportunity cost variance	1 020U	6 320U

Second half of April:		
Volume and mix forecast variance	55F	
Price and efficiency forecast variance	19 520U	
Volume and mix opportunity cost variance	475U	
Price and efficiency opportunity cost variance	1 020U	20 960U
Total variance		27 280U

In the above tabulation, the total variance is equal to the excess of the planned contribution for April (£51 680) over the actual contribution for April (£24 400). The interpretation of the four variances obtained for each half of April may be undertaken as follows:

1. While the volume and mix of production was forecast correctly for the first half of April, Araque's management forecast inaccurately by £55 the contribution it could potentially earn in the second half because it failed to specify correctly the optimum volume and mix of production in the second half.

   It should be noted that while this failure of forecasting happens to have given rise to a 'favourable' variance (because $C^p X^a < C^p X^p$), this failure is neither more nor less serious than would be a failure giving rise to an 'unfavourable' variance of £55.

2. The failure to forecast the extra time required to pass Fleur through Process B caused Araque's management to overestimate by £1 520 the contribution that could potentially be earned with the *ex ante* optimum volume and mix in the first half of April.

   This overestimation of the potential contribution from the *ex ante* optimal volume and mix rose to £19 520 in the second half of April because of the failure to forecast the price increase for Material R which took place then.

3. The volume and mix opportunity cost variances represent the loss of contribution arising from the divergence of the actual from the *ex post* optimal volume and mix of production.

   This divergence is valued by reference to *ex post* optimal contribution margins.

   In this case, Araque Perfumes fell £3 780 below the *ex post* optimum contribution in the first half and £475 below the *ex post* optimum contribution in the second half of April as a result of the divergence between X^o and X^p.

4. Finally, Araque Perfumes lost £1 020 in each half of April as a result of failing to earn optimal contribution margins per unit on their actual production.

   This failure to earn optimal margins arose entirely because of the excess usage of Material P in producing Fleur, giving rise to an adverse variance of 0.6 (£1 700) = £1 020 in each half of April.

Shortcomings of the ex post *approach*

Since *ex post* variance analysis has been subjected to sustained
criticism in the literature, it would be quite wrong to leave this
problem without outlining what are said to be its shortcomings.
The critique of *ex post* variance analysis may be summarised in
terms of five major lines of argument.

A very powerful attack may be mounted by concentrating on the
dependence of *ex post* analysis on a static optimising model.
Consideration of the material availability constraints in Araque
Perfumes makes it plain that if one of these is not binding, then
some of the material to which it relates will be left over at the end
of the month, and this in turn will change the value of the
right-hand side of the constraint for this material in the next
month. An example of this is provided by Material Q in April.
There are 40 000 litres of this material available, but only 31 440
litres are used up in producing April's actual output. If this
material is storable, then in May 1989 there will be 40 000 + (40
000 − 31 440) = 48 560 litres of Material Q available. The fact
that the right-hand side value for May's Material Q constraint is
48 560 not 40 000 may affect the optimal solution for May. This
immediately raises the general point that where decisions taken in
this period may affect a subsequent period's profitability, then
maximisation in this period may prove suboptimal overall. If,
then, it is inappropriate to use a static single-period model, it must
also be inappropriate to build a variance analysis system around
such a model, and especially inappropriate to use two single-
period models within one month yet assume that there is no
interaction between them (as was done for Araque Perfumes in
April).

A related point about modelling is that the *ex post* approach can
be applied only to situations in which an optimising model of some
kind (not necessarily involving linear programming) can be constructed. This approach is thus unsuited to situations in which the
production technology is very imperfectly understood, or in which
there is substantial dispute among management concerning organi-
sational objectives. Nor is it suited to situations of such complexity
that the cost of building optimising models would exceed the
benefits to be derived from them.

Turning next to the outputs of *ex post* analysis, the opportunity cost variances must always be negative, since they represent the losses arising either from failures to produce the optimum volume and mix of output or from failures to achieve the optimum contribution margins per unit. Managers may feel discouraged and resentful when faced always with adverse variances, relating their actual performance to a level of perfection unattainable in reality. An outlook may develop that since variances against optimality must always be unfavourable, perhaps the size of these variances does not matter too much.

These adverse motivational effects associated with perpetually unfavourable opportunity cost variances may be aggravated by a further restrictive assumption inherent in *ex post* analysis. This asserts that all uncontrollable changes in the parameters *A, b* and *C* must be deemed to occur at the very beginning of the budget period, with no further changes taking place during the course of the period. Suppose that this assumption were to be violated by an uncontrollable parameter change occurring near the end of a budget period. Insofar as this change influenced the *ex post* optimal budget, the difference it caused between this optimal budget and actual performance could not reasonably be treated as representing an opportunity loss applicable to the *whole* budget period, only to the period *after* the parameter change. However, the *ex post* approach treats the budget period as a unitary whole, and is not capable of adjusting for changes part-way through it. The opportunity loss associated with parameter changes late in the budget period will thus be mis-stated, giving rise to inaccurate measures of the opportunity cost variances. To the extent that these inaccuracies are visible, confidence in the *ex post* budgeting system may be lost.

There is no reason in principle why the *ex post* approach should not be modified to deal with this problem by recalculating the optimal solution every time a parameter change affects it, and comparing actual performance against this newly optimal perform-ance for the period between this parameter change and the next change affecting the optimal solution. However, this would be expensive to implement administratively, and would result in budget periods of uneven length unless parameter changes took place at regular and predictable intervals. If, though, parameter changes could be forecast with moderate accuracy, it would seem possible to incorporate them in *ex ante* budgets, thus largely avoiding the need for *ex post* analysis.

A fifth and last point is that, for managerial purposes, it would be useful to split the forecast variances into three parts, as follows:

1. The variance that would have arisen even had the best forecasting methods available been used throughout – as representing the unavoidable 'costs of uncertainty'.
2. The variance attributable to conscious decisions not to attempt to implement the *ex ante* optimal plan because of changes in expectations during the budget period.
3. The variance attributable to imperfections in the forecasting techniques employed in drawing up the *ex ante* optimal plan.

It is only part 3 of these variances which can really be described as a measure of forecast quality, yet there is a temptation to regard all of the forecast variances in this light. This is especially so since the measurement problems involved in breaking down forecast variances into components 1, 2 and 3 above are almost certainly insuperable.

Input–Output Analysis and Linear Programming

7A.1 Taumor Industries

Taumor Industries manufactures fine chemicals. Its Leamouth factory makes two products called Noractil and Penebor by means of four distinct processes. The processes are numbered I – IV, and the flow of product through them may be depicted as in Figure 7A.1.

FIGURE 7A.1
Taumor Industries – Product Flow

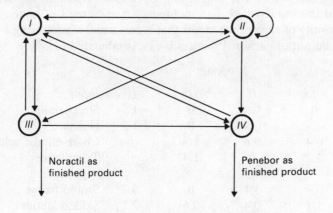

Noractil as
finished product

Penebor as
finished product

Each of these processes produces a single product; the output of Process I is called Product I, and so on (thus calling Noractil Product III and Penebor Product IV). Using the interrelationships shown in Figure 7A.1, the amount of each product used up to produce a unit of output of each of Products I to IV is tabulated as below. For Product II and III a unit of output is 1 litre, and for Products I and IV a unit of output is 1 kilogram. Hence this table shows (for example) that each kilogram of Product IV manufactured requires 0.3 kilograms of Product I, 0.25 litres of Product II and 0.6 litres of Product III.

Processes

I	II	III	IV	Products
0	0.7	0.4	0.3	I
0.4	0.15	0.5	0.25	II
0.2	0	0	0.6	III
0.1	0	0	0	IV

As well as using internally-supplied products, the processes use inputs of materials, machine time and labour. Of the three materials required, two of them (strepsamin and niamate) have the amount of their input measured in kilograms, and one (chlorsulfonic acid) has the amount of its input measured in litres. Two types of machine are employed, one to carry out the task of turbulence patterning and the other the task of strand fixing. Inputs from both types of machine are measured in terms of machine hours. The labour employed is divided into the skilled and the semi-skilled, and its inputs are measured in hours. The quantity of each of the inputs that is consumed in producing a unit of output of each of Products I – IV is tabulated below:

Processes

I	II	III	IV	Input
0	0.8	0	−1.5	Strepsamin
1.4	0.9	0	1.2	Niamate
0.4	0.6	1.8	0	Chlorsulfonic acid
2.2	0	1.4	0	Turbulence patterning
0.9	3.1	0	0.7	Strand fixing
1.1	0.4	0.6	2.1	Skilled labour
2.4	1.9	1.1	1.3	Semi-skilled labour

The negative number for strepsamin in Process IV indicates that 1.5 kilograms of strepsamin are *produced* (as a by-product) for each kilogram of Penebor manufactured. Strepsamin serves as an input to Process II, and any amount of it can be either bought or sold externally at a price of £3 per kilogram.

Niamate costs £8 per kilogram, and chlorsulfonic acid £6 per litre. Both are available in what are effectively unlimited quantities. The skilled labour is paid £3.50 per hour and the semi-skilled labour £2.75 per hour.

In April 1989, there are 900 hours of skilled labour and 2 000 hours of semi-skilled labour available. The turbulence patterning machines can work for no more than 1 100 hours in April, and the strand fixing machines for no more than 1 300 hours. These machines perform slow, precise operations consuming negligibly small amounts of electricity, and technical change relating to them is so rapid that they will be scrapped as obsolete long before they are physically worn out.

The management of Taumor Industries have set a price of £135 per litre for Noractil and £170 per kilogram for Penebor. They believe that they can sell all they can produce of either product at these prices, but existing contractual commitments mean that they must produce at least 70 litres of Noractil and 55 kilograms of Penebor during April.

You are required:

1. To advise the management of Taumor as to the number of litres of Noractil and kilograms of Penebor they should produce for sale during April.
2. To take this optimum volume and mix, and work out from it:
   (a) The number of units of Products I – IV that will need to be manufactured during April.
   (b) The amounts of each of the inputs that will be used up during April, including the net amount of strepsamin bought or sold.

7A.2   Analysis

Computation of variable costs

This problem is characterised by a complex system of product flows, in which (for example) Product I from Process I acts as an input to Processes II, III and IV, while Product II from Process II is fed back to Process I as an input, as well as entering into Processes III and IV. A further complication is that some of the Product II is fed back into the process of its own manufacture (Process II) as a raw material, perhaps to act as a catalyst. Given the dense interaction of the product flows, it is useful to be able to model them as an input–output system, from which to compute variable cost data for insertion in a linear programming format.

Since each process produces a single product, a unit of activity of a process may be defined as the amount of activity required to produce one unit (1 kilogram or 1 litre) of the product from that process. From the four processes and four products of this problem, a 4×4 matrix can be generated in which the processes make up the columns and the products the rows. Let q^o_{ij} represent the number of units of Product i ($i = 1 \ldots 4$) produced by a unit of activity within Process j ($j = 1 \ldots 4$). Values of q^o_{ij} are referred to collectively as output coefficients, and the matrix of these coefficients q^o is for this problem an identity matrix of order four, as shown below:

$$q^o = \begin{bmatrix} 1 & 0 & 0 & 0 \\ 0 & 1 & 0 & 0 \\ 0 & 0 & 1 & 0 \\ 0 & 0 & 0 & 1 \end{bmatrix}$$

Let q^i_{ij} represent the number of units of Product i consumed by a unit of activity of Process j in producing a unit of Product j. Values of q^i_{ij} are referred to collectively as input coefficients, and the values of these coefficients are given within the problem. Representing the matrix of these coefficients of q^i, it appears as below:

$$q^i = \begin{bmatrix} 0 & 0.7 & 0.4 & 0.3 \\ 0.4 & 0.15 & 0.5 & 0.25 \\ 0.2 & 0 & 0 & 0.6 \\ 0.1 & 0 & 0 & 0 \end{bmatrix}$$

Next, the net input–output coefficient q_{ij} must be defined as follows:

$$q_{ij} = q_{ij}^o - q_{ij}^i$$

In this equation, q_{ij} represents the net number of units of Product i either produced or consumed by one unit of activity of Process j. The matrix of net input–output coefficients q is obtained by subtracting q^i from q^o, and computation here yields:

$$q = \begin{bmatrix} 1 & -0.7 & -0.4 & -0.3 \\ -0.4 & 0.85 & -0.5 & -0.25 \\ -0.2 & 0 & 1 & -0.6 \\ -0.1 & 0 & 0 & 1 \end{bmatrix}$$

In the Taumor Industries problem, a tabulation is given of the seven 'external' inputs (three kinds of materials, two types of machine and two grades of labour) entering into production. Let:

d_{kj} represent the number of units of input $k(k = 1 \ldots 7)$ required by one unit of activity of Process $j(j = 1 \ldots 4)$

v_k represent the variable cost per unit of input k

Then a 7×4 matrix d, with elements d_{kj}, can be drawn up directly from the problem. Alongside this can be placed a 1×7 column vector v with elements v_k, again derived directly from the problem, to give:

$$d = \begin{bmatrix} 0 & 0.8 & 0 & -1.5 \\ 1.4 & 0.9 & 0 & 1.2 \\ 0.4 & 0.6 & 1.8 & 0 \\ 2.2 & 0 & 1.4 & 0 \\ 0.9 & 3.1 & 0 & 0.7 \\ 1.1 & 0.4 & 0.6 & 2.1 \\ 2.4 & 1.9 & 1.1 & 1.3 \end{bmatrix} \quad v = \begin{bmatrix} 3 \\ 8 \\ 6 \\ 0 \\ 0 \\ 3.5 \\ 2.75 \end{bmatrix}$$

Within the v vector, $v_1 = 3$ represents the £3 per kilogram price at which strepsamin can be either bought or sold. Also within that vector, the explanation of the elements $v_4 = 0$, $v_5 = 0$ is that the variable cost of a machine hour is zero, given that depreciation is a function of time, not of usage, and that the cost of power consumed is negligble.

Having derived the above matrices, the first use that may be made of them is to find the gross amount of each product which must be manufactured in order to support the net production of one unit of each of the products in turn. This information is given within the gross internal coefficient matrix q', obtained by inverting the input–output coefficient matrix q, so that:

$$q' = q^{-1}$$

Performing this inversion yields:

$$q' = \begin{bmatrix} 2.445 & 2.014 & 1.985 & 2.428 \\ 1.597 & 2.491 & 1.884 & 2.232 \\ 0.636 & 0.524 & 1.516 & 1.231 \\ 0.245 & 0.201 & 0.199 & 1.243 \end{bmatrix}$$

It may help in interpreting the q' matrix to focus on a single element within it, say q'_{11}. The figure here signifies that the production of 1 kilogram of net output of Product I requires a gross production of 2.445 kilograms of Product I. The remaining 1.445 kilograms of Product I is used up in the process of manufacturing Products II, III and IV, all of which require Product I for their manufacture and all of which are in turn required for the manufacture of Product I. Specifically, from the q' matrix, the production of 1 kilogram of net output of Product I requires the manufacture of 1.597 litres of Product II, 0.636 litres of Product III and 0.245 kilograms of Product IV.

The requirements for other products arising from the manufacture of a unit of net output of each product are thus represented respectively by the four columns of q' for Products I – IV. Given this information, it is possible to investigate the requirement for external inputs generated by the net production of 1 unit of product. This requirement is obtained by multiplying the amount of inputs required for a unit of each product by the number of units of each product required for a unit of *net* product. Put in another way, external input requirements per unit of net product are represented by taking the d matrix and postmultiplying it by the gross internal coefficient matrix q'. Calling the resulting matrix d', the equation involved is:

$$d' = dq'$$

Carrying out this multiplication (to three decimal places) for Taumor Industries yields the following result:

$$d' = \begin{bmatrix} 0.910 & 1.691 & 1.209 & -0.079 \\ 5.154 & 5.303 & 4.713 & 6.900 \\ 3.081 & 3.243 & 4.653 & 4.526 \\ 6.269 & 5.164 & 6.489 & 7.065 \\ 7.323 & 9.675 & 7.766 & 9.974 \\ 4.224 & 3.948 & 4.265 & 6.912 \\ 9.920 & 10.404 & 10.270 & 13.038 \end{bmatrix}$$

For the interpretation of entries within this matrix, consider the elements $d'_{14} = -0.079$ and $d'_{24} = 6.900$. These lie in the fourth column, and therefore relate to the input requirements associated with the manufacture of 1 kilogram of net output of Product IV. The negative figure in d'_{14} indicates that this manufacture gives rise to the net production of 0.079 kilograms of strepsamin (the by-product) and the d'_{24} figure shows it to require the input of 6.9 kilograms of niamate. Similarly, the net production of 1 litre of Product II requires 1.691 kilograms of strepsamin (from d'_{12}) and 10.404 hours of semi-skilled labour (from d'_{72}).

Once these physical requirements for external inputs per unit of net output have been obtained, costing them out is a fairly simple matter. The 7×1 column vector v carrying the cost structure of the external inputs can be converted by transposition into 1×7 row vector v^T. It then becomes possible to postmultiply v^T by d', thus converting the physical inputs per unit of net output into variable costs per unit of net output. Representing the row vector of variable costs per unit of net output as c^T, then:

$$c^T = v^T d'$$

By computation, for Taumor Industries this gives:

$$c^T = [104.51 \quad 109.38 \quad 112.42 \quad 142.17]$$

From left to right, these are the variable costs per unit of net output for each of Products I – IV, in a form amenable to insertion in a linear programming problem.

Solution by linear programming

To formulate Taumor Industries as a linear programming problem, it is first necessary to define variables as follows. Let:

X_1 represent the output (in litres) of Noractil for April
X_2 represent the output (in kilograms) of Penebor for April

From the c^T vector, the variable cost per unit of net output is £112.42 per litre for Noractil and £142.17 per kilogram for Penebor. The problem specifies selling prices of £135 per litre and £170 per kilogram respectively for Noractil and Penebor, so that the objective function is simply:

Maximise $22.58X_1 + 27.83X_2$

Drawing up the constraints involves picking out of the d' matrix the input requirements per net unit produced of Noractil and Penebor for each of the inputs in constrained supply. The bottom four rows of the d' matrix are the appropriate ones, with coefficients taken from the third and fourth columns of each row to represent respectively the consumption of inputs per net unit produced of Noractil and Penebor. The constraints are then as follows:

$$6.489X_1 + 7.065X_2 \leq 1\,100 \qquad (1)$$
$$7.766X_1 + 9.974X_2 \leq 1\,300 \qquad (2)$$
$$4.265X_1 + 6.912X_2 \leq 900 \qquad (3)$$
$$10.27X_1 + 13.038X_2 \leq 2\,000 \qquad (4)$$

Constraint (1) relates to turbulence patterning machine hours, constraint (2) to strand fixing machine hours and constraints (3) and (4) respectively to skilled and semi-skilled labour hours.

Finally, there are two contractual commitment constraints, of the form that:

$$X_1 \geqq 70 \tag{5}$$
$$X_2 \geqq 55 \tag{6}$$

This completed linear programming problem has a solution of $X_1 = 96.76$, $X_2 = 55$ to give a contribution of £3 715.47. The optimum solution, therefore, is to manufacture for sale 96.76 litres of Noractil and 55 kilograms of Penebor during April 1989. It is important to note that these figures relate to *net* output, and that the total (gross) output of each of Products I – IV that will need to be manufactured during April is the subject of a subsequent question. To obtain the gross outputs, first let $\bar{Q}^T$ denote the row vector of optimal net outputs of Products I – IV, so that:

$$\bar{Q}^T = [0 \quad 0 \quad 96.76 \quad 55]$$

The gross internal coefficient matrix q' gives the gross amount of each product which must be manufactured to support the net production of a unit of each product. Consequently, the total production of each product required to support the output must be given by postmultiplying q' by $\bar{Q}$. Denoting the resulting (4 × 1) column vector as $\hat{Q}$, then:

$$\hat{Q} = q'\bar{Q}$$

Computation yields:

$$\hat{Q}^T = [325.61 \quad 305.06 \quad 214.39 \quad 87.62]$$

This vector shows that in order to yield the optimal outputs of Noractil and Penebor, it is necessary to produce in total 325.61 kilograms of Product I, 305.06 litres of Product II, 214.39 litres of Noractil and 87.62 kilograms of Penebor.

To find the volume of inputs which must be supplied to sustain this level of overall activity, it is simply necessary to postmultiply the d matrix by $\hat{Q}$. The resulting (7×1) column vector of input requirements may be labelled $\bar{D}$, where:

$$\bar{D} = d\,\hat{Q}$$

Performing the computations leads to a vector as follows:

$$\bar{D} = \begin{bmatrix} 112.6 \\ 835.6 \\ 699.2 \\ 1\,016.5 \\ 1\,300.0 \\ 792.8 \\ 1\,710.8 \end{bmatrix}$$

The $\bar{D}_{11}$ element above may be interpreted as showing that in order to sustain the optimum production it is necessary to purchase 112.6 kilograms of strepsamin (over and above that amount that arises as a by-product of Process IV). Similarly, the $\bar{D}_{51}$ element shows that the constraint on strand fixing machine hours is a binding one, with all the 1 300 hours available being used up.

As a final point, it is worth noting that the total variable cost of the optimum output may be represented by TV, where:

$$TV = c^{T}\hat{Q} = \text{£}18\,697.1$$

The contribution from the optimum output is thus given by (96.76) (£135) + (55) (£170) − £18 697.1 = £3 715.5, which agrees with the optimum value derived from the linear programming solution (apart from a slight rounding error).

Input–Output Analysis and Linear Programming 7B

with Purchasable Intermediate Products and Joint Final Products

7B.1 Salmedge Products

Salmedge Products is a small firm engaged in biotechnology. Its manufacturing activity involves three processes, numbered I – III. Process III gives rise to two joint products, Ramethos and Kegebrol, produced in fixed proportions; 0.6 kilograms of Ramethos are produced for each litre of Kegebrol made. Processes I and II each serve to manufacture a single product (Products I and II respectively). The flow of product through the processes may be depicted as in Figure 7B.1.

For Product I the unit of output is 1 litre, and for Product II it is 1 kilogram. Process III results in a unit of output made up of 1 litre of Kegebrol and 0.6 kilograms of Ramethos together. Using the interrelationships shown in Figure 7B.1 the amount of each product used up in producing a unit of output from each process may be tabulated as below:

	Processes		
I	*II*	*III*	*Products*
0.2	1.8	1.3	Product I
0.2	0	0.9	Product II
0	0	0	Kegebrol
0	0	0	Ramethos

79

FIGURE 7B.1
Salmedge Products – Product Flow

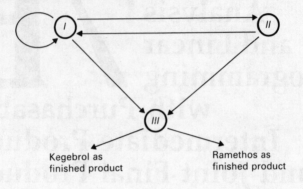

Kegebrol as
finished product

Ramethos as
finished product

As well as using internally supplied products, the processes use
two types of material and a single grade of labour; in addition they
all take up time on a centrifuge. The material called ninofane has
the amount of its input measured in kilograms, while the other
material, triglycol, has the amount of its input measured in litres.
Inputs of labour and of centrifuge time are measured in hours. The
amount of each of the inputs required to produce a unit of output
from each of the processes may be tabulated as below:

	Processes		
I	*II*	*III*	*Input*
0	1.4	1.3	Ninofane
2.2	0	2.6	Triglycol
1.1	1.6	3.1	Labour
1.4	1.1	1.9	Centrifuge time

In January 1989, there are 700 hours of labour and 500 hours of
centrifuge time available. The variable costs of centrifuge operation may be taken as negligible. Ninofane can be bought for £4 per
kilogram, and triglycol for £2 per litre; both are available in
virtually unlimited quantities. Labour is paid £3 per hour.

Instead of manufacturing Product I in Process I and Product II in Process II, it is possible to buy either of these products on the open market. Product I costs £28 per litre and Product II costs £38 per kilogram.

The management of Salmedge have set a selling price of £60 per litre for Kegebrol and one of £52 per kilogram for Ramethos. They feel that they can sell all they can produce of either product at these prices.

You are required to advise Salmedge as to:

1. The number of litres of Kegebrol and kilograms of Ramethos that should be produced for sale during January.
2. The number of units of Products I and II that will need to be manufactured during January.
3. The number of units of Products I and II that will need to be purchased during January.
4. The amount of each of the inputs that will be used up during January.

7B.2 Analysis

Formulation and solution by linear programming

This problem builds upon the techniques employed in dealing with the Taumor Industries problem, to which reference should be made. It is, however, rather more complex, in that the final process of manufacture in Salmedge Products gives rise to two joint products. A unit of activity for Process III in Salmedge consists of the amount of activity required to produce 1 litre of Kegebrol and 0.6 kilograms of Ramethos *together*. By contrast, in Processes I and II a unit of activity is the amount of activity required to produce one unit of the *sole* product of each process. Using the same terminology as in the Taumor Industries problem, the matrices of output coefficients, input coefficients and net input–output coefficients appear as follows:

$$q^o = \begin{bmatrix} 1 & 0 & 0 \\ 0 & 1 & 0 \\ 0 & 0 & 1 \\ 0 & 0 & 0.6 \end{bmatrix}$$

$$q^i = \begin{bmatrix} 0.2 & 1.8 & 1.3 \\ 0.2 & 0 & 0.9 \\ 0 & 0 & 0 \\ 0 & 0 & 0 \end{bmatrix}$$

$$q = \begin{bmatrix} 0.8 & -1.8 & -1.3 \\ -0.2 & 1 & -0.9 \\ 0 & 0 & 1 \\ 0 & 0 & 0.6 \end{bmatrix}$$

As the number of products exceeds the number of processes, q is not a square matrix, and thus cannot be inverted to obtain q'. In any event, the procedure used for Taumor Industries cannot be adopted here, because of the further complication arising from being able to buy the intermediate Products I and II on the open market. It is consequently necessary to adopt a different approach, involving some extra terminology as follows.

Let:

p_i represent the selling price of product i

$\tilde{c}_i$ represent the unit cost of product i purchased externally

$\tilde{Q}_i$ represent the optimum quantity of intermediate product i to be purchased externally

Then, from the information in the problem, 1×4 row vectors p^T and $\tilde{c}^T$ can be drawn up as follows:

$$p^T = \begin{bmatrix} 0 & 0 & 60 & 52 \end{bmatrix}$$
$$\tilde{c}^T = \begin{bmatrix} 28 & 38 & 0 & 0 \end{bmatrix}$$

Also from the information in the problem, the matrix of units of 'external' input per unit of activity d, and its associated vector of variable costs per unit of 'external' input v, can be drawn up as follows:

$$d = \begin{bmatrix} 0 & 1.4 & 1.3 \\ 2.2 & 0 & 2.6 \\ 1.1 & 1.6 & 3.1 \\ 1.4 & 1.1 & 1.9 \end{bmatrix} \quad v = \begin{bmatrix} 4 \\ 2 \\ 3 \\ 0 \end{bmatrix}$$

In this problem, the objective function to be maximised consists of the excess of total sales revenue over total variable cost. Sales revenue is given by the product of the selling price row vector p^T and the column vector of optimal net outputs $\tilde{Q}$. That is to say:

Sales revenue $= p^T \tilde{Q}$

Total variable cost may be divided up into the cost of intermediate products bought on the open market and the cost of 'external' inputs purchased. The column vector of input requirements in the optimum solution is $\tilde{D}$, so that total variable cost may be represented as follows:

Total variable cost $= \tilde{c}^T \tilde{Q} + v^T \tilde{D}$

Bringing together revenue and cost gives rise to an objective function:

$$\text{Maximise } p^T \hat{Q} - (\tilde{c}^T \tilde{Q} + v^T \bar{D})$$

It should be noted that the optimal solution will give not only the optimal net output of each product in $\hat{Q}$, but also the optimal outside purchases in $\tilde{Q}$ and the input requirements in $\bar{D}$. In fact, it will also give the total (gross) production of each product $\hat{Q}$ required to sustain the optimal net output $\hat{Q}$, because $\hat{Q}$ enters into the first set of constraints. The basis of this set is that the net output of any product must equal the amount sold less the amount purchased externally. It may be represented symbolically as below:

$$q\hat{Q} - \hat{Q} + \tilde{Q} = 0$$

Within the $\hat{Q}$ vector, the optimal net output of any product i is represented by the element Q_i. Since Products I and II are not sold by Salmedge Products, $Q_1 = Q_2 = 0$, and since neither Kegebrol nor Ramethos may be purchased $\tilde{Q}_3 = \tilde{Q}_4 = 0$. With these values, and inserting the elements from the net input–output coefficient matrix in the general form of the constraint above, four constraints may be constructed for this problem as follows:

$$0.8\hat{Q}_1 - 1.8\hat{Q}_2 - 1.3\hat{Q}_3 + \tilde{Q}_1 = 0 \tag{1}$$
$$-0.2\hat{Q}_1 + \hat{Q}_2 - 0.9\hat{Q}_3 + \tilde{Q}_2 = 0 \tag{2}$$
$$\hat{Q}_3 - Q_3 = 0 \tag{3}$$
$$0.6\hat{Q}_3 - Q_4 = 0 \tag{4}$$

The second set of constraints states that the total requirement for inputs $d\hat{Q}$ generated by production must be equal to the quantity purchased and used in the optimal solution $\bar{D}$. Rearranging this, and representing it in symbolic terms, gives:

$$d\hat{Q} - \bar{D} = 0$$

Within the $\bar{D}$ vector, the quantity of input i purchased and used is represented by the element D_i. Inserting values from the d matrix above enables the construction of the following four constraints:

$$1.4\hat{Q}_2 + 1.3\hat{Q}_3 - D_1 = 0 \tag{5}$$
$$2.2\hat{Q}_1 + 2.6\hat{Q}_3 - D_2 = 0 \tag{6}$$
$$1.1\hat{Q}_1 + 1.6\hat{Q}_2 + 3.1\hat{Q}_3 - D_3 = 0 \tag{7}$$
$$1.4\hat{Q}_1 + 1.1\hat{Q}_2 + 1.9\hat{Q}_3 - D_4 = 0 \tag{8}$$

The final set of constraints specifies that the usage of inputs in restricted supply must not exceed the maximum quantity of them available. Applied to labour hours and hours of centrifuge time, this gives rise to constraints as follows:

$$D_3 \leqq 700 \tag{9}$$
$$D_4 \leqq 500 \tag{10}$$

Having formulated the objective function algebraically, it remains only to specify it numerically by reference to the information given above. This yields an objective function as follows:

Maximise $\quad 60Q_3 + 52Q_4 - 28\tilde{Q}_1 - 38\tilde{Q}_2 - 4D_1 - 2D_2 - 3D_3$

Maximising this function subject to constraints (1)–(10) above gives rise to a contribution for January 1989 of £1 489.52, obtained with the following values:

$\hat{Q}_1 = 194.6$	$D_1 = 155.7$
$\hat{Q}_3 = 119.8$	$D_2 = 739.5$
$Q_3 = 119.8$	$D_3 = 585.3$
$Q_4 = 71.9$	$D_4 = 500$
$\tilde{Q}_2 = 146.7$	

From this information, the optimal production in January is 119.8 litres of Kegebrol (Q_3) together with 71.9 kilograms of Ramethos (Q_4). To obtain this output, it will be necessary to produce 194.6 litres of Product I ($\hat{Q}_1$) during January. Process II should not be run at all, since $\hat{Q}_2$ does not enter into the optimal solution; instead, 146.7 kilograms of Product II ($\tilde{Q}_2$) should be purchased during January. The usage of inputs will be 155.7 kilograms of ninofane (D_1), 739.5 litres of triglycol (D_2), 583.5 labour hours (D_3) and 500 hours of centrifuge time (D_4). Sensitivity analysis may be performed on this solution in the usual way, to point out (for example) that an increase of 1 hour in the amount of centrifuge time available would increase contribution by £2.98 over the range from 500–598 hours available.

Use of Information Theory to Isolate Substantial Variances

8

8.1 Heversham Horticulture Ltd

Heversham Horticulture sells its products over two sales areas, one centred on Dudsworth and the other centred on Ambleside. Each of these areas sells three groups of products – tools, fertilisers and plants. The budgeted and actual sales for January–March 1989 were as follows:

	Budgeted Sales		
	Dudsworth	Ambleside	Total
	£	£	£
Tools	8 977	20 842	29 819
Fertilisers	93 424	83 870	177 294
Plants	79 538	70 435	149 973
	181 939	175 147	357 086

	Actual Sales		
	Dudsworth	Ambleside	Total
	£	£	£
Tools	8 476	30 568	39 044
Fertilisers	83 303	76 589	159 892
Plants	63 759	62 441	126 200
	155 538	169 598	325 136

You are required to consider analytically the variances of actual from budgeted sales for January–March 1989, with a view to identifying those variances which seem relatively substantial.

8.2 Analysis

Fundamentals of information theory

In the consideration of either a cost variance or a revenue variance, there are two factors which (amongst others) must enter into any judgement as to whether the variance concerned is substantial or negligible:

1. The proportion by which the actual cost or revenue diverges from budget.
   A divergence of 50 per cent from budget in either direction is likely to be a more substantial matter than a divergence of 10 per cent.
2. The proportion of total cost or total revenue to which the variance relates.
   A variance of 10 per cent of actual relative to budget for an item accounting for 1 per cent of total cost or revenue is likely to be of much less significance than is the same proportional variance of 10 per cent applied to an item accounting for 20 per cent of total cost or revenue.

The feature that these two factors have in common is that they both relate not to the absolute sizes of variances, but to variances expressed as *proportions*. When a proportion is converted to a decimal, its value must lie between zero and one – the same range of values as is occupied by a measure of probability. If the information content of a message is taken as relating to the change in *probabilities* before and after that message is received, this suggests that the information content of a variance may perhaps be expressed in terms of the change in *proportions* as between a budget and an actual financial statement.

This is the approach which will be taken in analysing the Heversham Horticulture problem. But before the idea of information as proportion change is explored, it is necessary first to say something about the better-established concept of information as probability change. Here, the central argument is that the information content of a message that an event E has occurred depends on the previous belief concerning the probability p that E would occur. The lower was p, the greater is the information content of the message. A message that an event has occurred which previously had a probability p of occurrence is said to have an information content of $h(p)$, where:

$$h(p) = -\log_2 p \qquad (8.1)$$

The use of logarithms to the base two has the advantage that the information content of a message that an event which had a probability of 0.5 has in fact happened is $-\log_2 0.5 = 1$. This one unit of information arising from the occurrence of a $p = 0.5$ event is referred to as 'one bit'. More generally, if a message transforms the probability of an event E from p to q, then the information content of that message may be expressed as:

$$h(p) - h(q) = -\log_2 p + \log_2 q = \log_2 q/p \qquad (8.2)$$

It is worth noting that if $q = 1$, then since $\log_2 1 = 0$, the information content of the message becomes $-\log_2 p$, as in equation (8.1).

A difficulty here is that the information content of a message about an event cannot be known for certain until that event has happened. If, for example, a message is received saying that the probability of event E has changed from p to q, where $q < p$, then the application of equation (8.2) would suggest that this message has a negative information content, in the sense of being 'worth' a negative number of bits. But the consequent inference that the message is misleading can be supported only by the actual occurrence of the event E; if E occurs, the message had a negative information content, if E does not, it did not. However, once E has occurred (or ceased to be capable of occurrence) then the question of what the information content was of a previous message about E ceases to be of much interest.

For this reason, the focus of information theory is on the expected value of information in a message (called its 'information expectation'), not on the actual value of information. To illustrate the computation of the information expectation, consider a situation in which there are n possible events, $E_1 \ldots E_n$, one of which must happen. Initially, the probabilities associated with these events respectively are $p_1 \ldots p_n$; then a message is received changing them respectively to $q_1 \ldots q_n$. In advance of knowing which of the events $E_1 \ldots E_n$ actually occurred, the information content of this message is given by weighting the information values from equation (8.2) for each event by the revised probability for the event concerned. Calling the information expectation of the overall message I, this gives:

$$I = \sum_{i=1}^{n} q_i \log(q_i/p_i) \tag{8.3}$$

In equation (8.3), the base of the logarithm is not specified. This is because one base is as good as another, so that the choice of base is purely a matter of convenience. On the whole, it is most convenient to use logarithms to base e (natural logarithms), because of their ready availability, especially on computers. They will be denoted by 'ln' to distinguish them from logarithms to any other base. The information measure to which they give rise is called a 'nit'.

From probabilities to proportions

As has already been pointed out, proportions resemble probabilities in that both measures run on a scale from zero to one. In the Heversham Horticulture problem, the proportions which are of concern are the proportions borne by budgeted sales for each product and each area to total budgeted sales, and by actual sales for each product and each area to total actual sales. A notation for these proportions may be developed as follows: Let:

p_{ij} represent the budgeted sales of product i in area j as a proportion of total budgeted sales

q_{ij} represent the actual sales of product i in area j as a proportion of total actual sales

X represent the classification of sales by product, so that if there are m products these are labelled $X_1 \ldots X_m$

Y represent the classification of sales by area, so that if there are n areas these are labelled $Y_1 \ldots Y_n$

With sales areas making up the columns and products making up the rows, let the marginal column totals for budgeted sales be $p_{01} \ldots p_{0n}$ and the marginal row totals for budgeted sales be $p_{10} \ldots p_{m0}$. Similarly, let the marginal column totals for actual sales be $q_{01} \ldots q_{0n}$ and the marginal row totals for actual sales be $q_{10} \ldots q_{m0}$. Then computations of budgeted and actual proportions for the Heversham Horticulture problem yield the following results:

	$Y_1(Dudsworth)$	$Y_2(Ambleside)$	Total
X_1 *(Tools)*	$p_{11} = 0.0251$	$p_{12} = 0.0584$	$p_{10} = 0.0835$
X_2 *(Fertilisers)*	$p_{21} = 0.2616$	$p_{22} = 0.2349$	$p_{20} = 0.4965$
X_3 *(Plants)*	$p_{31} = 0.2228$	$p_{32} = 0.1972$	$p_{30} = 0.4200$
Total	$p_{01} = 0.5095$	$p_{02} = 0.4905$	1

	$Y_1(Dudsworth)$	$Y_2(Ambleside)$	Total
X_1 *(Tools)*	$q_{11} = 0.0261$	$q_{12} = 0.0940$	$q_{10} = 0.1201$
X_2 *(Fertilisers)*	$q_{21} = 0.2562$	$q_{22} = 0.2356$	$q_{20} = 0.4918$
X_3 *(Plants)*	$q_{31} = 0.1961$	$q_{32} = 0.1920$	$q_{30} = 0.3881$
Total	$q_{01} = 0.4784$	$q_{02} = 0.5216$	1

By analogy with equation (8.3), but substituting proportions for probabilities, the information expectation for m products and n sales areas is given by:

$$I(X,Y) = \sum_{i=1}^{m} \sum_{j=1}^{n} q_{ij} \ln (q_{ij}/p_{ij}) \qquad (8.4)$$

Hereafter, all measures of information content will be given in units of 10^{-4} nits. With this unit of measure for Heversham Horticulture, computation indicates that $I(X,Y) = 109.7$. The statistic $I(X,Y)$ has three important properties:

1. It is always either zero or a positive number, being zero for the case where $q_{ij} = p_{ij}$ for all i and j.
2. As the difference between budgeted and actual proportions q_{ij} and p_{ij} increases, so the value of $I(X,Y)$ increases.
3. Each component of $I(X,Y)$ is weighted by q_{ij}, reflecting the proportion which actual sales for the product and area con-

cerned bore to total actual sales; financially important product/ area combinations are consequently given a heavy weighting relative to those of lesser financial importance.

The second and third of these considerations mirror the two factors outlined at the beginning as helping to determine whether a particular variance is substantial or negligible. A time series of $I(X, Y)$ values may help to indicate whether in aggregate actual sales performance is becoming more or less divergent from budgeted performance over time, but of more immediate interest are the various breakdowns of the total information expectation $I(X, Y)$. These are dealt with below.

Geographical variation in a product's sales

It may be thought desirable to obtain a measure of the proportional variance of sales by area for a given product i. This involves computing the number of nits that are represented by the difference between the actual proportion of product i's sales that arose in each area and the budgeted proportion of that product's sales which should have arisen in each area. To do this, it is necessary to express the p_{ij} and q_{ij} values for product i not as proportions of the total sales but as proportions of the total sales of product i – that is, as proportions of p_{i0} and q_{i0}. The information expectation of sales of product i by area is given by $I(Y|X_i)$, where for n sales areas:

$$I(Y|X_i) = \sum_{j=1}^{n} (q_{ij}/q_{i0}) \ln[q_{ij}/q_{i0})/(p_{ij}/p_{i0})] \qquad (8.5)$$

For Heversham Horticulture, calculation of the information expectation for each product over sales areas gives rise to the following results:

$$I(Y|X_1) = 178.3; \ I(Y|X_2) = 0.7; \ I(Y|X_3) = 12.7$$

Suppose that the responsibility for budgeting were to be located with area managers, so that the budget as a whole was aggregated from their area budgets. If these area managers could budget accurately, they would be able to say what proportion of a product's total sales would take place in each of their areas (demanding a knowledge of each area's relative propensity to purchase that product). To measure their budget accuracy, what would be required would be to sum the nit values for each individual product over all the m products, weighting these values by the proportion of actual sales for all products represented by each individual product. The formula for this is:

$$I(Y|X) = \sum_{i=1}^{m} q_{i0} \, I(Y|X_i) \tag{8.6}$$

For Heversham Horticulture, computation gives:

$$I(Y|X) = 26.7$$

Variation of sales by product for a given area

The converse of the approach just taken involves focusing on areas rather than products. Specifically, the question here is one of how many nits are represented by the difference between the actual proportion of area j's sales that arose from each product and the budgeted proportion of that area's sales that should have arisen from each product. Summing down the m products gives rise to the information expectation of sales in area j by product, denoted by $I(X|Y_j)$, as follows:

$$I(X|Y_j) = \sum_{i=1}^{m} (q_{ij}/q_{0j}) \ln [(q_{ij}/q_{0j})/(p_{ij}/p_{0j})] \tag{8.7}$$

For Heversham Horticulture, calculation of the information expectation for each sales area in relation to products yields the following results:

$$I(X|Y_1) = 15.9; \; I(X|Y_2) = 158.6$$

If the responsibility for budgeting were to be located with product managers, then their remit would involve forecasting what proportion of an area's sales would be represented by each of their products. This would demand a knowledge of the relative importance of each product in comparison to the other products sold by the firm. To measure the budget accuracy of product managers, it would be necessary to weight the nit value for each sales area by the proportion of total actual sales represented by that area, and then to sum those weighted values. This would give rise to:

$$I(X|Y) = \sum_{j=1}^{n} q_{0j} I(X|Y_j) \qquad (8.8)$$

For Heversham Horticulture, computation gives:

$$I(X|Y) = 90.4$$

Univariate variances

Comprehensiveness requires that two other information expectations be computed, relating to the marginal row and column proportions. These are as follows:

$$I(X) = \sum_{i=1}^{m} q_{i0} \ln(q_{i0}/p_{i0}) \qquad (8.9)$$

$$I(Y) = \sum_{j=1}^{n} q_{0j} \ln(q_{0j}/p_{0j}) \qquad (8.10)$$

For Heversham Horticulture $I(X) = 83.0$ and $I(Y) = 19.3$, indicating that the proportion of total sales accounted for by each area was predicted more accurately in the budget than was the proportion of total sales accounted for by each product. This should be seen in the context that $I(X|Y) > I(Y|X)$, implying that the distribution of each product's sales over areas was much more accurately forecast than was the distribution for each area of sales by products. Put simply, the budget predicted quite well the area mix of sales for each of the products, but was much less good at predicting the product mix of sales for each of the areas.

Breakdown to individual areas and products

Probably the most concrete application of information theory to this problem lies in the highlighting of individual sales areas and products. An elaboration of the notation is necessary for this purpose. Let:

$$I(Y|X_{ij}) = (q_{ij}/q_{i0}) \ln[(q_{ij}/q_{i0})/(p_{ij}/p_{i0})] \qquad (8.11)$$

Equation (8.11) can be used to simplify equation (8.5) to the following form:

$$I(Y|X_i) = \sum_{j=1}^{n} I(Y|X_{ij}) \qquad (8.12)$$

Similarly, let:

$$I(X|Y_{ij}) = (q_{ij}/q_{0j}) \ln[(q_{ij}/q_{0j})/(p_{ij}/p_{0j})] \qquad (8.13)$$

Equation (8.13) can be used to simplify equation (8.7), giving:

$$I(X|Y_j) = \sum_{i=1}^{m} I(X|Y_{ij}) \qquad (8.14)$$

Using this notation, a breakdown of the computations in equations (8.5) and (8.7) can be undertaken, as below:

$$
\begin{aligned}
I(Y|X_1) &= I(Y|X_{11}) &&+ I(Y|X_{12}) \\
178.3 &= -709.8 &&+ 888.1 \\
I(Y|X_2) &= I(Y|X_{21}) &&+ I(Y|X_{22}) \\
0.7 &= -59.1 &&+ 59.8 \\
I(Y|X_3) &= I(Y|X_{31}) &&+ I(Y|X_{32}) \\
12.7 &= -245.2 &&+ 257.9 \\
I(X|Y_1) &= I(X|Y_{11}) &&+ I(X|Y_{21}) &&+ I(X|Y_{31}) \\
15.9 &= 54.1 &&+ 225.6 &&- 263.8 \\
I(X|Y_2) &= I(X|Y_{12}) &&+ I(X|Y_{22}) &&+ I(X|Y_{32}) \\
158.6 &= 748.3 &&- 264.7 &&- 325.0
\end{aligned}
$$

A key point to observe from this breakdown is that a shortfall of actual below budgeted sales does not necessarily give rise to a negative information expectation. Consider, for example, the sales of fertilisers in the Dudsworth area. Here, there has been a shortfall of nearly £10 000, but the information expectation is given by:

$$I(X|Y_{21}) = \left(\frac{0.2562}{0.4784} \right) \ln \left[\left(\frac{0.2562}{0.4784} \right) \bigg/ \left(\frac{0.2616}{0.5095} \right) \right]$$

The expression in the square brackets is $\ln 1.04 = 0.0392$. Since this is positive, the whole information expectation must be positive. This arises because the proportion of actual sales in the Dudsworth area accounted for by fertilisers exceeded the budgeted proportion. As a consequence, the information expectation is positive even though fertiliser sales fell short of their budget target.

This illustration implies that information expectation figures may not serve as good guides for management control, and this implication is easily reinforced. In Heversham Horticulture, the total shortfall of January sales below budget was £31 950. A major contributory factor to this shortfall was the £25 900 making up the combined adverse variances on fertilisers and plants in the Dudsworth area. Yet the information expectation for this area $I(X|Y_1)$ is very small, as is the information expectation $I(Y|X_3)$ relating to plants, despite the £23 773 shortfall of actual below budgeted sales for this product group.

The information theory approach, however, is not concerned with management control. It measures the accuracy of budgets considered as forecasts about the proportional distribution of revenue (or expenditure) across categories. In this problem, the large information expectations $I(Y|X_1)$ and $I(X|Y_2)$ serve to signal that the distribution of sales revenue from tools over the two areas was an unexpected one, and that the distribution of sales revenue in the Ambleside area over the three products sold there was also an unexpected one. This may well be important information from the point of view of allocating marketing effort to areas and products. It may also act as a valuable input to the budget setting process, inasmuch as it indicates those products and areas for which it is unsafe to base a future budget on the proportional distributions of sales revenue contained in the budget for the first quarter of 1989.

In relation to either of these uses, it is unlikely to be advantageous to produce the further breakdown of the analysis in equations (8.5) and (8.7) carried out here after equation (8.14). This was done for illustrative purposes only; what matters in the practical application of information theory to the evaluation of budget forecasts is the predictability of proportions within the entire category represented by either an area or a product, not the predictability of the proportion represented by a single product within an area or a single area within a product category.

The practice of management control at Heversham Horticulture requires that attention should be focussed on the breakdown into price, volume and mix variances of the total sales variances, with especial reference to the variances on fertilisers and plants in the Dudsworth area. From a forecasting point of view, however, the distribution and relative importance of tool sales seems to have proved difficult to predict within the budget, as does the distribution and relative importance of sales in the Ambleside area. It is upon these two issues that the analysis using information theory has focused.

The Single-period Cost Variance Investigation Decision

9

9.1 Alston Glassworks

Alston Glassworks uses a small electric arc furnace for fusing silica. When the air vents on the furnace are properly open, its electricity cost takes the form of a normal distribution with a mean of £2 200 per week and a standard deviation of £400; when the vents are not properly open the furnace's electricity cost again takes the form of a normal distribution, but with a mean of £2 800 per week and a standard deviation of £1 400.

The furnace is used only during the week, and is permitted to cool down at weekends. On Friday evenings, before the work force leave for the weekend, either of two types of investigation of the furnace can be carried out. The alternatives are called 'hot' and 'cold' investigations, the difference between them being that a hot investigation does not involve spraying the furnace with water to cool it completely, while a cold investigation does. The need to reheat the furnace from scratch makes a cold investigation more expensive than a hot one, but it is also much more thorough. If the air vents are not properly open, there is only a 0.5 probability that a hot investigation will find this out, but a cold investigation will always do so. A hot investigation involves incurring an incremental cost of £70, while the incremental cost of a cold investigation is £200. In the event of either type of investigation showing that the vents are not properly open, extra overtime costs of £40 have to be incurred in order to open them correctly.

Over the weekend, the cooling of the furnace causes the metal in its air vents to contract, thus moving the vents of their own accord. If the vents are properly opened on Friday evening, there is a 0.2 probability that they will not be properly opened by Sunday evening. Conversely, if the vents are not properly opened on Friday evening, there is a 0.4 probability that they will be properly opened by Sunday evening.

When the furnace stopped work on Friday 4 March, the foreman believed that there was a 0.8 probability that its vents were properly opened. He was then told that the electricity cost for the week ending on 4 March was £3 050; this changed his judgement of the probability that the vents were properly opened sufficiently to induce him to carry out a hot investigation. However, this investigation did not discover anything indicating conclusively that the vents were not properly opened; in fact, nothing found by the investigation changed the foreman's judgement in any way. However, at the end of Friday 11 March he was told that the electricity cost for the week which began on Monday 7 March was £3 120.

You are required:

1. To comment on the foreman's decision to carry out a hot investigation on Friday 4 March.
2. To advise the foreman as to whether he should carry out an investigation on Friday 11 March, and if so whether this investigation should be a hot or a cold one.
3. To indicate how your advice in 2 above would change if the facts in the problem were altered in the following two respects:

   (a) That hot investigations were ruled out for safety reasons, leaving a choice only of having a cold investigation or none at all
   (b) That the electricity cost for the week beginning on Monday 7 March was £1 340.

9.2 Analysis

Establishment of terminology

In approaching the Alston Glassworks problem, the initial requirement is to establish some terminology. Let:

S_1	represent the state of being 'in control', arising for the furnace when its air vents are properly open
S_2	represent the state of being 'out of control', arising for the furnace when its air vents are not properly open
a_1	represent the act of ordering a cold investigation
a_2	represent the act of ordering a hot investigation
a_3	represent the act of ordering no investigation at all
$f_n(S_j)$	represent the probability of state j at the beginning of the weekend following week n For dating purposes, let $n=1$ on Friday 4 March
$f'_n(S_j)$	represent the probability of state j at the end of the weekend following week n
C	represent the incremental cost of a comprehensive study of the air vents, so that here $C = 200$ for a cold investigation
C'	represent the incremental cost of a limited study of the air vents, so that here $C' = 70$ for a hot investigation
M	represent the cost of correcting an out of control state, so that here $M = 40$
L	represent the cost of failing to correct an out of control state On the arguable assumption that such a state will persist for one more week if it is not corrected, then on average $L = 2\,800 - 2\,200 = 600$
h	represent the probability that a hot investigation will find that the air vents are not properly open, if in fact this is the case Here, $h = 0.5$

The terminology now created is sufficient to address the problem at hand.

Break-even probabilities

To obtain the break-even probabilities – that is, those at which the foreman should be indifferent as between one act and another – it is necessary first to work out the expected costs associated with each of the three possible acts. Undertaking an investigation involves incurring a cost of C or C', together with a further cost M if an out of control state is found. If an out of control state exists but is not detected, a cost L is incurred. Weighting these costs by the probability of existence of an out of control state $f_n(S_2)$ gives rise to expected costs as follows:

Act	Expected cost
a_1	$C + M[f_n(S_2)]$
a_2	$C' + [L(1-h)+hM]\ [f_n(S_2)]$
a_3	$L[f_n(S_2)]$

Let the break-even probability as between a_1 and a_2 be $f_a(S_2)$, where:

$$C' + [L(1-h)+hM]\ [f_a(S_2)] = C + M[f_a(S_2)]$$

Hence

$$f_a(S_2) = \frac{C-C'}{L(1-h)+M(h-1)} \tag{9.1}$$

Let the break-even probability as between a_2 and a_3 be $f_b(S_2)$, where:

$$C' + [L(1-h)+hM]\ [f_b(S_2)] = L[f_b(S_2)]$$

Hence $f_b(S_2) = \dfrac{C'}{(L-M)h}$ \hfill (9.2)

For the Alston Glassworks data, $f_a(S_2) = 0.464$ and $f_b(S_2) = 0.250$. It will generally be true that $f_a(S_2) > f_b(S_2)$, but not invariably so; if $f_b(S_2) > f_a(S_2)$ then a limited investigation of the form of a_2 should never be undertaken.

Revision of prior probabilities

Having computed the break-even probabilities, the next step is to compare them against the probabilities of being in control or out of control on Friday 4 March. In symbolic terms, this involves deriving $f_1(S_1)$ and $f_1(S_2)$ from the foreman's prior probabilities. If $f_0(S_j)$ is taken as representing the prior probability assigned to state j, then for Alston Glassworks $f_0(S_1) = 0.8$ and $f_0(S_2) = 0.2$. The question resolves itself into one of how to revise these prior probabilities to allow for the fact that the electricity cost for the week ending Friday 4 March was £3 050. This revision involves the use of Bayes' Theorem, and requires the establishment of some further terminology as follows. Let:

x	represent the observed cost level, so that here $x = 3050$
μ_j	represent the mean cost associated with state j, so that here $\mu_1 = 2200$ and $\mu_2 = 2800$
σ_j	represent the standard deviation of cost associated with state j, so that here $\sigma_1 = 400$ and $\sigma_2 = 1400$
$f_u\left(\dfrac{x-\mu_j}{\sigma_j}\right)$	represent the value in a table of the ordinates of the unit normal density function associated with $(x-\mu_j)/\sigma_j$

The table referred to above shows the height of the standard normal density function associated with a value of a standardised variable. Since the standard deviation of cost associated with state j is σ_j not unity, to obtain the probability density for state j it is necessary to correct by multiplying the standardised ordinate value by the reciprocal of the standard deviation for state j. Let:

$f_x(x|S_j)$ represent the probability density for state j, so that these densities for $j=1$ and $j=2$ give the relative likelihood of observing the cost level x under the two possible states

Then, in symbolic terms, the correction required is given below:

$$f_x(x|S_j) = \frac{1}{\sigma_j} f_u \left(\frac{x-\mu_j}{\sigma_j} \right) \tag{9.3}$$

By the application of Bayes' Theorem:

$$f_1(S_j|x) = \frac{f_x(x|S_j)f_0(S_j)}{\sum\limits_{j=1}^{2} f_x(x|S_j) f_0(S_j)} \tag{9.4}$$

Applying equation (9.4) to the figures in Alston Glassworks gives rise to the following computation:

$$f_1(S_1|x) =$$

$$\frac{\left(\dfrac{1}{400}\right) f_u \left(\dfrac{3\,050 - 2\,200}{400}\right) (0.8)}{\left(\dfrac{1}{400}\right) f_u \left(\dfrac{3\,050 - 2\,200}{400}\right)(0.8) + \left(\dfrac{1}{1\,400}\right) f_u \left(\dfrac{3\,050 - 2\,800}{1\,400}\right)(0.2)}$$

$$= 0.60$$

Hence

$$f_1(S_2|x) = 0.40$$

This figure is such that $f_b(S_2) < f_1(S_2|x) < f_a(S_2)$, suggesting that the foreman's decision to carry out a hot investigation on Friday 4 March was correct. In evaluating the outcome of this investigation, some further terminology is required. Let:

    hnf represent the outcome 'hot investigation finds nothing to suggest an out of control state'

    hf represent the outcome 'hot investigation finds air vents not properly opened'

The problem specifies that $f(hnf|S_2) = 0.5$ and $f(hf|S_2) = 0.5$. Since an out of control state must prevail if the vents are not properly opened, it must be the case that $f(hf|S_1) = 0$ and $f(hnf|S_1) = 1$. In fact, the outcome hnf occurred, and can be used to revise $f_1(S_1|x)$ and $f_1(S_2|x)$ as follows:

$$f_1(S_1|hnf) = \frac{f(hnf|S_1)f_1(S_1|x)}{f(hnf|S_1)f_1(S_1|x) + f(hnf|S_2)f_1(S_2|x)} \quad (9.5)$$

$$= \frac{(1)(0.6)}{(1)(0.6) + (0.5)(0.4)} = 0.75$$

If $f_1(S_1|hnf) = 0.75$, then it must follow that $f_1(S_2|hnf) = 0.25$. The wording of the problem suggests that the foreman did not revise his probabilities $f_1(S_1|x)$ and $f_1(S_2|x)$ in response to the fact that the hot investigation produced hnf. If he did not carry out this revision he acted incorrectly, because although the outcome hnf is not conclusive, the fact that no evidence was found indicating that the air vents might not be properly opened increases the probability that they were in fact properly opened from 0.6 to 0.75.

The hot investigation took place at the beginning of the weekend, so that the probabilities associated with each state were subject to change over the weekend, as the cooling of the furnace caused the metal in the air vents to contract. On Sunday 6 March, the probabilities for each state are given by $f_1'(S_1)$ and $f_1'(S_2)$. They depend upon the transition probabilities from one state to another over the weekend. A matrix of these transition probabilities can be drawn up, first in general terms and then with the specific probabilities for Alston Glassworks inserted, as follows:

$$
\begin{array}{cc}
 & S_1 \text{ at } n' \quad S_2 \text{ at } n' \\
\begin{array}{c} S_1 \text{ at } n \\ S_2 \text{ at } n \end{array} &
\begin{bmatrix} (1-p) & p \\ g & (1-g) \end{bmatrix} =
\begin{bmatrix} 0.8 & 0.2 \\ 0.4 & 0.6 \end{bmatrix}
\end{array}
$$

If this matrix of transition probabilities is premultiplied by $[f_1(S_1|hnf) \; f_1(S_2|hnf)]$, the resulting vector gives the probabilities associated with the in control and out of control states on Sunday 6 March. The calculation is:

$$[0.75 \quad 0.25] \begin{bmatrix} 0.8 & 0.2 \\ 0.4 & 0.6 \end{bmatrix} = [0.7 \quad 0.3]$$

The prior probabilities for the analysis of the next week are thus given by $f'_1(S_1) = 0.7$ and $f'_1(S_2) = 0.3$. These priors have to be modified to reflect the electricity cost over week $n=2$ of £3 120. The general formula for deriving posterior probabilities for each state at the end of the nth week is given by:

$$f_n(S_j|x) = \frac{f_x(x|S_j)\, f'_n(S_j)}{\sum\limits_{j=1}^{2} f_x(x|S_j)\, f'_n(S_j)} \tag{9.6}$$

Applying equation (9.6) to the figures for the week ending on Friday 11 March produces the following computation:

$$f_2(S_1|x) =$$

$$\frac{\left(\dfrac{1}{400}\right) f_u \left(\dfrac{3\,120 - 2\,200}{400}\right)(0.7)}{\left(\dfrac{1}{400}\right) f_u \left(\dfrac{3\,120 - 2\,200}{400}\right)(0.7) + \left(\dfrac{1}{1\,400}\right) f_u \left(\dfrac{3\,120 - 2\,800}{1\,400}\right)} \tag{0.3}$$

The resulting figures are $f_2(S_1|x) = 0.373$ and $f_2(S_2|x) = 0.627$. Because $f_2(S_2|x) > f_a(S_2)$, expected cost will be minimised by carrying out a cold investigation. Two relatively high weekly electricity costs in succession have had the cumulative effect of confirming the need for a comprehensive study of the furnace's air vents.

The quadratic equation approach

In the final part of the Alston Glassworks problem, the issue is simplified by eliminating the possibility of carrying out a hot investigation. The acts which remain available may be relabelled as follows. Let:

a_1 represent the act of ordering a cold investigation, hereafter referred to simply as 'investigating'

a_2 represent the act of ordering no investigation at all

The fact that a hot investigation is now ruled out means that the revision of probabilities in equation (9.5) can no longer take place. Hence the probabilities $f_1'(S_1)$ and $f_1'(S_2)$ are obtained by premultiplying the matrix of transition probabilities by $[f_1(S_1|x) \; f_1(S_2|x)]$ to give the following calculation:

$$[0.6 \quad 0.4] \begin{bmatrix} 0.8 & 0.2 \\ 0.4 & 0.6 \end{bmatrix} = [0.64 \quad 0.36]$$

From this calculation, $f_1'(S_1) = 0.64$ and $f_1'(S_2) = 0.36$.

Because only two alternative acts are available, another approach to the problem in week $n=2$ becomes feasible. This involves working out the cost level(s) at which the foreman should be indifferent as to whether or not to investigate. In locating these cost level(s), it is necessary to define three new terms, a, b and c as follows:

$$a = \left(\frac{1}{2}\right)\left(\frac{1}{\sigma_1^2} - \frac{1}{\sigma_2^2}\right)$$

$$b = -\left(\frac{\mu_1}{\sigma_1^2} - \frac{\mu_2}{\sigma_2^2}\right)$$

$$c = \log_e\left[\left(\frac{L-M-C}{C}\right)\left(\frac{f_n'(S_2)}{f_n'(S_1)}\right)\left(\frac{\sigma_1}{\sigma_2}\right)\right] + \left(\frac{1}{2}\right)\left(\frac{\mu_1^2}{\sigma_1^2} - \frac{\mu_2^2}{\sigma_2^2}\right)$$

In their paper (see Appendix 2) Capettini and Collins employ these terms to advance a decision rule as follows:

'Investigate if $ax^2 + bx + c > 0$; otherwise do not investigate'

The cost level(s) for which the foreman should be indifferent as to whether or not to investigate are given by the values of x for which

$ax^2 + bx + c = 0$; there may be two positive numbers for which this equality is satisfied, or one, or none at all. If there are none, then it is either always better to investigate or never so, depending on whether or not $ax^2 + bx + c > 0$; if there is one positive number, then this is the break-even cost observation as between investigating or not. The interpretation if there are two positive values of x for which $ax^2 + bx + c = 0$ will be dealt with below.

Before coming to this, however, it is worth noting that the value(s) of x need to be recalculated every time the prior probabilities change, because the most recently updated prior probabilities enter into the formula for c above. Inserting the figures as they were at the beginning of week $n=2$ gives the following values for the parameters a, b and c:

$$a = 2.869 \times 10^{-6} \; ; b = -0.01232; c = 11.8847$$

The quadratic equation $ax^2 + bx + c = 0$ has roots given by:

$$x = -\frac{b}{2a} \pm \frac{\sqrt{b^2 - 4ac}}{2a}$$

When substitution is carried out, the result obtained is:

$$x = 2\,147 \pm 684$$

For values of x in the range $x = 2\,147 \pm 684$, $ax^2 + bx + c < 0$. Hence the conclusion reached by the Capettini–Collins decision rule for week $n=2$ may be expressed as follows:

'Do not investigate if the electricity cost for this week lies in the range between £1 463 and £2 831'

Light can be thrown on this decision rule by considering an act a_j and two threshold values of cost r_1 and r_2, where $r_1 < r_2$. Let the level of cost actually observed be c. If the act a_j is optimal when $c < r_1$ and when $c > r_2$, but not when $r_1 < c < r_2$, then the act a_j is said to have a disjoint region between r_1 and r_2. The decision rule for week $n=2$ above implies that there is a disjoint region between £1 463 and £2 831 for the act of investigating the air vents. Since the cost observation for week $n=2$ of £1 340 lies outside this disjoint region, expected cost will be minimised if an investigation is carried out in response to this relatively low electricity cost. On the face of it, though, this conclusion would seem contrary to common sense; why initiate an investigation in response to what seems to be a very good cost performance?

In fact, the conclusion to investigate is not illogical. When the air vents are not properly opened, the probability distribution of costs is much more widely spread than it is when the vents are properly opened; the standard deviation is 3.5 times as large in the out of control state as it is in the in control state. Consequently, an extreme cost reading, whether a very large one or a very small one, is more likely to come from the out of control distribution than it is to come from the in control distribution. It is thus optimal to investigate after either very large or very small cost observations, but not to investigate in response to observations in between – hence the disjoint region.

It is fairly easy to think of real life situations in which a very low electricity cost might be associated with an out of control state. Suppose, for example, that the air vents on the furnace were to be almost closed, so that sufficient oxygen was available to support only a very sluggish combustion. Relatively little electricity would be consumed in this out of control state, because the furnace would fail to reach anything approaching the required temperature. It may thus be seen that the existence of a disjoint region may well reflect an aspect of industrial reality.

Expected cost for a decision rule

The expected cost associated with implementing decision rule d in week n is given by EC_n (rule d), where:

$$EC_n \text{ (rule } d) = \quad [f'_{n-1}(S_1)] \ (C) \ \phi \ (a_1|S_1, \text{ rule } d) + \\ [f'_{n-1}(S_2)] \ [(C+M) \ \phi \ (a_1|S_2, \text{ rule } d) + \\ (L)\phi(a_2|S_2,\text{rule } d)]$$

(9.7)

In equation (9.7), $\phi(a_j|S_j$, rule $d)$ represents the probability that rule d will cause action a_j to be taken when the process is actually in state S_j. For week $n=2$, the expected cost associated with the optimal decision rule 'investigate unless £1 463 $\leqq x \leqq$ £2 831', where x is the week's cost observation, can be computed as follows:

EC_2 (a_1 unless $1\,463 \leqq x \leqq 2\,831$) =
$(0.64)(200)(1 - \text{Prob. of } 1\,463 \leqq x \leqq 2\,831 \text{ if } \bar{x} = 2\,200, s = 400)$
$+ (0.36) [(240)(1 - \text{Prob. of } 1\,463 \leqq x \leqq 2\,831 \text{ if } \bar{x} = 2\,800, s = 1\,400) + (600)(\text{Prob. of } 1\,463 \leqq x \leqq 2\,831 \text{ if } \bar{x} = 2\,800, s = 1\,400)]$

The probabilities in the round brackets above can be obtained from a table of areas under the standardised normal distribution. For example, the probability of obtaining a value outside the range $2\,147 \pm 684$ when sampling from a normal distribution with a mean of $2\,200$ and a standard deviation of 400 is equivalent to the probability of obtaining a z value greater than $(2\,831 - 2\,200)/400$ or less than $(1\,463 - 2\,200)/400$, which is $0.057 + 0.033 = 0.09$. By inserting probabilities in this way, calculation shows that:

$EC_2(a_1 \text{ unless } 1 \leqq x \leqq 2\,831) = £141.85$

It is interesting to contrast this expected cost against the cost for a decision rule which is identical except that it ignores the existence of the disjoint region – the 'common sense' rule of 'investigate if x > £2 831'. This rule may be referred to as the best one-sided decision rule, as compared with the best two-sided rule discussed above. A decision rule is one-sided if it has only one cost observation representing a point of indifference as between investigating and not investigating; a two-sided rule has two such points. The expected cost for the best one-sided decision rule at the end of week $n=2$ is given by:

EC_2 (a_1 if x > $2\,831$) = £159.66

The excess of this expected cost over the expected cost of £141.85 for the best two-sided rule represents the expected cost of ignoring the existence of the disjoint region; here it is £17.81.

The Multi-period Cost Variance Investigation Decision

10

10.1 Fitzroy Paper Products

At its Ashdown factory, Fitzroy Paper Products has a large pulp steaming machine, which is worked for two 8-hour shifts each day. During the remaining 8 hours of the day, any defect which has developed during the 16-hour operating period can be corrected. The task of checking for a defect involves the dismantling of the machine's heating mechanism; this work is done by the machine's operatives, and costs £290 in overtime payments each time it is undertaken. In addition, further overtime payments of £140 are required if the checking procedure finds a defect which needs to be corrected; different defects require slightly different levels of expenditure to deal with them, but these differences are small enough to be ignored in practice.

A further simplification arises from the relatively short period of operation between one machine shutdown and the next. Because the operating period is only 16 hours, the fact that defects can gradually develop *during* this period may be ignored for analytical purposes. Hence, for each operating period the machine may be treated either as being in a 'defective' or a 'non-defective' state throughout. From experience, the pulp steaming machine supervisor knows that once the machine becomes defective, it will remain so until its heating mechanism is dismantled and the fault put right. He also knows that if the machine is not defective at the end of an operating period, there is about one chance in five that it will become defective very soon after the beginning of the next operating period.

While the machine is in operation, it continuously feeds data on its consumption of raw materials and of electricity into the Ashdown factory's computer. This computer then converts the data from physical units into costs, and supplies the machine's supervisor with a report on the operating cost incurred for the day as soon as the second shift finishes. The cost level so reported may be taken as relating exclusively either to a process which is in control (not defective) or out of control (with a defect). However, the level of operating cost is not governed solely by the presence or absence of a machine defect. It is also subject to substantial random variations, arising largely from differences in the quality and texture of the pulp being steamed. The machine's supervisor has managed to build up the following probability distributions for the cost per operating period associated with the process being respectively in control and out of control:

Process in control		Process out of control	
Cost per period £	Probability	Cost per period £	Probability
500–600	0.10	700–800	0.05
600–700	0.35	800–900	0.15
700–800	0.35	900–1 000	0.25
800–900	0.10	1 000–1 100	0.25
900–1 000	0.05	1 100–1 200	0.25
1 000–1 100	0.05	1 200–1 300	0.05

Each day, at the end of the operating period, the question arises as to whether or not the machine's heating mechanism should be dismantled. This question cannot simply be left to the judgement of the machine's supervisor on every occasion, as there will inevitably be some days when he will be away on other business, on holiday, ill or otherwise unavailable. What is needed is the development of a rule specifying a level of cost for an operating period which, if it is exceeded, should automatically give rise to dismantling of the heating mechanism.

You are required:

1. To work out what rule would have the property of minimising the long-term expected cost per day arising from the pulp steaming machine, and to compute the level of this expected cost.
2. To compare this minimum long-term expected cost with the long-term expected cost associated with the following alternative policies:
   (a) Never dismantle the heating mechanism, and thus avoid any costs of either investigation or defect correction
   (b) Dismantle the mechanism and check for a defect at the end of every operating period.
3. To find what the long-term expected cost per day for the pulp steaming machine would be if a fault-diagnosing mechanism were to be fitted to it, indicating accurately the presence or absence of a defect.
   Ignore any costs associated with the fitting of this mechanism, and assume that it provides information on the state of the machine only once per day, at the end of that day's operating period.

10.2   Analysis

Introduction

In the discussion of the Alston Glassworks problem, the adjective 'arguable' was applied to the measurement of the variable L, which represents the cost of failing to correct an out of control state. The difficulty here may be expressed in the following way. If a process is out of control in a period j, and is not corrected in that period, it is likely to remain out of control in the next period $j+1$. There will be a further opportunity to correct the process in period $j+1$, but if this opportunity is not taken the process may remain out of control in period $j+2$, and so on. The presence of a sequence of opportunities for correction means that L cannot represent the present value of the extra costs associated with an out of control state continuing forever. At the same time, however, it is not strictly valid to assume that because an out of control state is not corrected in period j it *must* be corrected in period $j+1$, so that L can represent the extra cost associated with an out of control state persisting for one period only. The magnitude of L *depends on* when in the future the out of control state is corrected.

But the magnitude of L also *determines* when the out of control state will be corrected. Suppose that an investigation will always detect an out of control state if one is present, so that, in the terminology employed for the Alston Glassworks problem, $h=1$. Then, with symbols as in equation (9.2) for that problem, the break-even probability as between investigating and not investigating is given by $f_b(S_2)$, where:

$$f_b(S_2) = \frac{C}{L-M}$$

L thus determines $f_b(S_2)$, but also depends on it in that the higher is the break-even probability $f_b(S_2)$, the longer will an out of control state go uncorrected, and the larger will L be. If an assumption is made about how long an out of control state will go uncorrected in order to arrive at a value of L, then that value of L will change $f_b(S_2)$, giving rise to a change in L, which will in turn change $f_b(S_2)$ again, and so on forever.

A controlled Markov process

The problem of measuring L only arises because the objective in making a single-period cost variance investigation decision is to minimise the present value of the costs arising from *this period's* decision. An alternative approach is to specify the objective as being one of minimising the *long-term* expected cost per period incurred in operating, investigating and correcting the process concerned. This multi-period approach will be implemented by the use of Markov chains. Their use avoids the heavy computation associated with Bayesian revision, and does not require the restrictive assumption that the probability distributions of cost associated with the process being in control and being out of control are both normal. This approach also has the advantage of giving rise to a boundary between 'investigate' and 'do not investigate' which is represented by a single cost figure. This clear division implies that, with a Markov chain approach, cost variance investigation decisions can be taken by relatively junior staff without asking them to exercise a great deal of personal judgement.

The starting point for the analysis is a 'process transition matrix' containing the transition probabilities as between two states, $i=1$ representing 'in control' and $i=2$ representing 'out of control'. It is assumed that the process cannot revert back to being in control by itself once it has become out of control. Such a return to being in control can be achieved only by managerial investigation and defect correction. The process transition matrix is given below, both in symbolic terms and with the probabilities inserted for the Fitzroy Paper Products problem:

$$
\begin{array}{cc}
 & \begin{array}{cc} i=1 & i=2 \end{array} \\
\begin{array}{c} i=1 \\ i=2 \end{array} &
\begin{bmatrix} g & (1-g) \\ 0 & 1 \end{bmatrix}
\end{array}
=
\begin{bmatrix} 0.8 & 0.2 \\ 0 & 1 \end{bmatrix}
$$

At the end of each operating period, the computer at Fitzroy generates an observation $\bar{x}$ of the cost incurred by the pulp steaming machine in that period. Two cumulative probability functions can be drawn up showing the proportion of cases in which an operating period's cost falls below a level x; one of these functions relates to the absence of a defect (the in control state) and the other to the presence of a defect (the out of control state). The functions are as follows:

$$\text{Prob. } (\bar{x} \leq x|i) = F_i(x) \qquad (i=1,2)$$

where $E(\bar{x}|i) = \mu_i$
and $\Delta\mu = \mu_2 - \mu_1$

For example, from the in control distribution in the Fitzroy problem it may be seen that Prob. $[\bar{x} \leq 700 \mid (i=1)] = 0.45$. Computing the means of the two distributions gives $\mu_1 = 730$, $\mu_2 = 1\,015$, $\Delta\mu = 285$.

In the problem, any movement by the process from the in control to the out of control state may be taken as occurring at the very beginning of each operating period, so that the cost reported for a period relates exclusively to the state (in or out of control) arrived at through the mechanism of the transition probabilities. Once the machine's supervisor receives a cost report, he must decide whether or not to incur a fixed cost $I = £290$ by dismantling the heating mechanism and investigating. If an investigation takes place, it will find out what (if anything) is wrong with the mechanism. Then if a defect is present, its correction will involve a further outlay $K = £140$.

The objective to be attained is the finding of that cost level x which is such as to minimise the long-term expected cost per day of controlling the machine according to a decision rule which stipulates 'investigate if and only if $\bar{x} > x$'. Two kinds of error could arise from implementing this rule, with the following probabilities:

$$\begin{aligned}
\text{Prob.[Investigate} \mid \text{in control]} &= \text{Prob. } [\bar{x} > x \mid (i=1)] \\
&= 1 - \text{Prob.}[\bar{x} \leq x \mid (i=1)] \\
&= 1 - F_1(x) \qquad (10.1)
\end{aligned}$$

Prob. [Don't investigate $\mid$ out of control] =
Prob. $[\bar{x} \leq x \mid (i=2)] = F_2(x) \qquad (10.2)$

Since the process cannot go out of control whilst lying idle between operating periods, if it finishes an operating period in state $i=1$ it must start the next operating period in state $i=1$. If, however, the process is in state $i=2$ at the end of an operating period, and a cost report is received, there is a probability $F_2(x)$ that this report will show a cost observation $\bar{x}$ which is less than the critical value of x, leading to a decision not to investigate the process, so that it starts the next operating period in state $i=2$. On the other hand, there is a probability of $1-F_2(x)$ that the cost report will show $\bar{x} > x$, and lead to an investigation causing the process to start the next operating period in state $i=1$. All this information on the probabilities of movements between states during the interval between two operating periods can be summarised in a matrix in which the rows represent the states at the end of an operating period and the columns the states at the start of the next period. This matrix is called the 'control transition matrix' because it represents the outcome of the exercise of control. It appears as follows:

$$
\begin{array}{cc}
 & \begin{array}{cc} i=1 & \quad\quad i=2 \end{array} \\
\begin{array}{c} i=1 \\ i=2 \end{array} &
\left[\begin{array}{cc} 1 & 0 \\ 1-F_2(x) & F_2(x) \end{array} \right]
\end{array}
$$

If this control transition matrix is premultiplied by the process transition matrix given above, the 'controlled process transition matrix' is created. This shows the probabilities of moving from one state to another over an entire cycle from the beginning of one operating period to the beginning of the next, covering both changes of state by the process itself and control responses to those changes. Its form is as follows:

$$
\begin{array}{cc}
 & \begin{array}{cc} i=1 & \quad\quad\quad i=2 \end{array} \\
\begin{array}{c} i=1 \\ i=2 \end{array} &
\left[\begin{array}{cc} 1-(1-g)F_2(x) & (1-g)F_2(x) \\ 1-F_2(x) & F_2(x) \end{array} \right]
\end{array}
$$

The only problems of interpretation here are those posed by the element relating to the probability of moving from state $i=1$ at the beginning of one operating period to $i=1$ at the beginning of the next. This can be done either by:

1. The process never moving out of control, which has a probability of g, *or*
2. The process moving out of control, with probability $(1-g)$, and then control action being taken to move it back again, with probability $1-F_2(x)$, giving a compound probability of $(1-g)[1-F_2(x)]$.

The sum of these two probabilities is $g+(1-g)[1-F_2(x)]$, which simplifies to $1-(1-g)F_2(x)$ as in the matrix.

Steady-state probabilities

Consider a given value of x within the decision rule 'investigate if and only if $\bar{x} > x$'. The steady-state probabilities $\pi_1(x)$ and $\pi_2(x)$ are the probabilities of the process being respectively in states $i=1$ and $i=2$ for that critical cost x at the start of period n, where n is large. They are obtained from the controlled process transition matrix by the simultaneous solution of two equations, as follows:

$$\pi_2(x) = [(1-g)F_2(x)]\pi_1(x) + F_2(x)\pi_2(x) \qquad (10.3)$$
$$\pi_1(x) + \pi_2(x) = 1 \qquad (10.4)$$

Equation (10.3) represents a result from Markov chain theory, while equation (10.4) simply reflects the fact that the probabilities of states $i=1$ and $i=2$ must add up to unity. Solving these equations gives:

$$\pi_1(x) = \frac{1-F_2(x)}{1-gF_2(x)} \quad \text{and} \quad \pi_2(x) = \frac{(1-g)F_2(x)}{1-gF_2(x)} \qquad (10.5)$$

Because the controlled process transition matrix refers to states at the beginning of an operating period, the above steady-state probabilities have to be postmultiplied by the process transition matrix in order to obtain the steady-state probabilities $s_1(x)$ and $s_2(x)$ which prevail during an operating period. This is done as follows:

$$[\pi_1(x) \quad \pi_2(x)] \begin{bmatrix} g & (1-g) \\ 0 & 1 \end{bmatrix}$$

$$= [\pi_1(x)g \qquad (1-g)\pi_1(x) + \pi_2(x)]$$

Hence:

$$s_1(x) = \pi_1(x)g \quad \text{and} \quad s_2(x) = (1-g)\pi_1(x) + \pi_2(x) \qquad (10.6)$$

Substituting from (10.5) above in the expression for $s_2(x)$ gives:

$$s_2(x) = \frac{1-g}{1-gF_2(x)} \tag{10.7}$$

The relationships in (10.5) and (10.6) above constitute expressions for the probabilities of being in states $i=1$ and $i=2$ after the process has been run with a critical cost x for a long time. These probabilities can be used to find the long-term average cost per period of running the process using any given value of x in the decision rule. Then the value of x associated with the minimum long-term cost represents the optimum value of x to insert in the decision rule determining whether or not to investigate.

Determining long-term average cost per period

Let the long-term average cost per period incurred in operating a process with a given value of x in the decision rule be $C_0(x)$. Then $C_0(x)$ is obtained by weighting the mean operating costs per period for each of the states $i=1,2$ by the steady-state probabilities of each of these states being present during an operating period. This gives rise to:

$$C_0(x) = \mu_1 s_1(x) + \mu_2 s_2(x)$$

Substituting for $s_1(x)$ and $s_2(x)$ from the relationships in equation (10.6), then using equation (10.4) and the definition of $\Delta\mu$ enables the above equation to be expressed as:

$$C_0(x) = \mu_2 - g\pi_1(x)\Delta\mu \tag{10.8}$$

The probability that in any period $\bar{x} > x$ so that an investigation takes place is given by the conditional probability that $\bar{x} > x$ for each state $i=1,2$ multiplied by the steady-state probability of occurrence of that state. In symbolic terms:

$$\text{Prob.}(\bar{x} > x) = \text{Prob.}[\bar{x} > x|(i=1)]s_1(x) + \text{Prob.}[\bar{x} > x|(i=2)]s_2(x) \tag{10.9}$$

Substituting from equations (10.1) and (10.2) for the square-bracketed probabilities, then substituting by means of the relationships in equations (10.6) and (10.7) respectively for $s_1(x)$ and $s_2(x)$, and finally substituting $\pi_1(x)$ from its relationship in equation (10.5) gives:

$$\text{Prob.}(\bar{x} > x) = \pi_1(x)[1 - gF_1(x)]$$

Every time an investigation takes place, a fixed cost I is incurred. Hence the long-term average cost of investigation per period $C_I(x)$ is given by:

$$C_I(x) = \pi_1(x)[1 - gF_1(x)]I \tag{10.10}$$

Finally, the long-term average cost of correcting defects per period $C_K(x)$ is given by the probability that an investigation takes place in state $i=2$, multiplied by the cost of correction, which is K. The probability required is given by the second term on the right-hand side of equation (10.9). Substituting within this term from equations (10.2) and (10.7), then substituting $\pi_1(x)$ from its relationship in equation (10.5) gives:

$$C_K(x) = \pi_1(x)(1 - g)K \tag{10.11}$$

The long-term expected cost per period of controlling the process $C(x)$ is given by $C(x) = C_0(x) + C_I(x) + C_K(x)$. Substituting from equations (10.8), (10.10) and (10.11), and then simplifying, gives rise to:

$$C(x) = \mu_2 + \pi_1(x)[a - bF_1(x)] \tag{10.12}$$

where $a = (1 - g)K + I - g\Delta\mu$ (10.13)

and $b = gI$ (10.14)

It is worth noting that since g is a probability, $0 < g < 1$, and since I is a cost, $I > 0$. Consequently, it is always the case that $b > 0$.

Costs with extremal policies and with perfect information

The 'extremal policies' are those of never investigating at all, and always investigating at the end of every operating period. Their costs will now be dealt with in turn:

1. Never investigating is equivalent to setting $x = \infty$ in the decision rule 'investigate if and only if $\bar{x} > x$'. With $x = \infty$, $F_2(x) = 1$, hence $\pi_1(x) = 0$. If $\pi_1(x) = 0$, then $C(x) = \mu_2$.
2. Always investigating is equivalent to setting $x = 0$ in the above decision rule.
   With $x = 0$, $F_1(x) = F_2(x) = 0$.
   Because $F_2(x) = 0$, $\pi_1(x) = 1$, and substituting for $\pi_1(x)$ and $F_1(x)$ in equation (10.12) gives $C(x) = \mu_2 + a$.

If the pulp steaming machine supervisor in the Fitzroy problem had perfect information – in the sense of possessing advance knowledge of whether the process was in control or not – then he would never order an investigation unnecessarily, nor would he ever fail to investigate when this was required. This may be expressed as:

Prob.(Investigate | in control)=0, so that $F_1(x)=1$
Prob.(Don't investigate | out of control)=0, so that $F_2(x)=0$

Under perfect information, no decision rule as such would be required; a decision rule represents a response to uncertainty. Hence there would be no value of x under certainty, enabling long-term expected cost in this case simply to be labelled as C^*. To derive C^*, note that if $F_2(x) = 0$, then $\pi_1(x) = 1$. By substitution for $F_1(x)$ and $\pi_1(x)$ in equation (10.12), it is found that $C^* = \mu_2 + a - b$. This formula represents the minimum attainable long-term expected cost per period of controlling the process.

Solving the Fitzroy problem

The question now is how to find $C(x)$ for $x \neq 0$ and $x \neq \infty$. For any given problem, μ_2, a and b are all constants, so that from equation

(10.12) the magnitude of $C(x)$ for any given x must depend upon $\pi_1(x)$ and $F_1(x)$. From equation (10.5), it may be seen that $\pi_1(x)$ depends on $F_2(x)$ but not on $F_1(x)$. The probability $F_2(x)$ is simply the probability of a cost observation $\bar{x}$ falling below x for the out of control state. Referring back to equation (10.12), since $b > 0$ it must follow that cost is minimised for a given value of x when $F_1(x)$ is maximised. Since $F_1(x)$ is the probability of a cost observation $\bar{x}$ less than x for the in control state, this implies that it is necessary to read from the in control distribution the probability of obtaining any $\bar{x}$ value up to a very small amount below x. The probability thus obtained is referred to as Max.$F_1(x)$.

The first step in solving the Fitzroy problem is to discretise the two probability distributions of cost by taking the midpoints of their class intervals as being representative of the whole class. Thus, for example, the 0.1 probability of a cost per day lying between £500 and £600 if the process is in control is discretised by saying that there is a 0.1 probability that the cost will be exactly £550. The discretised distributions appear as follows:

	Process in control		Process out of control
Cost per period £	Probability	Cost per period £	Probability
550	0.10	750	0.05
650	0.35	850	0.15
750	0.35	950	0.25
850	0.10	1050	0.25
950	0.05	1150	0.25
1050	0.05	1250	0.05

It is then necessary to compute $C(x)$ for each discrete cost x from $x = 750$ to $x = 1150$. These limits are determined by the fact that for $x < 750$, $F_2(x) = 0$, and for $x < 1150$, Max.$F_1(x) = 1$. Performing the computation requires the evaluation of the parameters μ_2, a and b. For the Fitzroy data, $\mu_2 = 1015$, $a = 90$ and $b = 232$. Using these parameters, a table can be drawn up as on p. 121. In it, the heading 'control limit' refers to the level of observed cost below which no investigation should be undertaken, and the value of $C(x)$ is obtained by substitution within equation (10.12).

Control Limit	$F_2(x)$	$\pi_1(x)$	Max.$F_1(x)$	$C(x)$
$x < 750$	0	1	0.45	1 000.6
$x < 850$	0.05	0.990	0.80	920.4
$x < 950$	0.20	0.952	0.90	901.9*
$x < 1 050$	0.45	0.859	0.95	903.0
$x < 1 150$	0.70	0.682	1	918.2

The asterisk in the above table denotes the minimum value of $C(x)$, which is associated with a decision rule 'investigate if the reported operating cost for a period is equal to or greater than £950'. This answers the first part of the Fitzroy problem, although it is worth noting that using £1 050 instead of £950 in the decision rule would raise the long-term expected cost associated with the pulp steaming machine by just over £1 per day. If, for example, there are elements of inconvenience associated with dismantling the machine's heating mechanism which are not fully reflected in the £290 cost figure for doing this, then it may be preferable to substitute £1 050 for £950 in the decision rule.

The Fitzroy problem goes on to ask for the costs associated with the policies of 'always investigating' and 'never investigating'. These costs are given by the formulae in 1 and 2 at the beginning of the previous section, and are as follows:

(a) For 'never investigate', $C(x) = \mu_2 = £1 015$ per day
(b) For 'always investigate', $C(x) = \mu_2 + a = £1 105$ per day

The final part of the problem asks what the long-term expected cost per day would be if perfect information were available, so that investigation decisions were made optimally throughout. From the formula in the previous section, $C^* = \mu_2 + a - b = £873$ per day.

Approximation to optimality of a fixed decision rule

There is a clear contrast between the use of a fixed critical cost level for investigation here, and the employment of cost observations for the Bayesian revision of state probabilities in the procedure applied to the Alston Glassworks problem. In the introduction to this problem, the point was made that the single-period orientation of the Bayesian approach could not produce a wholly satisfactory measure of the cost of failing to correct an out of control situation. The Markovian approach taken in the Fitzroy problem is not the only way of addressing this difficulty; Kaplan in his (1969) paper (see Appendix 2) advocated an elaborate alternative involving a multi-period Bayesian model, in which a dynamic programming computation is used to minimise the present value of expected costs incurred up to an infinite time horizon.

While this dynamic programming approach produces lower-cost solutions than does the Markovian approach, its practical application gives rise to very severe computational problems. A paper by Dittman and Prakash in the *Journal of Accounting Research*, April 1979 (see Appendix 2) compared the Markovian and dynamic programming approaches by means of simulation. They found that the difference between the minimum long-run expected costs per period obtainable under the two approaches was quite small, except in the case in which the standard deviation of the probability distribution of cost for the in control state was large both in relation to $\Delta\mu$ and to the corresponding standard deviation for the out of control state. However, this situation is probably uncommon; the standard deviation will normally be greater for an out of control state (which can arise from a variety of causes having widely differing effects on costs) than for an in control state (where the very fact that the process is working as intended would seem likely to impose some uniformity on costs incurred).

Stochastic Cost–Volume–Profit Analysis and Decision Theory

11

11.1 William Lehman Timber Ltd

William Lehman Timber Ltd (WLT) are importers and distributors of wood and forest products. WLT have extensive yards at the port of Goole, and are contemplating the installation (on currently unused space within the Goole yards) of plant for the distillation of fusel oil. Considerations of cash flow make it strongly in WLT's interests to lease this plant rather than purchase it outright. Two types of fusel oil distillation plant are available for leasing; direct distillation (DD) plant is being quoted with lease payments of £320 000 per annum, while the more sophisticated catalysis-assisted (CA) plant is being quoted with lease payments of £490 000 per annum. Because these plants are based on quite distinct technologies, they carry out the process of distillation with widely differing efficiencies. CA plant is capable of producing fusel oil at a variable cost of £0.17 per litre, while DD plant is capable of producing only at a variable cost of £0.28 per litre. WLT is part of a vertically-integrated forest products group, and sells solely through 250 'captive' wholesalers belonging to this group. These wholesalers do not currently stock fusel oil, but will all be required to do so when WLT makes it available to them. The price to the wholesaler is determined by competitive considerations, and will be 55p per litre irrespective of whether the fusel oil is produced by CA plant or DD plant.

Although there is no doubt within WLT as to the appropriate price to the wholesaler, there is considerable uncertainty as to the volume of demand that will be generated at that price. WLT have other possible uses for the space the distillation plant would occupy, and consequently feel that the project to produce fusel oil would need to yield a profit of 'certainly not less than' £100 000 per annum in order to justify itself. Here, profit is arrived at by deducting lease payments and variable production costs from the sales revenue obtained from wholesalers. On the basis of their limited experience of selling wood-derived chemicals, the best that WLT's management can do by way of predicting the demand for fusel oil is to say that there is an even chance that it will lie between 4 000 and 8 000 litres per wholesaler per annum. In view of this extreme uncertainty, WLT have undertaken detailed negotiations to obtain firm orders for a year's supply of fusel oil from a sample of their wholesalers. These negotiations involved five wholesalers, and the orders they obtained were for a mean of 6 350 litres with a standard deviation of 1 630 litres.

An opportunity has arisen to conduct negotiations with a further sample of six wholesalers, but this would cost an extra £5 800. The management of WLT believe that the standard deviation of fusel oil sales per annum as between wholesalers will be of the order of 1 700 litres.

You are required to advise WLT's management as to their most appropriate course of action.

11.2 Analysis

Elimination of the DD plant option

Before proceeding to the analysis of the data in this problem, it is necessary to be clear as to what constitutes the problem itself. Three mutually exclusive alternatives exist, which may be labelled as below. Let:

a_1 represent the act of leasing the DD plant
a_2 represent the act of leasing the CA plant
a_3 represent the act implicit in not proceeding with the fusel oil distillation project

Some further terminology required may be obtained by letting:

S represent the average sales of fusel oil, in litres per wholesaler per annum
$C(a_j,S)$ represent the cost per annum associated with act a_j for a given value of S

Initially, the focus of the enquiry will be on the choice between acts a_1 and a_2. Cost functions for these acts (in pounds per annum) may be drawn up as below:

$$C(a_1,S) = 320\,000 + (0.28)(250)S$$
$$C(a_2,S) = 490\,000 + (0.17)(250)S$$

These cost functions are made up of the sum of fixed cost plus the variable cost per litre of fusel oil produced, applied to the average sales in litres and multiplied by the 250 wholesalers under consideration. The break-even point for S as between a_1 and a_2 may be represented by S_b, and computed as $S_b = 170\,000/[250(0.28-0.17)] = 6\,182$ litres per wholesaler per annum.

This figure may be compared with that sales level at which the minimum acceptable profit of £100\,000 per annum would be earned with the DD plant. If this level is represented by S_d, then the relevant calculation is $S_d = 420\,000/[250(0.55-0.28)] = 6\,222$ litres per wholesaler per annum. Since $S_d > S_b$ for an opportunity cost of £100\,000 per annum incurred in using the Goole site space for fusel oil distillation, it must follow that the DD plant cannot be preferred to the CA plant at this opportunity cost level. By the definition of S_b, for sales levels in excess of 6 182 litres per wholesaler per annum the CA plant is preferred, while for sales levels below this figure the minimum acceptable profit is not earned and the project does not proceed.

By this line of argument, the DD plant would seem to be eliminated from further consideration, the more so since the problem stipulates the minimum acceptable profit on the project as being 'certainly not less than' £100 000 per annum. It should be noted, however, that if for any reason the opportunity cost figure were actually to lie below £100 000 per annum, act a_1 would immediately re-enter the analysis. For an opportunity cost of £75 000 per annum, $S_d = 5 851$ and for an opportunity cost of £50 000 per annum, $S_d = 5 481$. With figures of this order, where actual sales S were such that $S_d < S < S_b$, the DD plant would be preferred. While estimates of opportunity cost are inherently imprecise, the case where $S_d < S_b$ will not be pursued further here, since it would transform the issue into a 'three-action problem' of considerable complexity.

Posterior analysis

Attention will be focused on the choice between acts a_2 and a_3. The CA plant would earn the minimum acceptable profit of £100 000 per annum at a sales level of $S_c = 590 000/[250(0.55-0.17)] = 6 210$ litres per wholesaler per annum. The question is one of how the likelihood of attaining this level has been affected by the information that has already been obtained from the sample of five wholesalers. The study of this effect involves an approach called posterior analysis. If a very large number of samples of five observations were to be drawn from the population of 250 wholesalers, the means of these samples could be plotted to form a sampling distribution of the mean for samples of size five. The Central Limit Theorem indicates that even for samples as small as this, the sampling distribution will be approximately normal unless the population is extremely skewed. Let:

$\bar{x}$ represent the sample mean
s represent the standard deviation of the sample

n represent the sample size

$\sigma_{\bar{x}}$ represent the standard deviation of the sampling distribution

Then since $s = 1630$ and $n = 5$ here:

$$\sigma_{\bar{x}} = s/\sqrt{n} = 729.0$$

The term $\sigma_{\bar{x}}$ is referred to as the standard error of the mean. Its computation does not involve a finite population correction, since the sample constitutes only 2 per cent of the population.

Before any sample information was obtained, WLT's management had in their minds a prior distribution of demand per wholesaler per annum, drawn from their knowledge and experience of the forest products industry. Assuming this distribution to be normal in form, let:

$E_0(\mu)$ represent the mean of the prior distribution

σ_0 represent the standard deviation of the prior distribution

For this problem, $E_0(\mu) = 6000$, but σ_0 is not given, and has to be inferred. All that WLT's management can say about the spread of the prior distribution is that they feel there to be an even chance that demand will lie within the range from 4000–8000 litres per wholesaler per annum. More formally, WLT's management can be taken as asserting (for example) that there is a 0.25 probability that demand will exceed 8000 for a normal distribution with a mean of 6000 and an unknown standard deviation. Some 25 per cent of the area under a standardised normal distribution lies to the right of $z = 0.675$. The standardised value (or z score) of a reading of 8000 from the normal prior distribution must thus be 0.675. This makes it possible to find the unknown standard deviation σ_0 by solving the following equation:

$$(8000-6000)/\sigma_0 = 0.675, \text{ hence } \sigma_0 = 2963$$

The calculation required for posterior analysis involves revising a normal prior distribution with mean $E_0(\mu) = 6000$ and standard deviation $\sigma_0 = 2963$ by reference to the sample findings, which gave an estimate of the mean sales $\bar{x} = 6350$ subject to a standard error $\sigma_{\bar{x}} = 729$. The distribution obtained from the revision of a prior distribution by reference to sample data is referred to as the posterior distribution. If the prior distribution is normal, then so also will be the posterior distribution. Let:

$E_1(\mu)$ represent the mean of the posterior distribution

σ_1 represent the standard deviation of the posterior distribution

Then the following are standard results from statistical decision theory:

$$E_1(\mu) = \frac{E_0(\mu)\,\sigma_{\bar{x}}^2 + \bar{x}\sigma_0^2}{\sigma_{\bar{x}}^2 + \sigma_0^2} \tag{11.1}$$

$$\sigma_1 = \sqrt{\frac{\sigma_0^2\,\sigma_{\bar{x}}^2}{\sigma_0^2 + \sigma_{\bar{x}}^2}} \tag{11.2}$$

The normality of the prior distribution has already been assumed, but in any event so long as the variance of the prior distribution σ_0^2 is large in relation to the sampling variance of the mean $\sigma_{\bar{x}}^2$, then the posterior distribution can be taken as being normal even if the prior distribution is not normal. In this problem, with $\sigma_0^2 = 16.5\sigma_{\bar{x}}^2$, it would require an exceedingly skewed prior distribution to prevent the posterior distribution from being normal.

By computation, for this problem $E_1(\mu) = 6\,330$ and $\sigma_1 = 707.9$. Since $E_1(\mu) > S_c$, on the basis of the information in the first sample act a_2 is to be preferred. However, the question which now arises is one of whether it is worth obtaining any more information before proceeding to a final decision as between acts a_2 and a_3. This question is handled by means of an approach named preposterior analysis.

Preposterior analysis

Since the cost of sampling a further six wholesalers is known, the question of whether this is worthwhile resolves itself into one of finding the expected value of sample information associated with the sample of six. Some further terminology is required, as follows. Let:

σ'^2 represent the variance prior to the new sample, so that from the calculations above $\sigma'^2 = 707.9^2$

σ''^2 represent the variance posterior to the new sample

σ^2 represent the estimated variance of the population, given in the problem as $\sigma^2 = 1\,700^2$

In the absence of any information from the new sample, the approach of equation (11.2) may be employed, but with the estimated variance of the population taking the place of the variance obtained from sample information. This gives rise to:

$$\sigma''^2 = \frac{\sigma'^2\,\sigma^2}{\sigma^2 + n\sigma'^2} \tag{11.3}$$

Let σ^{*2} represent the reduction in variance due to a sample of size n, so that:

$$\sigma^{*2} = \sigma'^2 - \sigma''^2 \tag{11.4}$$

Substituting from equation (11.3) for σ''^2 in equation (11.4) and simplifying produces the following relationship:

$$\sigma^{*2} = \frac{n\sigma'^4}{\sigma^2 + n\sigma'^2} \tag{11.5}$$

With $n = 6$, and given the values for σ'^2 and σ^2 shown above, computation yields $\sigma^* = 505.5$. From the form of equation (11.5), it will be noted that the value of σ^* is fairly insensitive to errors in estimating the variance of the population, unless n is very small. It is next necessary to define a standardised variable D^* as follows. Let:

D^* represent the absolute distance, in terms of σ^* units, that separates $E_1(\mu)$ from the break-even value

Then:

$$D^* = \left| \frac{S_c - E_1(\mu)}{\sigma^*} \right| = 0.24$$

A pair of functions must now be defined representing the opportunity losses associated with the incorrect decisions to abandon the project if $S > S_c$, and to proceed with CA plant if $S_c > S$. These functions appear as follows:

$$(0.55 - 0.17)(250)(S - S_c) \text{ for } S > S_c$$
$$(0.55 - 0.17)(250)(S_c - S) \text{ for } S_c > S$$

Let L represent the rate of change of these opportunity loss functions, so that here $L = 95$.

The final step in building up the equation for the expected value of sample information (EVSI) involves the unit normal loss integral $L_N(D^*)$, defined as below:

$$L_N(D^*) = \int_{D^*}^{\infty} (\theta - D^*) f_N(\theta) \, d\theta \tag{11.6}$$

In equation (11.6), $f_N(\theta)$ represents the value of the standard normal density function associated with θ. It is not in practice necessary to carry out the integration on the right-hand side of equation (11.6), since tables from which the unit normal loss integral can be read for given values of D^* are readily available. The expected value of sample information is given by the following equation:

$$\text{EVSI} = L\sigma^* L_N(D^*) \tag{11.7}$$

From tables, $L_N(0.24) = 0.2904$, and the expected value of sample information for a further sample of six wholesalers is found to be £13 946. The cost of sampling six wholesalers is stated in the problem to be £5 800, and when this is subtracted from the EVSI an expected net gain from sampling (ENGS) of £8 146 is obtained. As this ENGS figure is positive, it seems worthwhile to take a further sample of six wholesalers before deciding between acts a_2 and a_3 – leasing the CA plant or abandoning the project.

However, this conclusion is dependent upon the accuracy of the £100 000 figure for the opportunity cost of using the vacant space in the Goole yards for fusel oil distillation. Since this £100 000 can be no more than a rough estimate, sensitivity analysis of the above conclusion favouring further sampling is needed.

The sensitivity analysis required is of a fairly simple kind. If the opportunity cost per annum were to be £125 000 instead of £100 000, then $S_c = 6474$, and if it were to be £150 000 then the corresponding figure would be $S_c = 6737$. Inserting these S_c values into the computation of D^*, and recalculating the EVSI and ENGS figures with the new values of D^* obtained, gives rise to the following results. (Brackets denote negative figures).

Opportunity cost per annum	EVSI	ENGS
£	£	£
125 000	13 281	7 382
150 000	5 671	(129)

The conclusion to be drawn is that if the opportunity cost of the space in the Goole yards lies below £150 000 per annum, then it will be worthwhile to take the further sample of six wholesalers preparatory to a final decision as between acts a_2 and a_3. If, however, the opportunity cost lies at or above the £150 000 per annum level, then with $S_c > E_1(\mu)$ and a negative ENGS, it will neither be worth proceeding with the fusel oil distillation project nor worth taking the further sample of six wholesalers. Unless some cheaper form of sampling is available, with a sample size of less than six, act a_3 will be optimal prior to further sampling. In these circumstances the project should be abandoned immediately.

Stochastic Cost–Volume– Profit Analysis: Satisficing with Short Product Lives

12

12.1 Knowsley Medical Products

Knowsley Medical Products (KMP) is a major manufacturer of drugs for human and veterinary use. Its researchers have developed two new vaccines which provide protection against a highly contagious disease afflicting sheep. These vaccines are called Murax and Diprofyl. Their chemical compositions and costs of manufacture are different, and they confer differing degrees of protection against the disease. However, it is clear to KMP's management that Murax and Diprofyl would compete against one another to an extent making it impossible to cover the additional fixed costs that would be involved in manufacturing both of them. It is a commercial proposition to manufacture only one of the vaccines, abandoning the exploitation of the other one.

In choosing which vaccine to manufacture, KMP's management have extensive experience upon which to draw. A study of their sales records has shown that frequency distributions for the number of packs of a vaccine demanded per week usually conform quite closely to the normal distribution. Either Murax or Diprofyl will replace an existing KMP product, and only a small capital investment will be required to adapt its production line for either of the new products. The Product Planning and Market Research departments within KMP have together drawn up estimates for Murax and Diprofyl costs and revenues as follows:

	Murax	*Diprofyl*
Mean sales (in packs) per week	1 300	1 400
Standard deviation of sales	450	700
	£	£
Avoidable fixed costs of manufacture per week	6 000	6 000
Variable cost per pack produced	28	33
Sales revenue per pack sold for veterinary use	39	47
Sales revenue per pack sold to Kalumon PLC	24	24
Present value of future profit lost per unsatisfied order for a pack	5	7

The last three entries in the above table require explanation. It is possible to manufacture only one batch of either sheep vaccine per week, because of the extreme fragility of the production equipment and the stringency of the quality control requirements. Both Murax and Diprofyl are chemically unstable, deteriorating quite rapidly in storage. If a pack of either vaccine is not sold after a week has elapsed since its production, it is said to have become 'stale'. The contents of a stale pack must not be put to veterinary use, but can readily be sold by KMP to Kalumon PLC, a large company located nearby and engaged in the manufacture of fine chemicals. Kalumon will buy any amount of either Murax or Diprofyl that KMP cares to supply, to use as a substitute for dibutane sulphate, an intermediate product in the manufacture of a chemical completely unrelated to sheep vaccine. As substitutes for dibutane sulphate, Murax and Diprofyl are chemically indistinguishable, and Kalumon will pay the same £24 per pack price for either of them.

It is not economic for a sheep farmer to innoculate every new-born lamb with either Murax or Diprofyl. These vaccines will be demanded only when the disease against which they protect has actually broken out, and they will then be required with extreme urgency. Existing vaccines manufactured by KMP's competitors offer some protection against the disease, and vets faced with an outbreak of the disease will buy and use these vaccines if KMP cannot meet their orders within a day. If a week's batch of vaccine has been sold out completely, KMP cannot hope to keep any further orders received in that week waiting until the next week's batch of vaccine becomes available. KMP feel that turning away vets' orders (and thus compelling them to use the less effective vaccines of their competitors) will generate ill-will toward KMP from both vets and farmers. This will be particularly true if it is orders for the especially effective Diprofyl which are frustrated. While KMP are conscious of the difficulty of estimating the present value of future profit lost as a result of an unsatisfied order for a pack of vaccine, they feel that this factor is so important that they have provided the 'guesstimates' in the table above.

A final note may be helpful regarding the 'avoidable fixed costs' entry in this table. The variable costs of sheep vaccine production are mainly composed of raw material costs; a large part of the labour costs, and all of the costs of support services such as maintenance and sterilisation, do not vary with the volume of vaccine output. These costs are nonetheless substantial, and appear in the table above as 'avoidable fixed costs'. They constitute cash outlays which could only be avoided by shutting down the sheep vaccine production line entirely.

By reference to the above facts, **you are required:**

1. To compute the expected profit per week from each vaccine if output is set at the profit-maximising level.
   The figures for expected profit should be taken net of any (notional) costs of ill-will arising from inability to meet orders for vaccine.
2. To specify which of Murax or Diprofyl would be the riskier product financially.
   This should be done by reference to the probability of at least breaking even at the profit maximising output, and by reference to the probability of earning at least £5 000 of profit (net of costs of ill-will) per week at the profit-maximising output.
   KMP's management have said that they will produce whichever vaccine yields the higher expected profit at its profit-maximising level of output. They are worried, however, that producing at

this level of output may involve too great a financial risk, and are seeking advice about this.

You are required to answer the following further questions posed by KMP:

3. For the vaccine chosen according to the criterion in the preceding paragraph, what level of output would maximise the probability of earning at least a 'satisfactory' £5 000 of profit (net of costs of ill-will) in a given week?

   What would the probability of earning at least this amount in a given week be at that output?

4. How would the output level which maximised the probability of earning at least £5 000 in a given week change in response to an increase from £6 000 to £6 500 per week in the avoidable fixed costs of manufacture?

12.2   Analysis

Introduction

There are two assumptions implicit in most stochastic cost–volume–profit analyses which have far-reaching consequences, and thus merit serious examination. The first of these is that, in the face of uncertain demand, attention should be focused on the *average* demand per period. So long as there is a sufficiently high probability that this average demand figure will be acceptable, the implication is that no concern need be expressed about fluctuations in demand from one period to another. Underlying this approach is an assumption that production can be expanded very rapidly to meet abnormally high demand, while in periods of abnormally low demand products can be stored for a long time without incurring significant incremental costs. The second implicit assumption is that the firms is concerned to maximise profit rather than to maximise the probability of earning a certain acceptable level of profit. Here, the implication is that managerial behaviour is characterised by optimising rather than satisficing.

In dealing with the Knowsley Medical Products (KMP) problem, both of the above assumptions will be relaxed. It is not appropriate to focus on average demand over many periods where the product concerned is perishable and where a significant loss of future business may arise from failures to fill orders immediately. Both of these conditions apply to KMP, giving rise to a risk of serious loss if the output level is inappropriately chosen. In order to present the level of risk from becoming unacceptably high, KMP's managers may well opt for a satisficing than for an optimising policy. These policies will be explored in turn, taking optimising first.

Maximisation of expected profit

Before commencing the analysis, it is necessary initially to define some terms, as follows. Let:

X represent the output level of a vaccine, in packs produced per week

X^* represent the value of X for which profit is maximised

c represent the contribution margin per pack sold for veterinary use

h represent the holding cost per pack not sold for veterinary use

For a perishable product, the holding cost is given either by the sum of the variable cost of manufacture and the cost of disposal, or by the difference between the variable cost of manufacture and the salvage value obtainable on resale after perishing.

In the KMP problem, the act of 'salvage' involves selling a stale pack for £24 to Kalumon PLC for use in chemical manufacture. Thus for Murax $h = 28-24 = 4$ and for Diprofyl $h = 33-24 = 9$.

s represent the opportunity cost arising from inability to supply a pack of vaccine, measured in terms of the present value of future profit sacrificed as a result of the ill-will generated by this frustrated order

D represent the demand for a vaccine, in packs per week

Z represent a vaccine's profit per week net of all costs, including those arising from ill-will

To maximise profit, the expected holding cost of the last unit of production must be equated to the sum of its expected contribution margin and the expected opportunity cost saving arising from its manufacture. Using the symbol P to represent the probability of a particular demand level, the above relationship may be expressed as:

$$h[1-P(D \geqq X^*)] = (c+s) [P(D \geqq X^*)] \qquad (12.1)$$

Expanding equation (12.1), and isolating out the terms in P gives:

$$P(D \geqq X^*) = h/(c+h+s) \qquad (12.2)$$

For the Murax vaccine, $h = 4$, $c = 11$ and $s = 5$, so that the profit-maximising output X^* is that for which the probability of demand being in excess of output is $4/(4+11+5) = 0.2$. Demand for Murax can be taken as normally distributed, with mean $\mu =$

1 300 and standard deviation $\sigma = 450$. Inspection of a table of the inverse normal function shows that 0.2 of the area under a standardised normal distribution lies to the right of $z = 0.8416$. X^* is then given by:

$$X^* = \mu + \sigma z \tag{12.3}$$

Substitution in equation (12.3) shows that for Murax $X^* = 1\,679$ packs per week.

In determining X^* it was not necessary to take into account the 'avoidable fixed costs', but they do enter into the determination of the profit level Z. Let:

> F represent the avoidable fixed costs of manufacture per week, so that for Murax $F = 6\,000$

The level of profit Z earned for any output X depends on the behaviour of demand D. Specifically:

$$\text{If } D \geqq X, \text{ then } Z = cX - s(D-X) - F \tag{12.4}$$

All of the output X is sold for veterinary use in this case, and opportunity costs are incurred in respect of the excess, unsatisfied demand.

$$\text{If } D \leqq X, \text{ then } Z = cD - h(X-D) - F \tag{12.5}$$

Only D packs of vaccine are here sold for veterinary use, and the holding cost h is incurred for each pack produced in excess of the veterinary demand.

Letting $f(D)$ represent the probability density function for demand, and combining equations (12.4) and (12.5), an expression for the expected profit $E(Z)$ at output level X is obtained:

$$E(Z) = \int_{X}^{\infty} [cX - s(D-X)]f(D)dD + \int_{0}^{X} [cD - h(X-D)]f(D)dD - F \tag{12.6}$$

Terminology may now be employed as below. Let:

> $f_N(z)$ represent the value of the standard normal probability
> density function at z, with $z = (X-\mu)/\sigma$
> $\Phi(z)$ represent the probability that a standard normal ran-
> dom variable is less than or equal to z

With this terminology, it can be shown that equation (12.6) is
equivalent to:

$$E(Z)=(c+s)X-(c+s+h)[(X-\mu)\Phi(z)+\sigma f_N(z)]-s\mu-F \quad (12.7)$$

For an output of Murax vaccine of $X^* = 1\,679$ packs per week,
substituting in equation (12.7) gives rise to $E(Z) =$ £5 777.
Carrying out the calculations of this section for the Diprofyl
vaccine yields a profit-maximising output of $X^* = 1\,767$ packs per
week, associated with an expected profit of $E(Z) =$ £6 281. Hence,
on the basis of expected profit, it would seem better for KMP to
manufacture Diprofyl rather than Murax. However, the expected
profit figures are fairly close to one another, which means that
particular attention needs to be paid to the question of which of
the two vaccines is the riskier to manufacture from a financial
standpoint.

Analysis of financial risk

'Financial risk' is here expressed in terms of the probability of
earning not less than a given amount of profit in a week by
producing a vaccine at that level of output for which expected
profit is a maximum. New 'target' variables may be defined as
below. Let:

> Z_t represent the minimum acceptable level of profit
> Y_t represent the minimum acceptable contribution level

It then follows that:

$$Y_t = Z_t + F \tag{12.8}$$

In a given week, there are two ways of earning a profit of exactly Z_t while producing at an output level of X^*, depending upon the relationship between X^* and D. Firstly, if over the week $D \geqq X^*$, then from equation (12.4) it follows that a profit of exactly Z_t can be earned if D is such that:

$$Z_t = cX^* - s(D - X^*) - F \qquad (12.9)$$

The level of D for which equation (12.9) holds will be referred to as D_U. Here, the subscript U is employed to signify that D_U represents the upper limit on a week's demand consistent with earning a profit of not less than Z_t in that week. At levels of demand above D_U, the costs of ill-will associated with frustrated orders bring profit down below Z_t. Substituting D_U for D in equation (12.9), isolating D_U and simplifying by reference to equation (12.8) gives rise to:

$$D_U = \frac{(c+s)X^* - Y_t}{s} \qquad (12.10)$$

The second way of earning Z_t from an output of X^* arises in the case in which $D \leqq X^*$ over the week. Then equation (12.5) shows that a profit of exactly Z_t can be generated if D is such that:

$$Z_t = cD - h(X^* - D) \qquad (12.11)$$

The level of D satisfying equation (12.11) will be referred to as D_L, the subscript signifying that it represents the lowest level of demand at which a profit of not less than Z_t can be earned in a week. Substituting D_L for D in equation (12.11), isolating D_L and simplifying gives rise to:

$$D_L = \frac{hX^* + Y_t}{c+h} \qquad (12.12)$$

The probability of earning a week's profit of Z_t or more may be represented by the area under a standardised normal distribution between the values $z = (D_U - \mu)/\sigma$ and $z = (D_L - \mu)/\sigma$. Using the symbol Φ as it was used in equation (12.7), and representing the probability of earning Z_t or more at an output of X^* as $P_{X^*}[Z \geq Z_t]$, the relationship is given by:

$$P_{X^*}[Z \geq Z_t] = \Phi\left(\frac{D_U - \mu}{\sigma}\right) - \Phi\left(\frac{D_L - \mu}{\sigma}\right) \qquad (12.13)$$

Working through equations (12.8), (12.10), (12.12) and (12.13) for $Z_t = 0$ and $Z_t = 5\,000$ yields the following results for the case where each vaccine is produced to its profit-maximising output:

Murax	Diprofyl
$P_{1679}[Z \geq 0] = 0.84$	$P_{1767}[Z \geq 0] = 0.74$
$P_{1679}[Z \geq 5\,000] = 0.60$	$P_{1767}[Z \geq 5\,000] = 0.63$

Of the two vaccines, Diprofyl has an average profit per week which (at the profit-maximising output) is just over £500 larger than that for Murax. Diprofyl also has a higher probability of achieving a profit target of £5 000 in a given week than has Murax, comparing their performances at their profit-maximising outputs.

But if Diprofyl were to be produced at its profit-maximising output, the £5 000 profit target would on average be achieved in less than 13 weeks out of every 20, and on average a loss would be sustained in 1 week out of 4. This erratic performance, with frequent losses, may be unacceptable to managers who are held accountable for profit on a week-by-week basis. They may well prefer to select an output level for Diprofyl on the basis of maximising the number of weeks in which the £5 000 profit target is achieved, even at the expense of reducing the average profit. It is to this 'satisficing' approach that attention is now turned.

Maximising the probability of satisfactory profit

The problem of finding the 'satisficing' output level which maximises the probability of obtaining a profit from Diprofyl of at least £5 000 in any given week may be expressed formally as follows: Find that value X^{**} which is such as to maximise:

$$P_{X^{**}}(Z \geq 5000) = \Phi\left(\frac{D_U - \mu}{\sigma}\right) - \Phi\left(\frac{D_L - \mu}{\sigma}\right) \qquad (12.14)$$

Define the following terms:

$$\alpha = \frac{Y_t}{c+h} - \mu; \; \beta = \frac{h}{c+h}; \; \gamma = -\frac{Y_t}{s} - \mu; \; \delta = \frac{c+s}{s} \qquad (12.15)$$

$$K = (2\sigma^2) \{\log_e[(c+s)(c+h)/hs]\} \qquad (12.16)$$

Lau (1979, pp. 559–61) demonstrated that P is maximised at that output level X^{**} for which:

$$X^{**} = \frac{(\alpha\beta-\gamma\delta)+\sqrt{(\alpha\beta-\gamma\delta)^2-(\delta^2-\beta^2)(\gamma^2-\alpha^2-K)}}{\delta^2-\beta^2} \qquad (12.17)$$

For a target profit of £5 000 per week, Y_t = £11 000. Substituting the parameters for Diprofyl into equations (12.15) and (12.16) gives:

$$\alpha = -921.7 \; ; \; \beta = 0.3913 \; ; \; \gamma = -2971.4 \; ; \; \delta = 3 \; ; \\ K = 1\,996\,145$$

Substituting for these values in equation (12.17) yields $X^{**} = 1\,475$. Taking this value, and inserting it in equations (12.10) and (12.12) for $Y_t = 11\,000$ gives $D_U = 2\,853.6$ and $D_L = 1\,055.4$. Since Diprofyl has a mean demand per week $\mu = 1\,400$ with a standard deviation $s = 700$, the probability of earning at least £5 000 in a given week with an output of 1 475 packs of Diprofyl is given by:

$$P_{1475}[Z\geqq 5\,000]=\Phi\left(\frac{2\,853.6-1\,400}{700}\right)-\Phi\left(\frac{1\,055.4-1\,400}{700}\right)$$

$$= 0.67$$

Substituting $X^{**} = 1\,475$ in equations (12.10) and (12.12) for $Y_t = 6\,000$ gives $D_U = 3\,567.9$ and $D_L = 838.0$. Hence the probability of at least breaking even with this output in a given week may be computed as:

$$P_{1475}[Z\geqq 0]=\Phi\left(\frac{3\,567.9-1\,400}{700}\right)-\Phi\left(\frac{838-1\,400}{700}\right) = 0.79$$

By comparison with the profit-maximising strategy of producing 1 767 packs of Diprofyl per week, this satisficing strategy offers an increase in the probability of attaining an (acceptable) £5 000 profit from 0.63 to 0.67, and an increase in the probability of at least breaking even from 0.74 to 0.79. But there is a substantial cost associated with adopting the satisficing strategy, arising from the fact that this strategy makes improbable very high profit levels as well as very low ones. Denoting the expected profit per week associated with output level X as $E_X(Z)$, the position can be expressed as follows:

$$\text{Expected cost of satisficing strategy} = E_{X^*}(Z) - E_{X^{**}}(Z) \quad (12.18)$$

From the calculation immediately below equation (12.7), $E_{X^*}(Z)$ = £6 281. Then substituting X^{**} in the second term on the right-hand side of equation (12.18) and evaluating yields $E_{1\,475}(Z)$ = £5 628. The expected cost per week of adopting a satisficing strategy based on an acceptable profit level of £5 000 for Diprofyl is thus £6 281 − £5 628 = £653.

Fixed cost changes and satisficing decisions

The last part of the KMP problem asks what effect a £500 per week increase in avoidable fixed costs would have on the level of output X^{**} chosen so as to maximise the probability of earning £5 000 of profit in a given week. This involves recomputing X^{**} with Y_t = 11 500 instead of Y_t = 11 000, and produces a result of X^{**} = 1 497. From a satisficing point of view, the best level of output X^{**} is seen to have *risen* by 1 497 − 1 475 = 22 packs per week in response to an increase in *fixed* costs. This is in sharp contrast to decision-making using a profit-maximising criterion, in which the optimal output X^* is determined solely by incremental revenues and variable costs, being in no way influenced by changes in the level of fixed costs.

Studies in the theory of the firm under uncertainty have shown that to increase output in response to an increase in fixed costs is characteristic of managers who have increasingly risk-averse utility functions. To see what these represent, consider a manager who has acquired the right to undertake an investment with a 50–50 chance of increasing the firm's wealth by £$(x+h)$ or by £$(x-h)$. There must exist an amount £$(x-\pi)$ which he would regard as the minimum amount for which he would be willing to sell the right to undertake this investment. The magnitude π within this amount is referred to as the manager's 'risk premium'.

If, given a constant figure for h, the amount π specified by a particular manager increases as x increases, then that manager is said to have an 'increasingly risk-averse' utility function. In broad terms, a manager with this form of utility function is one who would be willing to pay more for insurance with a given coverage as corporate wealth increased. A fixed cost increase is equivalent to a diminution in wealth, and as wealth diminishes so risk-taking increases for this type of manager. Consequently, a fixed cost increase causes output to rise as calculated above, increasing the expected profit but diminishing the probability of breaking even in any given week.

Stochastic Cost–Volume– Profit Analysis: 13 Choice Among Combinations of Products

13.1 Barrow Gurney Orchards Ltd

Barrow Gurney Orchards Ltd (BGO) have pioneered a method of producing low-calorie cider, which they are able to make in low-strength, medium or full-strength versions. The low-strength version is designated X_1, the medium-strength version X_2 and the full-strength version X_3. After a study of markets and costs, BGO's management have derived the following data, with demand expressed in litres per week:

Product	Mean demand	Variance of demand	Price per litre	Variable cost per litre	Fixed manu- facturing cost outlay per week
			£	£	£
X_1	6 000	360 000	2.20	1.10	5 500
X_2	5 000	250 000	2.40	1.35	4 500
X_3	4 000	490 000	2.60	1.70	3 500

The correlation of demand among the three products is:

$r_{12} = 0.6; \ r_{23} = 0.6; \ r_{13} = 0.6$

Four strategies are currently under consideration:

	Strategy
1. To make products X_1 and X_2 only	A
2. To make products X_2 and X_3 only	B
3. To make products X_1 and X_3 only	C
4. To make products X_1, X_2 and X_3	D

You are required to answer the following questions:

(a) Which of the above strategies should be selected if it is desired to minimise the probability of failing to break even, and it is assumed that demand for each product is a normally distributed random variable?

(b) Suppose that the above data on demand for each product has been derived from a trial period of 30 weeks during which all three products were marketed.

What will be the 95 per cent confidence limits on the probability of at least breaking even for the strategy selected in part (a) above?

13.2 Analysis

Choice of a strategy

The issue which arises in this problem is one of choosing the optimal strategy for marketing some (or all) of the products within a group of related products. Since the products are related, the correlation of the demand for one product with the demand for another product has to be taken explicitly into account. Knowledge of both the levels of demand and of demand correlations as between products arises here from 30 weeks of test-marketing data. This data may be treated as a sample from the population of demand readings available over an indefinitely long period. Because demand per week is the only parameter subject to uncertainty, confidence limits can be attached to the probability of attaining a given level of profit from the adoption of a given strategy, without running into difficulties associated with the multiplication of probability distributions (as where a distribution for contribution margin per unit is multiplied by one for demand per period).

The problem involves three products, designated X_1, X_2 and X_3. Each product X_i is assumed to have a normally distributed probability density function for sales volume. Let:

$\hat{\mu}_i$ represent the (sample) mean demand for Product X_i

$\hat{\sigma}_i$ represent the (sample) standard deviation of demand for product X_i

r_{ij} represent the correlation of demand as between products X_i and X_j, computed from the sample data

A variance-covariance matrix may be drawn up showing the variances of demand for each of the three products, and the covariances between them, as follows:

	X_1	X_2	X_3
X_1	$\hat{\sigma}_1^2 = 360\,000$	$r_{12}\,\hat{\sigma}_1\hat{\sigma}_2 = 180\,000$	$r_{13}\,\hat{\sigma}_1\hat{\sigma}_3 = 252\,000$
X_2	$r_{21}\,\hat{\sigma}_2\hat{\sigma}_1 = 180\,000$	$\hat{\sigma}_2^2 = 250\,000$	$r_{23}\,\hat{\sigma}_2\hat{\sigma}_3 = 210\,000$
X_3	$r_{31}\,\hat{\sigma}_3\hat{\sigma}_1 = 252\,000$	$r_{32}\,\hat{\sigma}_3\sigma_2 = 210\,000$	$\hat{\sigma}_3^2 = 490\,000$

Along the principal diagonal of this matrix, from the top left-hand corner, are displayed the variances of each of the probability density functions for demand. The other elements in the matrix represent covariances, each covariance being repeated twice (since $r_{ij} = r_{ji}$) to form a pattern in which the covariances below the principal diagonal represent a mirror image of those above it. A more compact representation of the variance-covariance matrix is available using the following terminology. Let:

$$\hat{\sigma}_{ij} = \hat{\sigma}_i^2 \text{ if } i = j$$
$$\hat{\sigma}_{ij} = r_{ij}\, \hat{\sigma}_i\, \hat{\sigma}_j \text{ if } i \neq j$$

Then the matrix may be rewritten as below:

	X_1	X_2	X_3
X_1	$\hat{\sigma}_{11} = 360\,000$	$\hat{\sigma}_{12} = 180\,000$	$\hat{\sigma}_{13} = 252\,000$
X_2	$\hat{\sigma}_{21} = 180\,000$	$\hat{\sigma}_{22} = 250\,000$	$\hat{\sigma}_{23} = 210\,000$
X_3	$\hat{\sigma}_{31} = 252\,000$	$\hat{\sigma}_{32} = 210\,000$	$\hat{\sigma}_{33} = 490\,000$

Further symbols required may be obtained by letting:

c_i represent the contribution margin per litre for product X_i

f_i represent the outlay per week on fixed manufacturing costs for product X_i

$E(\hat{Y}_X)$ represent the estimated mean of the probability density function for profit associated with a given Strategy X

$V(\hat{Y}_X)$ represent the estimated variance of the probability density function for profit associated with a given Strategy X

If Strategy X involves the sale of n products, general formulae may be written as follows:

$$E(\hat{Y}_X) = \sum_{i=1}^{n} c_i\, \hat{\mu}_i - \sum_{i=1}^{n} f_i \qquad (13.1)$$

$$V(\hat{Y}_X) = \sum_{i=1}^{n} \sum_{j=1}^{n} \hat{\sigma}_{ij}\, c_i c_j \tag{13.2}$$

Let the estimated mean profit associated with Strategy A in this problem be $E(\hat{Y}_A)$, that associated with Strategy B be $E(\hat{Y}_B)$ and so on. Then:

$$E(\hat{Y}_A) = c_1\hat{\mu}_1 + c_2\hat{\mu}_2 - (f_1+f_2) = £1\,850$$
$$E(\hat{Y}_B) = c_2\hat{\mu}_2 + c_3\hat{\mu}_3 - (f_2+f_3) = £850$$
$$E(\hat{Y}_C) = c_1\hat{\mu}_1 + c_3\hat{\mu}_3 - (f_1+f_3) = £1\,200$$
$$E(\hat{Y}_D) = c_1\hat{\mu}_1 + c_2\hat{\mu}_2 + c_3\hat{\mu}_3 - (f_1+f_2+f_3) = £1\,950$$

Let the estimated variance of profit associated with Strategy A in this problem be $V(\hat{Y}_A)$, that associated with Strategy B be $V(\hat{Y}_B)$ and so on. Then:

$$V(\hat{Y}_A) = c_1^2\,\hat{\sigma}_{11} + 2c_1c_2\hat{\sigma}_{12} + c_2^2\,\hat{\sigma}_{22}$$

By computation, the standard deviation $\sqrt{V(\hat{Y}_A)} = £1\,061.6$

$$V(\hat{Y}_B) = c_2^2\,\hat{\sigma}_{22} + 2c_2c_3\,\hat{\sigma}_{23} + c_3^2\,\hat{\sigma}_{33}$$

By computation $\sqrt{V(\hat{Y}_B)} = £1\,034.1$

$$V(\hat{Y}_C) = c_1^2\,\hat{\sigma}_{11} + 2c_1c_3\,\hat{\sigma}_{13} + c_3^2\,\hat{\sigma}_{33}$$

By computation $\sqrt{V(\hat{Y}_C)} = £1\,153.9$

$$V(\hat{Y}_D) = c_1^2\hat{\sigma}_{11} + c_2^2\hat{\sigma}_{22} + c_3^2\hat{\sigma}_{33} + 2c_1c_2\hat{\sigma}_{12} + 2c_1c_3\hat{\sigma}_{13} + 2c_2c_3\hat{\sigma}_{23}$$

By computation, $\sqrt{V(\hat{Y}_D)} = £1\,555.6$

Since the probability density function for profit associated with a given Strategy X is normally distributed, a point estimate of the probability that this strategy will fail to break even is given by the area under a standardised normal distribution to the left of $z = [0-E(\hat{Y}_X)]/V(\hat{Y}_X)$. Applying this formula to Strategies A,B,C and D gives rise to the following tabulation, in which $P(Y_A < 0)$ refers to the probability of failing to break even with Strategy A, and so on.

Strategy	Point estimate of probability
A	$P(Y_A < 0) = 0.041$
B	$P(Y_B < 0) = 0.206$
C	$P(Y_C < 0) = 0.149$
D	$P(Y_D < 0) = 0.105$

From these figures, the application of a criterion of minimising the probability of failing to break even should lead to the selection of Strategy A. It is on this strategy that attention will be focused in addressing the second part of the problem.

Confidence limits for the break-even probability

In formal terms, what is required here is the computation of the 95 per cent confidence limits on $P(Y_A \geqq 0)$. A first step in this direction involves establishing the corresponding confidence limits for the expected profit $E(Y_A)$. The general formula for confidence limits around expected profit derived from a sample of m observations is given by:

$$E(\hat{Y}) - t_{m-1} \sqrt{\frac{V(\hat{Y})}{m}} < E(Y) < E(\hat{Y}) + t_{m-1} \sqrt{\frac{V(\hat{Y})}{m}} \quad (13.3)$$

In equation (13.3), t_{m-1} refers to the value of the Student t distribution with $m-1$ degrees of freedom at the specified significance level. For this problem, with $m = 30$ observations and 95 per cent confidence limits, the concern is with the t-value for 29 degrees of freedom which corresponds to an area of 0.05 in both tails of the t-distribution combined. Representing this by t_{29}, and substituting in the values for the estimated mean and variance of profit for Strategy A, the computation appears as:

$$1\,850 - t_{29} \sqrt{\frac{(1\,061.6)^2}{30}} < E(Y_A) < 1\,850 + t_{29} \sqrt{\frac{(1\,061.6)^2}{30}}$$

From tables, $t_{29} = 2.045$, and carrying out the computation yields 95 per cent confidence limits for $E(Y_A)$ of £1 453.64 $< E(Y_A) <$ £2 246.36.

A similar approach can be taken concerning confidence limits for the standard deviation of profits from Strategy A, represented by $\sqrt{V(Y_A)}$. The general formula for confidence limits around the standard deviation of profit is:

$$\frac{\sqrt{V(\hat{Y})}\ \sqrt{(m-1)}}{\sqrt{\chi^2_{m-1,q1}}} < \sqrt{V(Y)} < \frac{\sqrt{V(\hat{Y})}\ \sqrt{(m-1)}}{\sqrt{\chi^2_{m-1,q2}}} \qquad (13.4)$$

The terms in the denominators of the fractions in equation (13.4) are the quantiles of the chi-squared distribution for $m-1$ degrees of freedom. For a 95 per cent confidence interval, the relevant quantiles are $q1 = 0.975$ and $q2 = 0.025$. It is thus necessary to look up that value of a chi-squared distribution for which an area of 0.025 lies to the right, represented by $\chi^2_{29,0.975} = 45.72$, and that value for which an area of 0.025 lies to the left, represented by $\chi^2_{29,0.025} = 16.05$. Substituting these values in equation (13.4) yields 95 per cent confidence limits for $\sqrt{V(Y_A)}$ of £845.49 $< \sqrt{V(Y_A)} <$ £1 426.99.

Having obtained confidence limits for the expected mean and standard deviation of Strategy A, the question becomes one of how to combine them in order to find 95 per cent confidence limits for the probability of at least breaking even. It is convenient here to adopt the following terminology. Let:

$E(\hat{Y}_{0.025})$ and $E(\hat{Y}_{0.975})$ represent respectively the lower and upper limits of the 95 per cent confidence interval for the expected mean

$\sqrt{V(\hat{Y}_{0.025})}$ and $\sqrt{V(\hat{Y}_{0.975})}$ represent respectively the lower and upper limits of the 95 per cent confidence interval for the standard deviation

$P(Y \geq x)$ represent the probability of earning a profit level of at least x

Because the probability density function for profit associated with each of the strategies in this problem is normally distributed, the probability of achieving at least a given level of profit x may be expressed as:

$$P(Y \geq x) = 1 - P\left[z < \frac{x - E(\hat{Y})}{\sqrt{V(\hat{Y})}} \right] \qquad (13.5)$$

For a given x, the magnitude of the probability in equation (13.5) depends upon the values of $E(\hat{Y})$ and $\sqrt{V(\hat{Y})}$ on the right-hand side, and a 95 per cent confidence interval for this probability can be obtained by appropriate substitutions for these values. Specifically, the probability of falling below break-even would be least if the upper confidence limit for the mean happened to be the true value of the mean while the lower confidence limit for the standard deviation happened to be the true value of the standard deviation. Conversely, the probability of falling below break-even would be greatest if the lower confidence limit for the mean and the upper confidence limit for the standard deviation turned out to be their true values. From this, 95 per cent confidence limits for the probability of breaking even may be written out as follows:

$$1 - P\left[z < \frac{0 - E(\hat{Y}_{0.975})}{\sqrt{V(\hat{Y}_{0.025})}} \right] \geq P(Y \geq 0) \geq$$

$$1 - P\left[z < \frac{0 - E(\hat{Y}_{0.025})}{\sqrt{V(\hat{Y}_{0.975})}} \right] \qquad (13.6)$$

For Strategy A, computation shows that the probability of breaking even lies between $(1-0.004)$ and $(1-0.154)$, where the second figure in each of these brackets relates to the probability of obtaining standardised normal scores of respectively less than $z = -2\,246.36/845.49$ and $z = -1\,453.64/1\,426.99$. The 95 per cent confidence limits for the probability of breaking even with Strategy A are thus $0.996 \geq P(Y_A \geq 0) \geq 0.846$, which are very broad limits indeed.

Short-term Investment of Cash Balances

14

14.1 Alvor Developments

At the end of March 1989, the Treasurer of Alvor Developments is faced with a problem concerning the investment of surplus cash. He has £50 000 in hand, most or all of which will be required to meet payments arising from a build-up in inventories over the next 4 months. These payments are made at the month-ends, but it is not possible for the Treasurer to forecast exactly the size of the payment that will be required at the end of any given month. The most that he can do toward such a forecast is to draw up a probability tree specifying twelve possible sequences of cash payments over the next 4 months, and to associate probabilities with each sequence. This probability tree is given below (Figure 14.1); on it March is referred to as month 0, April as month 1, and so on. Each sequence of payments is labelled with a number.

It is clear from the probability tree that a substantial part of the £50 000 may well not be required until the latter part of the 4-month period; this raises the possibility that cash not immediately wanted may be profitably employed in making short-term investments. In particular, the Treasurer is looking at the possibility of investing surplus cash in short-term municipal bonds. These bonds are issued with maturities of 1, 2, 3 or 4 months, and can readily be bought and sold on the money market. If a bond, once bought, is held to maturity, it will yield a return of 1.3 per cent per month, but if a bond is sold before maturity the return available on it drops to 0.8 per cent per month. Every purchasing or selling transaction for bonds of a given maturity involves a fixed cost of

£76 plus a variable cost of 0.4 per cent of the face value of the bonds being bought or sold (so that, for example, selling £20 000 worth of *n*-month bonds would involve a total transaction cost of £(76 + 80 = 156)). No transaction costs are, however, incurred when bonds mature and are redeemed at their face value.

Given that the Treasurer must meet payment commitments out of the £50 000 immediately these commitments arise, **you are required** to advise him as to how much of the £50 000 he should invest in municipal bonds, and as to what maturities of bonds he should purchase. In giving this advice, your concern should be with the maximisation of expected net income over the next 4 months.

14.2 Analysis

Introduction

The issue here is one of determining the most profitable division of
funds as between cash and bonds, subject to the need to have
sufficient cash available to meet a sequence of cash outflows, the
magnitude and timing of these flows being subject to uncertainty.
This uncertainty is expressed in the form of a probability tree (see
Figure 14.1). On this tree, the conditional probabilities of different
cash outflows in a particular month given the level of outflows in a
previous month (or months) are shown, against branches linking
together chance nodes.

A method has to be found of balancing the earning of interest
against the incurrence of transaction costs under conditions of
uncertainty. If none of the cash surplus were to be invested, no
interest would be earned. On the other hand, if insufficient cash
were to be available to meet a payment when it became due, then
a forced sale of bonds would be necessary to meet the cash deficit.
Selling bonds before they mature would involve both a reduction
in the interest earned from 1.3–0.8 per cent per month, and the
incurrence of an extra set of transaction costs which could have
been avoided had the bonds concerned been held to maturity. The
risk of forced sales could be minimised by concentrating investment in the shorter-term 1-month or 2-month bonds, but this
would involve incurring extra transaction costs if these investments
had to be renewed as the cash held in them was still not needed to
meet payments when they matured.

Simplifying from the probability tree

One of the apparent difficulties facing the analysis of Alvor
Developments is that a separate decision would seem to be
required on investment policy for each £1 of the £50 000 initial
balance. However, observation of the probability tree shows that
all the possible end-month cash requirements are in multiples of
£10 000, suggesting that it would be convenient to split the £50 000
into five 'layers' of £10 000 each. The first layer in this arrangement

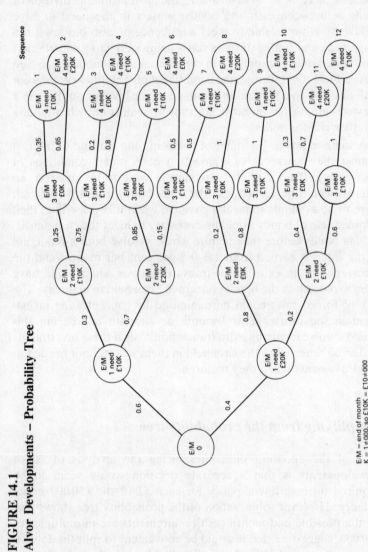

FIGURE 14.1
Alvor Developments – Probability Tree

E/M = end of month
K = 1≠000, so £10K = £10≠000

represents the first £10 000 to be used for cash payments, and so on through to the fifth layer which represents the last £10 000 to be paid out. In practice, the choice as to how to split the initial balance into layers will often be less clear-cut than it is here, but the accuracy of the analysis can be increased to any desired level by increasing the number of layers.

The layer concept enables the information in the problem to be presented more simply by replacing the probability tree with a statement of the probability that the cash in a layer will be required to meet payments in a given month. Some notation is necessary here. Let:

A_{jt} represent the cumulative requirement for cash by the end of the month t associated with the jth sequence of cash payments on the probability tree

For the jth sequence of payments, the kth layer of cash is said to be used up in month τ_{jk}, where τ_{jk} represents that value of t for which:

$$A_{jt} \geqq 10\,000k \text{ for } t = \tau_{jk}$$

and

$$A_{jt} < 10\,000k \text{ for } t = \tau_{jk} - 1$$

If the layer size had been other than £10 000, that other figure would have been substituted above.

The tabulation below shows the values of A_{jt} for each sequence j = 1 . . . 12 and each month t = 1 . . . 4. For each sequence j, the probability of its occurrence p_j is also shown. This is derived directly from the problem, by multiplying through the probabilities associated with each step within a payment sequence. The probability of Sequence 1 is thus given, from the probability tree, as $p_1 = (0.6)(0.3)(0.25)(0.35) = 0.01575$, and so on.

Cumulative cash demand A_{jt} for cash sequence j in month t

Cash sequence	Month $t = 1$	$t = 2$	$t = 3$	$t = 4$	Probability of sequence j
	£K	£K	£K	£K	(p_j)
$j=1$	10	20	20	30	0.01575
$j=2$	10	20	20	40	0.02925
$j=3$	10	20	30	30	0.02700
$j=4$	10	20	30	40	0.10800
$j=5$	10	30	30	40	0.35700
$j=6$	10	30	40	40	0.03150
$j=7$	10	30	40	50	0.03150
$j=8$	20	20	20	40	0.06400
$j=9$	20	20	30	40	0.25600
$j=10$	20	30	30	40	0.00960
$j=11$	20	30	30	50	0.02240
$j=12$	20	30	40	50	0.04800
					___
					1

From the table of A_{jk}, the values of τ_{jk} can be extracted simply by looking at the first month within each sequence in which a particular layer of cash is used up. Sequence 1 thus uses layer $k=1$ in month $t=1$, layer $k=2$ in month $t=2$ and layer $k=3$ in month $t=4$. It does not use either layer $k=4$ or $k=5$ at all, and these are consequently left blank in the τ_{jk} tabulation. This tabulation proceeds now:

Values of τ_{jk} for cash sequence j and cash layer k

Cash sequence	Cash layer				
	$k=1$	$k=2$	$k=3$	$k=4$	$k=5$
$j=1$	1	2	4	–	–
$j=2$	1	2	4	4	–
$j=3$	1	2	3	–	–
$j=4$	1	2	3	4	–
$j=5$	1	2	2	4	–
$j=6$	1	2	2	3	–
$j=7$	1	2	2	3	4
$j=8$	1	1	4	4	–
$j=9$	1	1	3	4	–
$j=10$	1	1	2	4	–
$j=11$	1	1	2	4	4
$j=12$	1	1	2	3	4

It is next necessary to introduce a new variable. Let:

Ω_{kt} represent that set of cash payment sequences for which cash layer k is first used up at the end of month t

For $k = 1$, $\Omega_{11} = 1 \ldots 12$, because cash layer $k = 1$ is used up at the end of the first month ($t = 1$) in each of the twelve possible cash payment sequences. For $k = 2$, $\Omega_{21} = 8 \ldots 12$, because only in Sequences $8 \ldots 12$ is the second cash layer used up in $t = 1$. In the remaining Sequences $1 - 7$ the second layer is used up in $t = 2$, so that $\Omega_{22} = 1 \ldots 7$. Continuing like this, it is possible to build up a tabulation of the sequences in Ω_{kt} as below. In this tabulation, the symbol ϕ refers to a cash layer which is not used up in a particular month in any one of the twelve cash payment sequences, so that for this combination of k and t Ω_{kt} is an empty set.

Sequences in Ω_{kt}

Cash layer	$t = 1$	$t = 2$	$t = 3$	$t = 4$
$k = 1$	[1 … 12]	ϕ	ϕ	ϕ
$k = 2$	[8 … 12]	[1 … 7]	ϕ	ϕ
$k = 3$	ϕ	[5,6,7,10,11,12]	[3,4,9]	[1,2,8]
$k = 4$	ϕ	ϕ	[6,7,12]	[2,4,5,8,9,10,11]
$k = 5$	ϕ	ϕ	ϕ	[7,11,12]

The values of Ω_{kt} can be used to find the probability that a particular cash layer will be required to meet payments in a particular month. Consider, for example, the cash layer $k = 2$. This will be required to meet payments at $t = 1$ if and only if one of Sequences 8–12 takes place. The probability of $k = 2$ being required for payments at $t = 1$ is thus given by the sum of the probabilities of occurrence of each of Sequences 8–12, that is, $p_8 + p_9 + p_{10} + p_{11} + p_{12} = 0.4$. Let:

π_{kt} represent the probability that the kth layer of cash will be used up in month t

Then in general terms:

$$\pi_{kt} = \sum_{j \in \Omega_{kt}} p_j \qquad (14.1)$$

This equation can be used to build up a tabulation of the values of π_{kt}, summarising the information in the probability tree and acting as a simpler substitute for it. The π_{kt} table is given below.

	Values of π_{kt} at $t = 0$			
Cash		Month		
layer	$t = 1$	$t = 2$	$t = 3$	$t = 4$
$k = 1$	1	0	0	0
$k = 2$	0.4	0.6	0	0
$k = 3$	0	0.5	0.391	0.109
$k = 4$	0	0	0.111	0.84625
$k = 5$	0	0	0	0.1019

The table shows it to be certain that cash layer $k = 1$ will be required at time $t = 1$. In the meantime, it may be invested in 1-month bonds, to yield a net income of £14, made up of the difference between interest (at £130) and the sum of the fixed and variable transaction costs of purchase (respectively at £76 and £40). The table also shows that since cash layer $k = 5$ cannot be required before $t = 4$, it may be invested in 4-month bonds to yield a net income of £404, on the same basis of calculation as above.

However, since there is only about one chance in ten that cash layer $k = 5$ will be required to meet payments at $t = 4$, the conclusion that it would be optimal to invest it in 4-month bonds can be justified only in terms of an objective of maximising net income up to a fixed planning horizon 4 months away. The balance of probability strongly favours the proposition that layer $k = 5$ will not be required until $t = 5$ (or later), so that reinvestment of it at $t = 4$ will be necessary, thus incurring transaction costs which could have been avoided with a longer-term investment (were one available). However, there is always a possibility that a plan which is optimal for a given planning horizon may be suboptimal for a longer horizon, and Alvor's Treasurer may wish to adhere to a 4-month horizon on the grounds that predictions of cash payment patterns more than 4 months ahead are too conjectural to be of value.

Expected returns for alternative maturities

Having dealt with cash layers $k = 1$ and $k = 5$, it is now necessary to focus on the more difficult issues posed by layers $k = 2$, $k = 3$ and $k = 4$. In analysing the optimal strategies for these cash layers, the first step is to specify the expected returns on the possible investments which could be made with them up to the planning horizon. Obviously, these cash layers could be invested at $t = 0$ in bonds with any maturities between 1 month and 4 months. But if at $t = 0$ one of the layers was invested in 1-month bonds, then at $t = 1$ the possibility would arise of reinvesting that layer in bonds of any maturity between 1 month and 3 months. All the possible patterns of investment and reinvestment have to be considered systematically for a given cash layer, in order to search out the optimal investment strategy for that layer in the face of uncertainty as to when it will be required to meet cash payments.

This uncertainty gives rise to an emphasis upon the expected net return for making an investment in bonds of a given maturity. The formulae for expected net return are derived as follows: Let:

M	represent the amount of a cash layer in pounds, so that here $M = 10\,000$
i_r	represent the interest per month available on bonds sold before maturity, so that here $i_r = 0.008$

i_m represent the interest per month available on bonds sold at maturity, so that here $i_m = 0.013$

F represent the fixed cost in pounds of purchasing or selling bonds, so that here $F = 76$

v represent the variable cost of purchasing or selling bonds expressed as a proportion of their face value, so that here $v = 0.004$

$r_{kt}(m_t)$ represent the expected net return from investing cash layer k at the end of month t in a bond maturing after m_t months

Three special cases have to be dealt with at the outset. These are as follows:

1. Where $m_t = 0$, a cash layer is being retained as cash with an expected net return of zero, so that $r_{kt}(0) = 0$.
2. Where $m_t = 1$ and $t = 0$, a cash layer is being invested in 1-month bonds at the start of the planning period. Since this cash cannot be required for payments before $t = 1$, the return on the one-month bonds is certain.
   It is given by:

$$r_{k0}(1) = (i_m - v)M - F \qquad (14.2)$$

3. Suppose a cash layer is invested in 1-month bonds at the end of month t, where $t > 0$. Since cash payments are required only at monthly intervals in this problem, if a cash layer is available for investment at the end of month t it cannot be required for payments before the end of month $t + 1$. Thus an investment in 1-month bonds need never be liquidated before it matures, and the only uncertain feature about its expected return is whether the cash layer concerned will be available at the end of month t to invest in it. The formula for the expected return on an investment in a 1-month bond taking place at the end of month t, where $t > 0$, is given by:

$$r_{kt}(1) = [(i_m - v)M - F]\left(1 - \sum_{w=1}^{t} \pi_{kw}\right) \qquad (14.3)$$

Having dealt with these three special cases, it is logical to proceed to the general formula for $m_t = 2 \ldots n-t$. This is given by:

$$r_{kt}(m_t) = \sum_{w=1}^{(m_t-1)} [Mwi_r - 2(F + Mv)] \, \pi_{k(t+w)}$$

$$+ \left[Mm_t i_m - (F + Mv) \right] \left[1 - \sum_{w=1}^{(t+m_t-1)} \pi_{kw} \right] \quad (14.4)$$

In order to locate the best investment strategy, it is necessary to draw up data on all the possible strategies. This involves computing the expected net return associated with each possible investment and reinvestment of each cash layer up to that layer's planning horizon. For any layer, its planning horizon is given by the sooner of the planning horizon for the problem as a whole, and the time by which it is certain that the cash layer concerned will have been used up. For cash layer $k = 2$, it is certain that this layer will be used up by $t = 2$, so that its planning horizon is thus 2 months. It will never pay to invest in a bond which matures after a cash layer's planning horizon, because such a bond must have a forced sale, with its associated penalties of a lower interest rate and the incurrence of an extra set of transaction costs.

Using equations (14.2), (14.3) and (14.4), the expected net returns $r_{kt}(m_t)$ for cash layers $k = 2,3,4$ may be computed. This computation yields the results tabulated below, with all figures in pounds:

Value of r_{kt} (m_t) for cash layer $k = 2$

Time of investment	Bond duration to maturity m_t (months)		
	0	1	2
$t = 0$	0	14	25.6
$t = 1$	0	8.4	
$t = 2$	0		

Value of $r_{kt}(m_t)$ for cash layer $k = 3$

Time of in-vestment	Bond duration to maturity m_t (months)				
	0	1	2	3	4
$t = 0$	0	14	144	101	11.16
$t = 1$	0	14	−4	−74.29	
$t = 2$	0	7	−43.74		
$t = 3$	0	1.53			
$t = 4$	0				

Value of $r_{kt}(m_t)$ for cash layer $k = 4$

Time of in-vestment	Bond duration to maturity m_t (months)				
	0	1	2	3	4
$t = 0$	0	14	144	274	360.04
$t = 1$	0	14	144	235.59	
$t = 2$	0	14	111.14		
$t = 3$	0	12.45			
$t = 4$	0				

Dynamic programming

The final step in the analysis of Alvor Developments involves using the values of $r_{kt}(m_t)$ to work out the optimal investment policy for each cash layer. This policy must cover the period up to the layer's planning horizon, so that it is a question of specifying a policy covering 2 months for cash layer $k = 2$ and 4 months for layers $k = 3$ and $k = 4$. To do this requires an elementary application of a technique called dynamic programming. At the outset, new variables must be defined by letting:

n represent the planning horizon (in months) for a given cash layer

f_t represent the maximum expected net return that can be obtained on a given cash layer at the end of month t

From these definitions, it may be observed that $f_t \geq 0$ for $t = 0 \ldots n-1$ and $f_t = 0$ for $t = n$. That is to say, the maximum expected net return must be either zero or positive for all month-ends prior to a layer's planning horizon, and must be exactly zero when that planning horizon is reached.

To compute the value of f_t for $t = 0 \ldots n-1$, it is necessary to use a recurrence relation of the following form:

$$f_t = \text{Max.} \left[\left\{ r_t(0) + f_{t+1} \right\}, \; m_t = 1, 2 \overset{max.}{\ldots} n-t \left\{ r_t(m_t) + f_{t+m_t} \right\} \right] \quad (14.5)$$

Working through it from left to right, this relation asserts that the maximum expected net return obtainable must be the larger of the following:

1. The expected net return obtainable by holding cash for 1 month plus the maximum net return that could be obtained at the end of month $t + 1$.
   This is given in symbolic terms by $r_t(0) + f_{t+1}$.
2. The expected net return that could be obtained by investing in bonds of maturity m_t months plus the expected net return that could then be obtained by reinvestment at the end of month $t + m_t$, where m_t has been chosen from the range $m_t = 1 \ldots n-t$ in such a way as to maximise the expected net return from this investment and reinvestment.

The recurrence relation in equation (14.5) is to be subjected to a process of backward solution, involving the successive computation of solutions for f_{n-1}, f_{n-2} and so on back to f_0. It is easiest to illustrate this process by solving first for the cash layer $k = 2$, since this layer has a short planning horizon of $n = 2$. The values of $r_{kt}(m_t)$ for cash layer $k = 2$ have been tabulated, and may be subjected to backward solution as follows:

$$f_2 = 0$$

$$f_1 = \text{Max.} \left[\left\{ r_1(0) + f_2 \right\}, \; m_1 = 1 \left\{ r_1(m_1) + f_{1+m_1} \right\} \right]$$

$$f_1 = \text{Max.} \left[(0+0), (8.4 + 0) \right] = 8.4, \text{ where } m_1 = 1$$

$$f_0 = \text{Max.} \left[\left\{ r_0(0) + f_1 \right\}, \; m_0 = \underset{\text{Max.}}{1,2} \left\{ r_0(m_0) + f_{m_0} \right\} \right]$$

$$f_0 = \text{Max.} \; [(0 + 8.4), \text{max}\{(14+8.4), (25.6+0)\}] = 25.6$$
where $m_0 = 2$

The optimal solution for cash layer $k = 2$ offers an expected net return of £25.60, and involves investing the £10 000 in 2-month bonds.

This solution did not really require the mechanism of dynamic programming, in that it could have been found by inspection. However, the computation for cash layer $k = 3$, with a planning horizon of $n = 4$, makes the need for a formal dynamic programming approach plainly apparent. It uses the values of $r_{kt}(m_t)$ for cash layer $k = 3$ tabulated above, and proceeds as follows:

$$f_4 = 0$$

$$f_3 = \text{Max.}\left[\left\{r_3\,(0) + f_4\right\}, \; m_3 = 1 \left\{r_3(m_3) + f_{3+m_3}\right\}\right]$$

$$f_3 = \text{Max.}[(0+0), (1.53 + 0)] = 1.53, \text{ where } m_3 = 1$$

$$f_2 = \text{Max.}\left[\left\{r_2(0) + f_3\right\}, \; m_2 = \underset{\text{Max.}}{1,2} \left\{r_2(m_2) + f_{2+m_2}\right\}\right]$$

$$= \text{Max.}[\;(0+1.53), \text{Max.}\{(7 + 1.53), (-43.74 + 0)\}] = 8.53, \text{ where } m_2 = 1$$

$$f_1 = \text{Max.}\left[\left\{r_1(0) + f_2\right\}, \; m_1 = \underset{\text{Max.}}{1,2,3} \left\{r_1(m_1) + f_{1+m_1}\right\}\right]$$

$$= \text{Max.}[(0+8.53), \text{Max.}\{(14 + 8.53), (-4+1.53), (-74.29+0)\}]$$

$$= 22.53, \text{ where } m_1 = 1$$

$$f_0 = \text{Max.}\left[\left\{r_0(0) + f_1\right\}, \; m_0 = \underset{\text{Max.}}{1,2,3,4} \left\{r_0(m_0) + f_{m_0}\right\}\right]$$

$$= \text{Max.} [(0+22.53), \text{Max.}\{(14+22.53), (144+8.53), (101+1.53), (11.16+0)\}]$$

$$= 152.53, \text{ where } m_0 = 2$$

The optimal solution for cash layer $k = 3$ gives rise to an expected net return of £152.53, and is as follows:

> 'Invest this £10000 in 2-month bonds, then if it is not required to meet payments at the end of month $t = 2$, invest it in 1-month bonds
> If it is still not required at the end of month $t = 3$, invest it in a further set of 1-month bonds'

Finally, it is necessary to deal with cash layer $k = 4$. The computations here, using the values of $r_{kt}(m_t)$ for layer $k = 4$ given above, are left to the reader as an exercise. The conclusion, however, is that this layer should be invested in 4-month bonds at $t = 0$, with an expected net return of £360.04.

These recommendations for cash layers $k = 3$ and $k = 4$ conclude the establishment of an optimal policy for the Alvor Developments problem. Cash layer $k = 1$ should be invested in 1-month bonds, layer $k = 2$ in 2-month bonds, layer $k = 5$ in 4-month bonds, and layers $k = 3$ and $k = 4$ treated as above. The sum of the expected net returns computed for each layer with this policy is £14 + £25.60 + £152.53 + £360.04 + £404 = £956.17. However, this figure is somewhat inaccurate, because of the incorrect treatment of fixed transaction costs arising from the separation of cash into layers. There is a fixed cost element of £76 per transaction in bonds of a given maturity, irrespective of the size of that transaction. Hence, since both of cash layers $k = 2$ and $k = 3$ are invested at $t = 0$ in 2-month bonds, a 'saving' of £76 arises on this joint purchase transaction which could not be allowed for in the separate computation of $r_{20}(2)$ and $r_{30}(2)$. An identical saving of £76 arises on the joint purchase, for cash layers $k = 4$ and $k = 5$, of £20000 of 4-month bonds at $t = 0$.

After $t = 0$, the savings on joint purchases or sales involving more than one layer of cash being invested or disinvested at the same time and in bonds of the same maturity generally become more difficult to calculate, because of the presence of uncertainty. However, the optimal policy for Alvor Developments does not give rise to the simultaneous purchase after $t = 0$ for different cash layers of bonds of the same maturity. Nor does it give rise to the simultaneous sale, prior to their date of redemption, of bonds of the same maturity from different cash layers. There are consequently no expected transaction cost savings on joint purchases or sales after $t = 0$, and the expected net return on the optimal policy for Alvor Developments is given by £956.17 + £76(2) = £1 108.17. This is just over 2 per cent of the initial sum available for investment, and represents a significant return for the effective management of short-term investments.

Payments Netting in Multinational Cash Management

15

15.1 Lintock Corporation

Lintock Corporation is a small multinational enterprise with a holding company and main operating subsidiary located in the United Kingdom, together with wholly-owned subsidiaries in France, Switzerland and Italy. At the end of June 1989, debts owed as between the British, French, Swiss and Italian subsidiaries were all translated into sterling at a common set of exchange rates. This enabled the following table to be drawn up, showing the amounts owed in units of £10 000. By way of illustration, note that the table shows the French subsidiary to have indebtedness to the British subsidiary of £190 000, while the British subsidiary's indebtedness to the French subsidiary amounts to £230 000.

Receiving companies	Paying companies				
	England	France	Switzerland	Italy	Total
England	–	19	17	11	47
France	23	–	6	14	43
Switzerland	11	22	–	13	46
Italy	8	19	7	–	34
Total	42	60	30	38	170

A table was also drawn up showing the transaction costs involved in transferring foreign exchange between the countries in which Lintock's subsidiaries were located. These transaction costs are expressed as a proportion of the sterling value transferred, so that for example the settlement of £x worth of debt owed by the French to the Italian subsidiary is shown by the table to involve £0.006x in transaction costs. The transaction costs table for June 1989 appeared as follows:

Transfer between	and	Cost as proportion of £ value transferred
England	France	0.008
England	Switzerland	0.0055
England	Italy	0.0075
France	Switzerland	0.007
France	Italy	0.006
Switzerland	Italy	0.0075

Lintock Corporation operates on the assumption that transaction costs do not vary with the direction of transfer as between two countries. For example, it is assumed that the transfer of £x worth of funds from Switzerland to Italy would involve incurring the same transaction costs (of £0.0075x) as would be incurred by the transfer of the same amount of funds from Italy to Switzerland.

You are required to advise Lintock Corporation as to the payments netting scheme which would minimise the transaction costs incurred in settling the inter-subsidiary debts outstanding at the end of June 1989.

15.2 Analysis

Introduction

When Subsidiary A of a multinational corporation, located in Country X, sends foreign exchange to Subsidiary B of that corporation, located in Country Y, to discharge a debt owed by A to B, in doing so it imposes transaction costs on the multinational as a whole. These costs arise from two major sources. Firstly, the act of changing currencies involves a cost arising from 'foreign exchange spread', which is the difference between the buying and selling rates offered by foreign exchange dealers. Secondly, a loss of interest, called 'float cost', arises while foreign exchange is in transit between countries. This is an *opportunity cost*, and is measured relative to the amount that would have been earned in interest if the amount remitted had remained within the bank account from which it was paid out. Taken together, foreign exchange spread and float cost can give rise to total transaction costs of between 0.25 per cent and 1.5 per cent of the value of funds transferred. Keeping these transaction costs to a minimum involves minimising the value of the funds transferred internationally, and progress can often be made in this direction by means of a technique called 'payments netting'.

Payments netting

Payments netting involves a systematic procedure whereby equal but opposite sums owed by subsidiaries to each other are cancelled out, so that only the net debt owed between subsidiaries is actually paid off by transactions involving the purchase of foreign exchange. Its operation may be illustrated by reference to a situation involving three subsidiaries called A, B and C. Their indebtedness position can be represented by a diagram like that in Figure 15.1, in which (for example) the number against an arrow running from A to B indicates the amount in thousands of pounds that A owes to B, while the arrow running from B to A indicates the amount that B owes A, and so on. With hypothetical figures inserted, Figure 15.1 is a typical initial diagram.

FIGURE 15.1
Initial Indebtedness

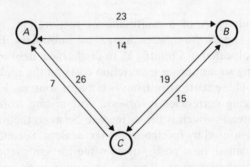

If all of the above debts were to be settled individually, in total
£104 000 worth of funds would have to be transmitted. The first
step in simplifying the situation is called bilateral netting, and
involves the cancellation of offsetting debts between each pair of
subsidiaries, to leave only the net amount of debt owed. Thus (for
example) A owes a net amount of £9 000 to B, being the £23 000
that it owes less the £14 000 that B owes it. The pattern of
indebtedness after bilateral netting has been completed is shown in
Figure 15.2.

FIGURE 15.2
Bilateral Netting

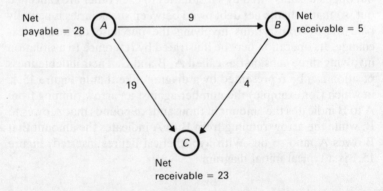

Bilateral netting leaves a total of £32 000 worth of funds requiring transmission to settle the inter-subsidiary debts. However, this figure can be reduced further by considering the indebtedness of each subsidiary to all the others taken together. A owes the other subsidiaries £28 000 in all, hence the words 'Net payable = 28' against it. Similarly, B is owed a net amount of £5 000 (the difference between £9 000 and £4 000) by A and C together, and C is owed £23 000 by A and B together. Each subsidiary can either pay what it owes or be paid what it is owed by the following transactions, involving multilateral netting (see Figure 15.3).

FIGURE 15.3
Multilateral Netting

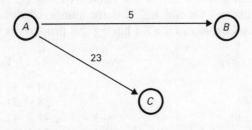

Here, a further £4 000 worth of funds transmission has been saved because A has been prevented from transferring £4 000 to B for further transfer on to C. But while the potential saving is quite easy to see in a three-subsidiary case like this, it becomes much more difficult to be certain that all the potential savings have been identified as the number of subsidiaries located in different countries increases. It is even more difficult to allow 'by eye' for the fact that different transfers involve different transaction costs per pound transferred, a fact not considered in the simple example above. As the issues grow more complex, a mathematical programming approach is to be preferred.

Mathematical programming and the Lintock problem

The Lintock Corporation problem can be tackled by formulating it in a manner akin to the transportation problem within linear programming. In doing this, the first step is to classify the subsidiaries into two groups, as below:

1. Those which owe more to other subsidiaries than other subsidiaries owe to them.

   When all debts are settled, these subsidiaries will have had a net outflow of cash.

   Representing the outflow of cash from the ith subsidiary by f_i, for a subsidiary in this group $f_i > 0$.

2. Those subsidiaries which are owed more by other subsidiaries than they owe to other subsidiaries.

   They will receive a net inflow of cash when all debts are settled, so that for a subsidiary i in this group $f_i < 0$.

Next, it is necessary to list the subsidiaries in such a way that the m subsidiaries for which $f_i > 0$ are numbered $i = 1 \ldots m$, and the $n-m$ subsidiaries for which $f_i < 0$ are numbered $i = m+1 \ldots n$. For Lintock Corporation, a list having this property is as follows:

Subsidiary	No.	f_i Value	
France	$i = 1$	$60 - 43 =$	17
Italy	$i = 2$	$38 - 34 =$	4
England	$i = 3$	$42 - 47 =$	-5
Switzerland	$i = 4$	$30 - 46 =$	-16

New variables a_i and b_i now need to be introduced, where:

$$a_i = f_i \text{ if } i = 1 \ldots m \tag{1}$$
$$b_1 = -f_i \text{ if } i = m+1 \ldots n \tag{2}$$

In this example, $a_1 = 17$, $a_2 = 4$, $b_3 = 5$, $b_4 = 16$. Let:

x_{ij} represent the amount of funds transferred from subsidiary i to subsidiary j, where $j = 1 \ldots n$ represents the same ordering of subsidiaries as did $i = 1 \ldots n$

These must in total be n constraints in the linear programming formulation, one for each subsidiary. The first m of these constraints must ensure that each of the m subsidiaries falling into the net debtor category has a net cash outflow equal to its indebtedness. These constraints therefore take the following form:

$$\sum_{\substack{j=1 \\ j \neq i}}^{n} x_{ij} = a_i \qquad i = 1 \ldots m \tag{3}$$

The remaining $n-m$ constraints must ensure that the inflow to each of the net creditor subsidiaries is equal to the net amount that it is owed. These constraints are of a form as follows:

$$\sum_{\substack{i=1 \\ i \neq j}}^{n} x_{ij} = b_j \qquad j = m+1 \ldots n \tag{4}$$

In the Lintock Corporation problem, $m = 2$, $n = 4$ and the individual constraints are as follows:

$$x_{12} + x_{13} + x_{14} = 17 \tag{5}$$
$$x_{21} + x_{23} + x_{24} = 4 \tag{6}$$
$$x_{13} + x_{23} + x_{43} = 5 \tag{7}$$
$$x_{14} + x_{24} + x_{34} = 16 \tag{8}$$

Taking as an example constraint (5) above, this asserts that the total of the French subsidiary's payments (from $i = 1$) to the other subsidiaries (to $j = 2 \ldots 4$) must be equal to the French subsidiary's net indebtedness. Similarly, constraint (7) asserts that the total of the English subsidiary's receipts ($j = 3$) from the other subsidiaries ($i = 1,2,4$) must be equal to the net amount that the English subsidiary is owed.

Next, let c_{ij} represent the transaction costs of transferring funds from subsidiary i to subsidiary j, expressed as a proportion of the sterling value transferred. Then, in the most general terms, the objective function can be expressed as:

$$\text{Minimise} \quad \sum_{\substack{i=1 \\ }}^{m} \sum_{\substack{j=1 \\ j \neq i}}^{n} c_{ij} x_{ij} + \sum_{\substack{i=m+1 \\ i \neq j}}^{n} \sum_{\substack{j=m+1 \\ }}^{n} c_{ij} x_{ij}$$

This simply represents the sum of all the possible amounts transferred x_{ij}, each weighted by its transaction cost c_{ij}. In detail the objective function for the Lintock Corporation problem is as below:

Minimise $0.006x_{12} + 0.008x_{13} + 0.007x_{14} + 0.006x_{21}$
$$+ 0.0075x_{23} + 0.0075x_{24} + 0.0055x_{43} + 0.0055x_{34} \quad (9)$$

When the linear programming problem of minimising (9) subject to constraints (5) – (8) above is solved, it gives the following result:

$$x_{13} = 1; \; x_{14} = 16; \; x_{23} = 4$$

In this solution, the only transfers that need take place are those of £10 000 worth of funds from France to England, £160 000 worth from France to Switzerland and £40 000 worth from Italy to England. Transfers of only £210 000 worth of funds in all suffice to discharge £1 700 000 worth of debt within Lintock Corporation, at a transaction cost of only £1 500. It is thus clear the administrative costs involved in setting up a payments netting system may well be justified in terms of the transaction cost savings to which such a system gives rise.

The Learning Curve and Financial Planning 16

16.1 Holt Electronics PLC

Holt Electronics has developed a novel design of noise reducer, called the Drigan filter, for use with satellite communications equipment. It will considerably improve reception by relay stations of satellite-reflected signals, and Holt anticipate that there will be a large market for it. However, as Holt has never assembled a filter anything like this one before, its management realise that there will be considerable scope for learning by the operatives engaged in its assembly. They feel that the first Drigan filter could take as long as 280 direct labour hours to assemble, but that the average assembly time per filter will drop by 10 per cent every time cumulative production doubles. Each filter sold will earn a contribution of £800 *before* deducting the cost of the direct labour supplied by assembly operatives, who are paid £4 per hour.

A facility has been set up for Drigan filter assembly, which will involve a cash outflow of £1 400 000 per annum to run, irrespective of the level of output that it produces. A skilled workforce is available, supplying 250 000 direct labour hours per year; the nature of the skills involved makes it difficult to contemplate expanding the workforce in anything but the long term. While the number of direct labour hours is fixed, the organisation of assembly labour is very flexible. In particular, it is possible to have either one high-speed production line using 250 000 labour hours per annum or two lower-speed production lines each using 125 000 hours per annum. This choice is purely a matter of layout, and has

no implications at all for the level of total costs. Using this
information, **you are required**:

1. To calculate the break-even level of output for each of the
   one-line and two-line alternatives over the first year of operation.
2. To calculate the level of output that will be achieved by each of
   the one-line and two-line alternatives over each of the first 2
   years of operation, assuming that the initial assembly time of
   280 hours has been correctly estimated, and that learning
   continues without interruption throughout both years.
3. To calculate the level of output that will be achieved by the
   one-line alternative over each of the first 2 years of operation if
   both the learning rate has been underestimated by 5 per cent
   and the initial assembly time has been underestimated by 5 per
   cent.

   On seeing the results 1 – 3 above, the Product Manager
   responsible for Drigan filters observes that he does not find
   them credible.

   When pressed for an explanation, he says that his general
   knowledge of filter assembly techniques convinces him that a
   Drigan filter cannot be assembled in less than 75 hours even
   when all the available savings from learning have been fully
   exploited.

Using this information, **you are also required**:

4. To compute the level of output at which learning effects will be
   exhausted for a single production line, assuming that both
   initial assembly time and the learning rate have been correctly
   estimated at the outset.
5. To compute the break-even level of output and the budgeted
   profit for each of the first and second years of operation if a
   single production line is employed, again assuming that both
   initial assembly time and the learning rate have been correctly
   estimated.

16.2   Analysis

Introduction

The issues here may be introduced by considering a model in which every time the cumulative amount produced doubles, the average number of direct labour hours spent per unit drops to $100R$ per cent of its level prior to that doubling of production. If, for example, $R = 0.8$, then after a doubling of the cumulative number of units that have been produced from (say) 16 to 32 units in total, average direct labour hours per unit will be at $100R$ per cent = 80 per cent of their level when 16 units had been produced. This relationship between cumulative production and average direct labour hours per unit is referred to as the 'learning curve' phenomenon, and the term R is referred to as the 'learning rate'. While other resources (such as direct materials) can enter into learning curve relationships of their own with cumulative production, this possibility does not enter into the Holt Electronics problem.

Although the magnitude of R often varies little over the life of a given product, it may vary greatly from one product to another. To incorporate R in a learning curve model requires the definition of terms as follows. Let:

a	represent the production time (in direct labour hours) required to manufacture the first unit of output
x	represent the cumulative number of units produced to date
y	represent the (cumulative) average production time (in direct labour hours) spent per unit after x units have been produced
b	represent the 'index of learning', which is given by log R/log 2
	The logarithms can be taken to any base, and here natural logarithms will be used, so that the index appears as ln R/ln 2
m	represent the number of times that production has doubled
	If, for example, $x = 4$, then production has doubled twice (from one unit to two, and from two units to four), thus giving $m = 2$

Using the above terms, the learning curve model can be expressed as:

$$y = aR^m \tag{16.1}$$

But from the definition of m:

$$x = 2^m \tag{16.2}$$

Converting both sides of equation (16.2) to natural logarithms and isolating out m gives:

$$m = \ln x / \ln 2 \tag{16.3}$$

Substituting for m in equation (16.1):

$$y = aR^{(\ln x/\ln 2)} \tag{16.4}$$

Converting both sides of equation (16.4) to natural logarithms gives:

$$\ln y = \ln a + (\ln x / \ln 2) \ln R \tag{16.5}$$

Substituting the index of learning on the right-hand side yields:

$$\ln y = \ln a + b \ln x \tag{16.6}$$

Suppose that observation of the start-up of a production process had supplied empirical data in the form of a series of pairs of values of x and y. Then equation (16.6) would represent the form in which these pairs of observations would be regressed against each other to obtain least squares estimates of the intercept term a and the index of learning b.

Taking antilogarithms of equation (16.6), it appears as:

$$y = ax^b \tag{16.7}$$

Equation (16.7) is probably the commonest way of expressing the learning curve, and serves as the foundation for dealing with the Holt Electronics problem.

Computing the break-even level with a single production line

In order to apply equation (16.7) to this problem, it is necessary to incorporate it within a financial framework. Some new terms are required for this, as follows. Let:

p	represent contribution per unit, after deducting all costs except those of direct labour
c	represent direct labour cost per hour
f	represent the cash outflow on fixed costs per annum
π	represent profit per annum

If in the first year x filters are produced, then the profit for the first year can be expressed by an equation of the form:

$$\pi = px - cyx - f \tag{16.8}$$

This simply asserts that profit is equal to contribution before deducting labour costs, *less* a second term representing labour costs and a third one representing fixed costs. Substituting for y from equation (16.7) gives:

$$\pi = px - cax^{b+1} - f \tag{16.9}$$

If there is only one production line, finding the break-even level of output over the first year is a fairly straightforward matter of solving equation (16.9) with $\pi = 0$. For the Holt Electronics problem, the values of the parameters in equation (16.9) are as follows:

$$p = 800; c = 4; a = 280; f = 1\,400\,000$$

The only parameter which requires computation is b, the index of learning. From the problem, if the average assembly time drops by 10 per cent every time production doubles, this is equivalent to a $(100 - 10)$ per cent = 90 per cent learning curve, so that here $R = 0.9$. The index of learning is thus given by:

$$b = \ln 0.9/\ln 2 = -0.152$$

Setting $\pi = 0$, and substituting the parameter values above, yields the following for equation (16.9) with $\pi = 0$:

$$800x - 1120x^{0.848} - 1\,400\,000 = 0$$

This equation may be solved by an iterative approach called the Newton–Raphson method. To illustrate this approach, consider its use to solve a general equation of the form $f(x) = 0$. This involves making an initial guess that the solution is $x = x_0$, then computing a new possible value for the solution x_1 such that:

$$x_1 = x_0 - \frac{f(x_0)}{f'(x_0)}$$

In the above equation, $f'(x_0)$ is the derivative of $f(x)$ at $x = x_0$. This process continues iteratively with the following general formula:

$$x_j = x_{j-1} - \frac{f(x_{j-1})}{f'(x_{j-1})}$$

The iterations are terminated when x_j and x_{j-1} differ from one another by an amount which is considered to be negligible. Substituting $x_j = x$ then produces an almost perfect solution to the equation $f(x) = 0$, though the solution can always be improved by tightening the specification of what constitutes a 'negligible' difference between x_j and x_{j-1}. The only cautionary note here is that occasionally the value of x_0 chosen may be such that this approach does not converge upon a solution, which necessitates restarting the process with a different x_0 value.

Applying the Newton–Raphson technique to the Holt Electronics parameters gives, for the first iteration:

$$x_1 = x_0 - \frac{(800x_0 - 1120x_0^{0.848} - 1\,400\,000)}{800 - 949.76x_0^{-0.152}}$$

It is very tedious to go through a long series of iterations to solve for x, and fortunately it is unnecessary. The simple computer program shown below (with the Holt Electronics data inserted) solves for x very quickly:

```
100   INPUT "VALUE OF X(0)"; X(0)
110   J=0
120   Y=800*X(J)−1120*X(J) ↑ .848−1400000
130   Z=800−949.76*X(J) ↑ −.152
140   J=J+1 :1F J>100 THEN 190
150   X(J)=X(J−1)−(Y/Z)
160   IF X(J)−X(J−1)>.1 THEN 120
170   IF X(J)−X(J−1)<−.1 THEN 120
180   ? "SOLUTION IS X=" : X(J): GOTO 200
190   ? "TRY ANOTHER VALUE OF X(0)"
200   END
```

This program has been written in BASIC for the Commodore PET computer. The accuracy of its solution can be improved by reducing the values in lines 160 and 170 from 0.1 to any desired value. It will work with any $f(x)$ and $f'(x)$ respectively inserted on the right-hand sides of the equations in lines 120 and 130.

Running the program with the Holt Electronics data gives a solution $x = 2\,990.33$, implying that the break-even point is almost exactly 2 990 filters over the first year. However, the interpretation of this break-even point depends upon what output is forecast to be over the first year of operation, a point which will be returned to later.

Computing the break-even level with multiple production lines

Suppose that, instead of one production line with a cumulative output of x units, there are n production lines each with a cumulative output of x/n units. Then the labour cost incurred by each line is a function of that line's cumulative output x/n. Substituting x/n for x in equation (16.9) gives rise to a new equation as follows:

$$\pi = px - nca \left(\frac{x}{n} \right)^{b+1} - f \tag{16.10}$$

Equation (16.10) implies that each production line is staffed by labour with the same initial skill level (so that a is a constant) and that the labour on each line learns at the same speed (so that b is a constant). In the first part of the Holt Electronics problem, the contrast is made between having one and two production lines. Suppose, therefore, that $n = 2$, and that the two assumptions just made both hold. Then the relevant equation for computing the break-even level over the first year becomes:

$$800x - 1\,244.4x^{0.848} - 1\,400\,000 = 0$$

The solution to this equation, by the Newton–Raphson method, is $x = 3\,216$. Having two production lines instead of one raises the break-even level in the first year from 2 990 to 3 216 filters. This is a completely general result. Because $b < 0$ always, and holding all the other parameters constant, the larger is the value of n the higher will be the value of x. As the fixed number of labour hours is spread over more and more production lines, the cumulative production achieved by each line over a given period will fall. Each line therefore have less experience, and thus be positioned higher up its learning curve, than would have been the case with fewer lines each employing more labour hours. The reservation here is that this result assumes that lines cannot learn from each other's experiences, by reason of geographical or temporal separation (as with day and night shifts).

Forecasting output over first year

To interpret the meaning of a break-even level, it must be compared with the forecast level of production over the period concerned. The attainable level of production depends upon the number of labour hours that are available. To produce x units requires xy labour hours. But y can be expressed in terms of x using equation (16.7), so that:

$$xy = ax^{b+1} \tag{16.11}$$

Let

T_{Li} represent the number of labour hours available to a production line in period i

Then, for $i = 1$, the forecast output x_1 for this first period is given by the value of x_1 which solves the equation:

$$ax_1^{b+1} = T_{L1} \tag{16.12}$$

Rearranging to isolate x_1 gives:

$$x_1 = (T_{L1}/a)^{1/(b+1)} \tag{16.13}$$

Applying the parameters from the Holt problem to obtain the first year's forecast output of filters with a single production line gives rise to:

$$x_1 = \left(\frac{250\,000}{280}\right)^{1/0.848} = 3\,018 \text{ filters}$$

For a first year's forecast output of $x = 3\,018$ filters, the budgeted profit is given by equation (16.9) as £14 354.

With two production lines running in the first year, each having 125 000 labour hours available, both lines together will produce a forecast amount x_1 given by:

$$x_1 = (2)\,(125\,000/280)^{1/0.848} = 2\,666 \text{ filters}$$

The combined forecast output of the two production lines is considerably less than the forecast output of a single line, for the input of the same number of labour hours. This reflects the fact that each of the two lines is placed higher up the learning curve at the end of the first year than a single line would be. Using equation (16.10), from two production lines the budgeted first year result is a loss of £267 439.

Forecasting output over subsequent years

Consider the problem of forecasting the level of output for any year subsequent to the first, on the assumption that the learning process continues unbroken throughout the year concerned. The forecast level of output is obtained by computing the cumulative forecast output from the start of production to the end of the year in question, and subtracting from that the cumulative output up to the beginning of the year in question. For the mth year, forecast output x_m is given by:

$$x_m = \left(\frac{1}{a} \sum_{i=1}^{m} T_{Li} \right)^{1/(b+1)} - \left(\frac{1}{a} \sum_{i=1}^{m-1} T_{Li} \right)^{1/(b+1)} \quad (16.14)$$

Equation (16.14) relates to a single production line; for n production lines, the T_{Li} figures relate to the labour hours available to each line, and each of the brackets on the right-hand side of the equation is multiplied by n.

To determine second-year output x_2 for the single-line case in Holt Electronics the computation is:

$$x_2 = \left(\frac{500\,000}{280} \right)^{1/0.848} - \left(\frac{250\,000}{280} \right)^{1/0.848} = 3\,815 \text{ filters}$$

For the two-line case, the computation is:

$$x_2 = (2) \left(\frac{250\,000}{280} \right)^{1/0.848} - (2) \left(\frac{125\,000}{280} \right)^{1/0.848} = 3\,369 \text{ filters}$$

Sensitivity analysis on output forecasts

The next task is to examine the sensitivity of the forecasts in the single-line case to errors in predicting both the initial assembly time and the learning rate. Two new symbols need defining here, as follows. Let:

δ_1 represent the proportional error in the learning rate, so that if (for example) R has been 5 per cent underestimated, putting Holt Electronics on a $100R\% = 95$ per cent learning curve not a 90 per cent one, then $\delta_1 = 1.05$

δ_2 represent the proportional error in the initial assembly time, so that if this too has been 5 per cent underestimated, then $\delta_2 = 1.05$

Then, for the mth year, the revised output forecast x'_m is given by:

$$x'_m = \left(\frac{1}{\delta_2 a} \sum_{i=1}^{m} T_{Li}\right)^{1/[\{\ln(\delta_1 R)/\ln 2\} + 1]}$$

$$- \left(\frac{1}{\delta_2 a} \sum_{i=1}^{m-1} T_{Li}\right)^{1/[\{\ln(\delta_1 R)/\ln 2\} + 1]} \tag{16.15}$$

From equation (16.15), for the single-line case in Holt Electronics:

$$x'_1 = \left[\frac{250\,000}{(1.05)(280)}\right]^{1/[\{\ln(1.05)(0.9)/\ln 2\} + 1]}$$

$$= (850.34)^{1.088} = 1\,549 \text{ filters}$$

$$x'_2 = \left[\frac{500\,000}{(1.05)(280)}\right]^{1.088} - 1\,549 = 1\,724 \text{ filters}$$

Steady-state conditions

It is often possible to forecast what the minimum production time per unit will be in the steady state, after all learning effects have been exhausted. Production time per unit in this state is referred to as the steady-state marginal time, and taking into account the steady state requires new symbols as follows. Let:

t_s represent steady-state marginal time

x_s represent the number of units produced until steady-state conditions are reached

y_s represent the cumulative average production time per unit after x_s units have been produced

T_s represent the total production time for the first x_s units

Then equation (16.11) can be rewritten as:

$$T_s = x_s y_s = a x_s^{b+1} \tag{16.16}$$

Another way of describing the steady-state marginal time is to say that it represents the rate of change of total time T_s with respect to output when x_s units have been produced. Thus t_s may be obtained by differentiating equation (16.16) with respect to x_s, giving rise to:

$$t_s = dT_s/dx_s = (b + 1) ax_s^b \qquad (16.17)$$

In the penultimate part of the Holt Electronics problem, t_s has been estimated and x_s must be computed from it. Isolating out x_s from equation (16.17) yields:

$$x_s = [t_s/a(b + 1)]^{1/b} \qquad (16.18)$$

Given that $t_s = 75$, then the computation proceeds as follows:

$$x_s = \left[\frac{75}{280(0.848)} \right]^{1/-0.152} = 1\,962 \text{ filters}$$

The steady-state assembly time of 75 hours is thus reached after just under 2 000 filters have been produced. It takes T_s labour hours to produce x_s units on a single production line, and from equation (16.16):

$$T_s = (280)(1\,962^{0.848}) = 173\,527 \text{ hr}$$

From this result, the learning effect is seen to be exhausted about two-thirds of the way through the first year of manufacture on a single production line. Where learning is exhausted part-way through the first year, the forecast output x_1 for that year may be derived as follows:

$$x_1 = (T_{L1} - T_s)/t_s + x_s \qquad (16.19)$$

Applying equation (16.19) to the data in Holt Electronics gives:

$$x_1 = (250\,000 - 173\,527)/75 + 1\,962 = 2\,982 \text{ filters}$$

The budgeted profit over the first year π is given by:

$$\pi = px - cT_s - ct_s(x - x_s) - f \qquad (16.20)$$

Substituting in the figures for Holt:

$$\pi = 800(2\,982) - (4)(173\,527) - (4)(75)(2\,982 - 1\,962)$$
$$- 1\,400\,000 = -14\,508$$

An output of 2 982 filters will thus give rise to a small loss of £14 508 over the first year of production. Clearly, the break-even point for the first year must exceed x_s. Where this is the case, the value of the break-even output can be found by setting $\pi = 0$ in equation (16.20) and solving it for x, as follows:

$$x = \frac{c(T_s - t_s x_s) + f}{p - ct_s} \tag{16.21}$$

For the first year's production:

$$x = \frac{(4)(173\,527) - (4)(75)(1\,962) + 1\,400\,000}{800 - (4)(75)} = 3\,011 \text{ filters}$$

For the second and subsequent years, with learning effects exhausted throughout, the break-even level x will be a constant obtained by dividing fixed cost by contribution, as below:

$$x = f/(p - cts) \tag{16.22}$$

In the Holt problem, this is simply:

$$x = 1\,400\,000/[800 - (4)(75)] = 2\,800 \text{ filters per annum}$$

Budgeted output in the second and subsequent years will be $250\,000/75 = 3\,333$ filters per annum, for a budgeted profit of £266 500 per annum.

Joint Product Decisions 17

17.1 Cydilla Separators Ltd

Cydilla Separators is a manufacturer of biological concentrates which accelerate the fruit ripening process. The basic raw material from which these concentrates are derived is called Marimol, and costs £14 per kilogram to make. From 4 kilograms of Marimol, it is possible by further processing to produce 2 kilograms of Aplintasarate and 2 kilograms of Ruthenase. This processing costs £9 per kilogram for the Aplintasarate and £7 per kilogram for the Ruthenase. Aplintasarate is a final product, but Ruthenase cannot be sold directly to Cydilla's customers. It must be left to cool, and then separated out in such a way that 2 kilograms of Ruthenase give rise to 1.5 kilograms of Lefcon and 0.5 kilograms of Grodyn. There is a large market for Lefcon, and Cydilla's production represents only a tiny proportion of the available supply of this product. Consequently, Cydilla can either buy or sell Lefcon, in what are for practical purposes unlimited quantities, at the market price of £17 per kilogram. From 1.5 kilograms of Lefcon, Cydilla can by chemical means synthesise 1 kilogram of a final product called Jantym; this process costs £12 per kilogram of Jantym produced.

Grodyn is a highly volatile product, and it is therefore unsafe to sell it to outside customers in this form. It has first to undergo a stabilisation process, which changes it into a related product called Questid. This process is costly, involving an outlay of £23 per kilogram of Questid manufactured. It also involves a considerable amount of wastage, such that each kilogram of Grodyn yields only 0.7 kilograms of Questid.

The markets in which Aplintasarate, Jantym and Questid are sold are all characterised by imperfect competition. For none of these three products is there any possibility of practising price discrimination, so that in each case extra sales can be obtained only by reducing the price per kilogram at which all sales are made. The management of Cydilla believe that it is reasonable to treat all the three demand functions as being approximately linear, and have derived the following estimates of sales (in kilograms per week) at alternative selling prices:

Aplintasarate		*Jantym*		*Questid*	
Price per kg £	*Sales level*	*Price per kg* £	*Sales level*	*Price per kg* £	*Sales level*
50	140	77	85	150	34
40	200	70	100	125	40

Using the above data, **you are required** to advise Cydilla as to what its weekly production and sales levels should be for Aplintasarate, Jantym and Questid, and as to the price per kilogram it should charge for each of these three products. **You are also required** to advise Cydilla as to whether it should sell Lefcon or purchase it from outside, and as to the quantities per week of Lefcon which should be bought or sold.

You may find it helpful, in visualising the production situation at Cydilla, to refer to the diagram in Figure 17.1. This shows how an initial amount of 4 kilograms of Marimol is transformed into the various finished products, and indicates the costs of each stage in this transformation.

FIGURE 17.1
Cydilla Separators Ltd – Products/Costs from 4 kg Maximol

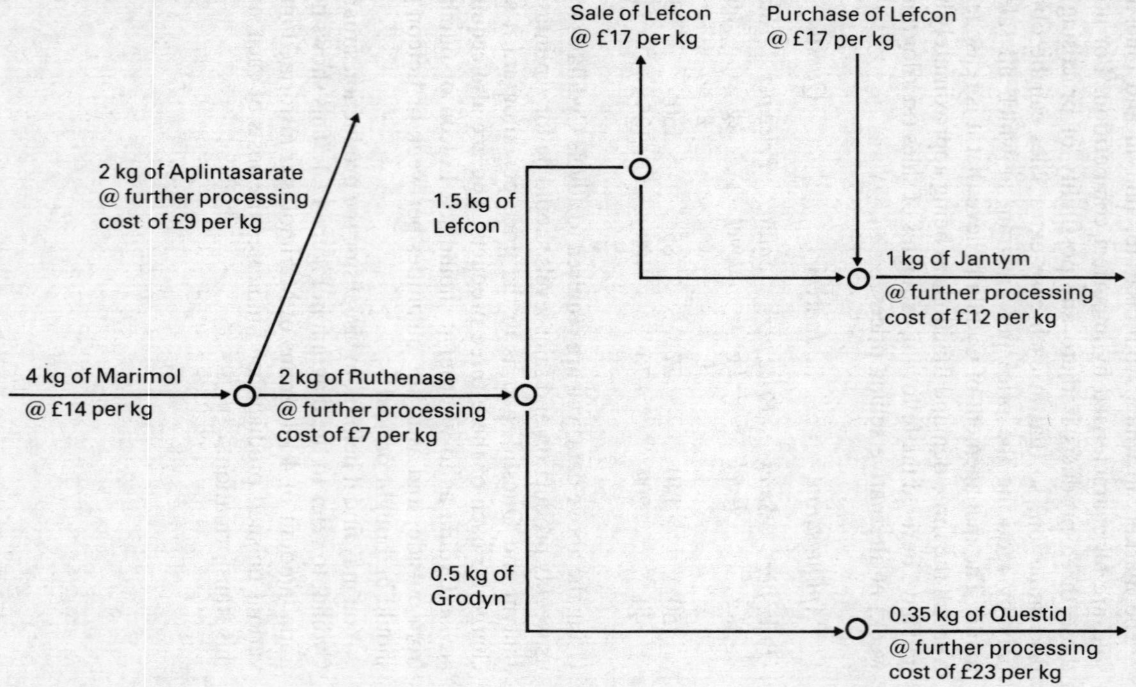

17.2   Analysis

Specification of demand functions

A preliminary step in dealing with the Cydilla Separators problem is to specify demand functions for the three final products sold in imperfectly competitive markets. For linear functions, the following terminology may be employed. Let:

P represent the price charged per kilogram
D represent the demand per week, in kilograms
b represent the gradient of the (downsloping) demand function
a represent the intercept term, being the notional price at which demand ceases to exist

The general form of the demand function is then:

$$P = a - bD \qquad\qquad (17.1)$$

For each of the three products, two pairs of D and P values have been estimated by Cydilla's management. Consequently, for each product two simultaneous equations can be set up in order to compute the two unknowns a and b. This gives the following results:

Aplintasarate	*Jantym*	*Questid*
$50 = a - 140b$	$77 = a - 85b$	$150 = a - 34b$
$40 = a - 200b$	$70 = a - 100b$	$125 = a - 40b$
Hence: $a = 73.3$	Hence: $a = 116.7$	Hence: $a = 291.7$
$b = 0.167$	$b = 0.467$	$b = 4.167$

Outline of the problem

Having dealt with this preliminary consideration, the next task is to define the terms that will be required in the analysis of this problem. Let:

P_A, P_J and P_Q represent respectively the selling prices per kilogram for Aplintasarate, Jantym and Questid

X_A, X_J and X_Q represent respectively the volume of sales (in kilograms per week) for Aplintasarate, Jantym and Questid

L_J represent the number of kilograms of Lefcon used per week in the production of Jantym

L_S represent the number of kilograms of Lefcon per week sold on the open market

L_P represent the number of kilograms of Lefcon per week bought on the open market

X_M represent the number of kilograms of Marimol processed per week

X_R represent the number of kilograms of Ruthenase processed per week

Using this terminology, the demand functions for the three products facing imperfect competition can be specified as follows:

$$P_A = 73.3 - 0.167X_A \tag{17.2}$$
$$P_J = 116.7 - 0.467X_J \tag{17.3}$$
$$P_Q = 291.7 - 4.167X_Q \tag{17.4}$$

The revenue obtained from selling Aplintasarate, Jantym and Questid is given by the sum of the products of unit price and quantity sold for each of them, that is by $P_A X_A + P_J X_J + P_Q X_Q$. To this must be added the revenue from net sales of Lefcon, represented by the excess of L_S over L_P, multiplied by its fixed market price of £17 per kilogram. Taken together, these yield an expression for total revenue per week R, where:

$$R = (73.3 - 0.167X_A)X_A + (116.7 - 0.467X_J) \, X_J \\ + (291.7 - 4.167X_Q)X_Q + 17(L_S - L_P) \tag{17.5}$$

The matching cost figure is given by the number of kilograms of each of the intermediate and final products processed per week, multiplied by the cost of processing per kilogram. Representing cost per week by C gives rise to:

$$C = 14X_M + 9X_A + 7X_R + 12X_J + 23X_Q \qquad (17.6)$$

The objective of Cydilla's management is to maximise profit, represented by the excess of R over C. If profit is denoted by π, then the expansion and simplification of equations (17.5) and (17.6) enables the following objective function to be drawn up:

Maximise $\pi = 64.3X_A - 0.167X_A^2 + 104.7X_J - 0.467X_J^2 + 268.7X_Q - 4.167X_Q^2 + 17L_S - 17L_P - 14X_M - 7X_R$

This maximisation is subject to five linear constraints as below:

$$X_A - 0.5X_M \leqq 0$$

This first constraint states that the amount of Aplintasarate produced and sold cannot exceed half the amount of Marimol produced.

$$X_R - 0.5X_M \leqq 0$$

This is a similar constraint, asserting that the amount of Ruthenase produced cannot exceed half the amount of Marimol produced.

$$L_J + L_S - L_P - 0.75X_R \leqq 0$$

This third constraint is somewhat more complex. It takes the amount of Lefcon which is either used in producing Jantym or is sold, which is given by $L_J + L_S$. The stipulation is then that this amount cannot exceed the sum of the amount of Lefcon purchased, L_P, and the amount of Lefcon produced within Cydilla, which is $0.75X_R$.

$$X_J - 0.667L_J \leqq 0$$

Here, what is being asserted is that the amount of Jantym produced and sold cannot exceed two-thirds of the amount of Lefcon used in the production of Jantym.

$$X_Q - 0.175X_R \leqq 0$$

This fifth constraint requires rather more detailed explanation. Denoting the amount of Grodyn produced by X_G, then $X_G = 0.25X_R$. Further, the amount of Questid available for sale cannot exceed 70 per cent of the amount of Grodyn produced, so that $X_Q \leqq 0.7X_G$. Substituting for X_G in this inequality gives rise to $X_Q \leqq (0.7)(0.25X_R)$, from which the fifth constraint above is obtained by simplification.

To complete the formulation of the problem, it is necessary only to note that none of the variables can sensibly take negative values, so that a non-negativity constraint should be associated with each one. Hence:

$$X_A, X_G, X_J, X_Q, X_M, X_R, L_J, L_S, L_P, \geqq 0$$

Having formulated the problem, the next question is how to go about finding its solution. It can be shown that maximising a quadratic objective function subject to five linear constraints is equivalent to maximising a function made up of the original objective function *less* the weighted sum of the expressions within each of the five constraints. The weights employed are referred to as Lagrangean multipliers, and the detailed reformulation of the problem in the Lagrangean mode makes it appear as below:

Maximise $M = 64.3X_A - 0.167X_A^2 + 104.7X_J - 0.467X_J^2 + 268.7X_Q - 4.167X_Q^2 + 17L_S - 17L_P - 14X_M - 7X_R - \lambda_1(X_A - 0.5X_M) - \lambda_2(X_R - 0.5X_M) - \lambda_3(L_J + L_S - L_P - 0.75X_R) - \lambda_4(X_J - 0.667L_J) - \lambda_5(X_Q - 0.175X_R)$

It can also be shown that a necessary condition for this maximisation to take place involves the satisfaction of requirements called Kuhn–Tucker conditions. These involve the partial differentiation of the function M for each of the variables within it, in turn. Partial differentiation is the process of finding the rate of change of a function with more than one variable with respect to one of its variables, all the other variables being considered constant. (It is denoted by the use of the Greek δ in place of the Roman d).

Written out in full, the Kuhn–Tucker conditions for this problem are as follows:

$$X_A \frac{\delta M}{\delta X_A} = 0 \qquad\qquad X_A \geqq 0$$

$$X_J \frac{\delta M}{\delta X_J} = 0 \qquad\qquad X_J \geqq 0$$

$$X_Q \frac{\delta M}{\delta X_Q} = 0 \qquad\qquad X_Q \geqq 0$$

$$X_M \frac{\delta M}{\delta X_M} = 0 \qquad\qquad X_M \geqq 0$$

$$X_R \frac{\delta M}{\delta X_R} = 0 \qquad\qquad X_R \geqq 0$$

$$L_J \frac{\delta M}{\delta L_J} = 0 \qquad\qquad L_J \geqq 0$$

$$L_S \frac{\delta M}{\delta L_S} = 0 \qquad\qquad L_S \geqq 0$$

$$L_P \frac{\delta M}{\delta L_P} = 0 \qquad\qquad L_P \geqq 0$$

$$\lambda_1 \frac{\delta M}{\delta \lambda_1} = 0 \qquad\qquad \lambda_1 \geqq 0$$

$$\lambda_2 \frac{\delta M}{\delta \lambda_2} = 0 \qquad\qquad \lambda_2 \geqq 0$$

$$\lambda_3 \frac{\delta M}{\delta \lambda_3} = 0 \qquad\qquad \lambda_3 \geqq 0$$

$$\lambda_4 \frac{\delta M}{\delta \lambda_4} = 0 \qquad\qquad \lambda_4 \geqq 0$$

$$\lambda_5 \frac{\delta M}{\delta \lambda_5} = 0 \qquad\qquad \lambda_5 \geqq 0$$

Complementary slackness conditions

In each of the (thirteen) equations immediately above, the partial differential of M with respect to a variable was multiplied by that variable, and the product equated to zero. Performing the partial differentiation within each equation gives rise to a set of simultaneous equations referred to as the complementary slackness conditions. These are as follows:

$$X_A \left[64.3 - 0.334X_A - \lambda_1 \right] = 0 \tag{17.7}$$

$$X_J \left[104.7 - 0.934X_J - \lambda_4 \right] = 0 \tag{17.8}$$

$$X_Q \left[268.7 - 8.334X_Q - \lambda_5 \right] = 0 \tag{17.9}$$

$$X_M \left[-14 + 0.5\lambda_1 + 0.5\lambda_2 \right] = 0 \tag{17.10}$$

$$X_R \left[-7 - \lambda_2 + 0.75\lambda_3 + 0.175\lambda_5 \right] = 0 \tag{17.11}$$

$$L_J \left[-\lambda_3 + 0.667\lambda_4 \right] = 0 \tag{17.12}$$

$$L_S \left[17 - \lambda_3 \right] = 0 \tag{17.13}$$

$$L_P \left[-17 + \lambda_3 \right] = 0 \tag{17.14}$$

$$\lambda_1 \left[0.5X_M - X_A \right] = 0 \tag{17.15}$$

$$\lambda_2 \left[0.5X_M - X_R \right] = 0 \tag{17.16}$$

$$\lambda_3 \left[0.75X_R + L_P - L_S - L_J \right] = 0 \tag{17.17}$$

$$\lambda_4 \left[0.667L_J - X_J \right] = 0 \tag{17.18}$$

$$\lambda_5 \left[0.175X_R - X_Q \right] = 0 \tag{17.19}$$

Each of equations (17.7) – (17.19) above can be solved in either of two ways. The expression within the square brackets can be set equal to zero, or the variable outside the brackets can be set equal to zero. Attention will first be focused on the former solution, which because it equates to zero the expression inside the brackets is referred to as the interior solution.

To find this solution involves solving a set of thirteen simultaneous equations, too much to cope with by hand but easily susceptible to computer analysis. However, it is obvious from the start that a pure interior solution is not feasible. This is because the expressions within the square brackets of equations (17.13) and (17.14) are identical save for a factor of -1, so that both equations have an interior solution of $\lambda_3 = 17$. It would appear, therefore, that there are here only twelve independent equations in thirteen variables, and that this system of simultaneous equations is consequently underdeterminate. However, since there can be no profit in buying Lefcon at £17 per kilogram for resale at exactly the same price, clearly either $L_P = 0$ or $L_S = 0$. That is, it is either profitable to buy Lefcon and not to sell it, or to sell Lefcon and not to buy it. Because one or other of L_P or L_S must be zero, the twelve equations within square brackets of which $\lambda_3 = 17$ is one relate to twelve variables only, and are therefore determinate.

An arbitrary initial choice may be made by assuming $L_P = 0$. Equation (17.14) is thus solved, and equation (17.17) may be rewritten as follows:

$$\lambda_3 \left[0.75 X_R - L_S - L_J \right] = 0$$

It is then a question of finding an interior solution to the twelve equations numbered (17.7)–(17.19) but excluding equation (17.14). Using a computer package for simultaneous equations, this interior solution is found to be:

$$X_A = 151.17; \ \lambda_1 = 13.81; \ X_J = 84.81; \ \lambda_4 = 25.49$$
$$X_Q = 26.45; \ \lambda_5 = 48.23; \ \lambda_2 = 14.19; \ \lambda_3 = 17$$
$$X_M = 302.34; \ X_R = 151.17; \ L_J = 127.15; \ L_S = -13.78$$

However, the last figure in this solution makes it unacceptable as a whole, because it violates the $L_S \geqq 0$ constraint. Put in another way, it directs Cydilla to sell a negative quantity of Lefcon, which is of itself impossible. None the less, this direction may be interpreted usefully as implying the sale of as little Lefcon as possible, represented by setting $L_S = 0$. This solves equation (17.13), and enables equation (17.17) to be rewritten as:

$$\lambda_3 \left[0.75 X_R + L_P - L_J \right] = 0$$

Computer analysis of the twelve equations numbered (17.7) – (17.19) but excluding equation (17.13) now gives a new interior solution. This is identical to the interior solution given above, except that $L_P = 13.78$ now replaces $L_S = -13.78$, thus rendering the overall solution feasible.

Substituting $X_A = 151.17$ in equation (17.2) yields $P_A = 48.05$, while substituting $X_J = 84.81$ in equation (17.3) yields $P_J = 77.09$ and substituting $X_Q = 26.45$ in equation (17.4) yields $P_Q = 181.48$. These results, together with those above, give rise to an optimal pricing, manufacturing and purchasing plan for Cydilla Separators as follows:

Product	Sales/Production level	Selling price
	(kg per week)	*(£ per kg)*
Marimol	302.34	–
Aplintasarate	151.17	48.05
Ruthenase	151.17	–
Lefcon	127.15 (manufactured)	–
Lefcon	13.78 (purchased)	–
Questid	26.45	181.48
Jantym	84.81	77.09

This solution gives rise to a profit of $\pi = £10\,091$ per week. Nowhere within it, though, is there any explanation of the meaning of the λ values obtained by solving equations (17.7) – (17.19). Hence these must be the focus of the final section.

Marginal conditions in the optimal solution

In general, λ_i represents the joint cost allocated to the ith product. This allocation has the special property that in the optimal solution the marginal revenue for each product will be equal to the sum of the joint cost λ allocated to that product and the separate processing cost incurred in respect of that product after its split-off point. Marginal revenue functions for each of the products are obtained by differentiating their total revenue functions. Let:

MR_A, MR_J and MR_Q represent respectively marginal revenue from the last kilogram sold of Aplintasarate, Jantym and Questid

Then differentiating separately the expressions for total product revenue in equation (17.5) relating to X_A, X_J and X_Q gives rise to three marginal revenue functions as follows:

$$MR_A = 73.3 - 0.334X_A \tag{17.20}$$

$$MR_J = 116.7 - 0.934X_J \tag{17.21}$$

$$MR_Q = 291.7 - 8.334X_Q \tag{17.22}$$

Substituting $X_A = 151.17$ in equation (17.20) yields $MR_A = 22.81$, while substituting $X_J = 84.81$ in equation (17.21) yields $MR_J = 37.49$ and substituting $X_Q = 26.45$ in equation (17.22) yields $MR_Q = 71.27$.

   Now let:

C_A, C_J and C_Q represent the separate processing costs incurred respectively for Aplintasarate, Jantym and Questid after their split-off points

From the data in the Cydilla problem, $C_A = 9$, $C_J = 12$ and $C_Q = 23$. Turning first to the allocated joint costs λ_1 and λ_2, these are given by $\lambda_1 = £13.81$, $\lambda_2 = £14.19$. Together they add up to £28, and in doing so represent an allocation of the cost of the two kilograms of Marimol to produce 1 kilogram of Aplintasarate (at an allocated cost of £13.81) and 1 kilogram of Ruthenase (at an allocated cost of £14.19). For Aplintasarate, the condition equating marginal revenue with the sum of allocated joint cost and separate processing cost is $MR_A = \lambda_1 + C_A = £22.81$. Similarly, for Jantym the marginal condition is $MR_J = \lambda_4 + C_J = £37.49$. Here, the value of

λ_4 (at £25.49) represents, with a small rounding error, the cost of 1.5 kilograms of Lefcon at its fixed market price of £17 per kilogram. The final marginal condition, for Questid, is given by $MR_Q = \lambda_5 + C_Q = $ £71.27, again with a small rounding error.

This last condition may be illuminated by showing how λ_5 is built up. The cost per kilogram of Ruthenase is given by the sum of λ_2 (the allocated joint cost to Ruthenase of Marimol) and £7 per kilogram cost of further processing of Ruthenase. With $\lambda_2 = 14.19$, Ruthenase is thus costed out at £21.19 per kilogram. It takes $(4)(10/7) = 5.714$ kilograms of Ruthenase to produce 1 kilogram of Questid, and from this amount of Ruthenase $0.75(5.714) = 4.286$ kilograms of Lefcon are derived. Valuing this Lefcon at its market price of £17 per kilogram, enough Ruthenase to produce one kilogram of Questid is seen to give rise to $(5.714)(£17) = $ £72.86 worth of Lefcon. With the cost per kilogram of Ruthenase given above as £21.19, enough Ruthenase to produce 1 kilogram of Questid will cost $(5.714)\ (£21.19) = $ £121.09. Then λ_5 is given by the difference between the £121.09 and £72.86 figures above, so that $\lambda_5 = $ £48.23. Aside from a small rounding error, the marginal condition $MR_Q = \lambda_5 + C_Q$ is seen to be satisfied.

Part II
Problems for
Self-study

Standard Costing and Matrix Algebra

1

Arconate Ltd

Arconate Ltd produces a very powerful antiseptic called Trikil. The production process necessitates mixing five chemicals. These chemicals fall into two groups, the ammoniate group and the oxidising group. The ammoniate group are solids – three of these are involved: hexachlorophene, paradichlorosol and bentonite. The oxidising group are liquids, ethyl acetate and carbon trimorphate. The mix of chemicals within either the ammoniate group or the oxidising group may be changed, but a larger input of a chemical in the oxidising group cannot be used to compensate for smaller input of a chemical in the ammoniate group, or vice versa. All of the chemicals are stored prior to use, and materials price variances are recorded at the time of their purchase. Three grades of labour are used in the production process; they may be substituted for one another but extra inputs of labour cannot serve to compensate for a reduction in the amount of any of the chemicals used.

The Trikil is produced in 100-kilogram batches, and the standard mixture with standard unit prices for a 100-kilogram batch is as follows:

	£ per kg
25 kg of hexachlorophene @	4.50
25 kg of paradichlorosol @	3.00
75 kg of bentonite @	0.80

	£ per l
20 l of carbon trimorphate @	2.50
50 l of ethyl acetate @	1.25

	£ per hr
18 hr of labour grade A @	4.20
26 hr of labour grade B @	3.15
31 hr of labour grade C @	2.80

During the month of January, the following materials were purchased:

	£ per kg
3 750 kg of hexachlorophene @	4.70
2 750 kg of paradichlorosol @	3.30
10 000 kg of bentonite @	0.70

	£ per l
2 500 l of carbon trimorphate @	2.95
6 000 l of ethyl acetate @	1.10

Production for January consisted of 10 700 kilograms of finished product, and there were no opening or closing stocks of work in progress. The following quantities of materials and labour were put into production:

2 625 kg of hexachlorophene
2 900 kg of paradichlorosol
9 240 kg of bentonite

2 200 l of carbon trimorphate
5 300 l of ethyl acetate

2 252 hr of labour grade A
2 660 hr of labour grade B
3 069 hr of labour grade C

At the beginning of January, there was a flat rate wage settlement of 60p per hour for labour grades B and C, raising the rate for grade B labour to £3.75 per hour and that for grade C labour to £3.40 per hour. The grade A labour was the subject of a separate settlement at the same time, raising its wage to £4.50 per hour.

Using matrix algebra techniques, **you are required** to calculate:

1. Where appropriate, price (rate of pay), quantity (efficiency) and mixed variances for materials and labour.
2. Mix and yield variances, but at the aggregate level only, not for individual inputs.

Stochastic Process Costing 2

Kleeford Distilled Compounds

Kleeford Distilled Compounds (KDC) are manufacturers of artificial flavourings and colourings for the food industry. One of their most important products is synthetic lemon oil, which is made by a three-stage distillation process. Each stage involves a prolonged period of heating, followed by a period in which the product settles into layers. This settlement must be completed before the product can be further processed; as a consequence, each of the three stages of distillation lasts a full working week.

At the end of Stage 1 distillation, the product separates into three layers. The top layer of Stage 1 distillation is called 'wash' and is thrown away as valueless; it amounts to 12 per cent of the output of Stage 1. The middle layer is referred to as 'Stage 1 main run' and amounts of 78 per cent of the output of Stage 1 – it is transferred to Stage 2. In the bottom layer of Stage 1 distillation is a product called 'heavy citron'. This amounts to 10 per cent of Stage 1 output, and while it cannot be transferred into Stage 2, it is still of value. If heavy citron is thoroughly mixed with the new fluid (called 'feed oil') which comes in each week as a raw material for synthetic lemon oil distillation, then this mixture can enter Stage 1 distillation so long as it has been 'balanced off'. The process of balancing off the input of Stage 1 involves mixing into it substances called 'two-light' and 'feed additive', respectively obtained from distillation in Stages 2 and 3 of the synthetic lemon oil manufacturing cycle. These substances are described below.

Stage 1 main run is one of the inputs to Stage 2 distillation, but there are two others. One of these is described later, the other is a by-product from another distillation process carried out elsewhere in KDC, and is called 'citric essence'. It differs from Stage 1 main run in that it is obtained from natural rather than synthetic products. However, it is almost identical chemically to Stage 1 main run, and can be mixed with it to produce a homogenous substance. This mixing, like that for the inputs to Stage 1, takes place over the weekend prior to the working week during which Stage 2 distillation takes place.

The output of Stage 2 distillation consists of four layers of product. 14 per cent of Stage 2 output makes up the top layer; this is the 'two-light' referred to above, and is returned to Stage 1 distillation for mixing with heavy citron, feed oil and feed additive. The bulk of Stage 2 output is called 'Stage 2 main run' and is transferred to Stage 3 distillation. 69 per cent of the output of Stage 2 falls into this second layer. Below it is a third layer called 'two-heavy', which is left in Stage 2 at the end of a working week. Its function is to balance off the citric essence in the weekend mixing process, and it thus serves as the third input to Stage 2 distillation. The proportion of Stage 2 output which falls into the 'two-heavy' layer is 11 per cent. In the bottom layer comes the remaining 6 per cent of Stage 2 output. This is referred to as 'grouts', and is discarded as worthless.

The only input to Stage 3 distillation is Stage 2 main run, so that no mixing process is required prior to the working week of distillation. At the end of this Stage 3 distillation process, three layers of product are separated. The top layer is referred to as 'feed additive'. It is too light to be saleable of itself, but it can be added to the feed oil entering Stage 1 of the distillation process. All the feed oil entering Stage 1 at the beginning of a working week is balanced off in part by having mixed with it the feed additive obtained from the Stage 3 distillation process at the end of the preceding week. When Stage 3 distillation has been completed, 9 per cent of the final product goes into the top (feed additive) layer.

Beneath this layer is a second layer called Stage 3 main run. This is the final product, and represents fully processed synthetic oil. 83 per cent of the output of Stage 3 distillation is main run, and KDC sells it in this form to the food industry. The remaining 8 per cent of the output of Stage 3 is a worthless residue called 'fallings', which is thrown away.

At the beginning of every weekend, a fresh consignment of 23 500 litres of feed oil enters the mixing process prior to Stage 1 distillation. There, this new supply is balanced off with the previous week's output of heavy citron, two-light and feed additive, before entering the Stage 1 distillation process on Monday morning.

Also on Monday morning, the week-long distillation operations of Stages 2 and 3 commence. Into Stage 2 goes the mixture of Stage 1 main run and two-heavy obtained from the previous week's distillation. The two-heavy serves to balance off an input, from outside the three-stage distillation process, of 3 900 litres of citric essence. As has been stated above, this comes from elsewhere in KDC. Finally, into Stage 3 goes the output of Stage 2 main run which was derived from that distillation operation at the end of the preceding week.

The variable cost of passing a litre of input through Stage 1 is £1.90, through Stage 2 is £2.75 and through Stage 3 is £2.20. Given these facts, **you are required** to answer the following questions:

1. In the steady state, what will be the mean and standard deviation of the volume of product undergoing each of the distillation processes during any given working week?
2. What will be the expected output of synthetic lemon oil, and what will be the average volume of wash, grouts and fallings together which are thrown away? Both quantities should be expressed in terms of litres per week.
3. What will be the expected variable cost per working week of operating each of the three stages of distillation?
4. In the steady state, what will be the standard deviations of the output of synthetic lemon oil per working week and of the volume of wash, grouts and fallings together thrown away per working week?
5. If it were desired to produce an average output of 21 000 litres of synthetic lemon oil per working week, and if the supply of citric essence was fixed at 3 900 litres per week, by how much would the volume of feed oil entering Stage 1 per week have to be expanded?

Credit Management and Markov Chains: Partial Balance Aging Method

3

Langdale Ltd

Langdale Ltd uses partial balance aging to classify the amounts of money owed to it. Over the last 3 months of 1989, the total of debts owed to Langdale Ltd increased in the following manner:

End of	Total owed (£)
October	764 927
November	871 464
December	912 960

The breakdown of these debts by reference to the period of time for which they had been outstanding is given below:

Time for which debt owed	End of October	End of November	End of December
Less than	£	£	£
1 month	511 401	662 666	672 390
1–2 months	94 853	79 261	103 722
2–3 months	53 711	55 212	43 685
3–4 months	26 108	12 471	42 433
Over 4 months	78 854	61 854	50 730

The Credit Control Manager of Langdale Ltd says that she thinks about 35 per cent of the debts in the 3–4 months' old category at any one time are paid during the next month. Langdale Ltd wrote off £19 901 in November and £14 108 in December in respect of bad debts. **You are required** to use Markov chain analysis to answer the following questions:

1. What would you forecast cash receipts to be in January 1990?
2. If forecast credit sales for January 1990 are £492 000, what would you forecast cash receipts to be in February 1990?

In answering these two questions, use an exponential smoothing formula in which the current transition matrix is given a weight of $\alpha = 0.8$.

Credit Management and Markov Chains: Modified Total Balance Aging Method

4

Firenza Associates

Firenza Associates produces highly specialised loudspeaker equipment for a very small number of customers, who purchase from it on credit. At the end of May 1989 it had twelve credit customers, whose accounts stood as follows, with all figures in thousands of pounds:

Customer account no.	Owed from May invoices	Owed from April invoices	Owed from invoices in or before March
1	10	–	–
2	9	2	–
3	–	–	7
4	5	6	3
5	6	11	–
6	13	15	2
7	–	8	16
8	7	4	–
9	–	–	12
10	16	–	4
11	–	10	–
12	7	14	5

The same accounts stood as follows at the end of June 1989:

Customer account no.	Owed from June invoices	Owed from May invoices	Owed from invoices in or before April
1	14	4	–
2	–	9	–
3	5	–	–
4	–	–	–
5	7	6	11
6	–	13	–
7	9	–	24
8	3	7	–
9	–	–	12
10	12	16	–
11	13	–	–
12	5	–	–

The management of Firenza Associates believe that all of the amounts owed at the end of June 1989 will ultimately be paid, with the exception of the £12 000 owed on Account 9. It was decided during June that this amount represented a bad debt. Excluding this bad debt, the total amounts owed at the end of June were as follows:

Owed from	£
June invoices	68 000
May invoices	55 000
Invoices in or before April	35 000
	158 000

Using this data, **you are required**:

1. To compute the expected value of receipts from the £158 000 owed at the end of June.
2. To compute the provision for bad debts that should be made in respect of the £158 000 owed.

This provision should be such that, given a normal distribution for the amount of bad debts, there is only a 0.01 probability that the actual amount of bad debts will exceed the amount provided for them.

3. To compute the present value of receipts from the £158 000 given a rate of discount of 1½ per cent per month.

4. To estimate the size of the investment in debtors that Firenza Associates will have in the steady state if it acquires new debts at a constant rate of £65 000 per month.

Linear Programming and Decisions on Internal v. External Purchases of Services

5

Remosense PLC

Remosense PLC is a company specialising in the detection of mineral deposits by the use of aerial surveys. It is based in the United Kingdom, but the nature of its work requires it to maintain an elaborate communications network on a worldwide basis. The company is divided up into two parts, a Communications Division and an Operations Division. Within the Communications Division there are four service departments numbered S_1 (telephones), S_2 (telex), S_3 (document transmission) and S_4 (electronic data transfer). These service departments support the Operations Division, but they also provide services to one another (for example, some of the electronic data transfer is carried out down private lines operated by the telephone department). The amounts and proportions of services consumed in the departments and provided to the Operations Division in 1989 may be tabulated as follows, with all figures in thousands of units:

From/To	S$_1$	S$_2$	S$_3$	S$_4$	Operations division	Total
S$_1$	0	42	31	9	230	312
	–	13.5%	9.9%	2.9%	73.7%	(h)
S$_2$	5	0	62	28	195	290
	1.7%	–	21.4%	9.7%	67.2%	(h)
S$_3$	26	108	0	67	820	1 021
	2.5%	10.6%	–	6.6%	80.3%	(facsimile pages)
S$_4$	22	121	94	0	408	645
	3.4%	18.8%	14.6%	–	63.2%	(m of printout)

During 1989, the variable operating costs incurred in the service departments were as follows:

	£
S$_1$ (telephones)	873 600
S$_2$ (telex)	551 000
S$_3$ (document transmission)	408 400
S$_4$ (electronic data transfer)	387 000

At the end of 1989, Remosense were approached by an international communications company called Transferincorp, with a proposal that they should perform some of the services currently carried out by the Communications Division. Since the work of the Communications Division does not involve the incurrence of avoidable fixed costs on any significant scale, Remosense feel justified in evaluating any offer made by Transferincorp solely in terms of its impact on variable operating costs.

You are required to advise Remosense as to how it should respond to an offer by Transferincorp to supply electronic data transfer services at a cost of £0.75 per metre of printout, and document transmission services at a cost of £0.55 per facsimile page.

Linear Programming, Opportunity Losses and *ex post* Budgeting

6

Shalmirane Ltd

Shilmirane Ltd is a small, specialist manufacturer of extremely expensive radar-reflecting paints for military use. These paints are made up of two ingredients, and the distillation of these ingredients constitutes the only manufacturing process within Shalmirane. The ingredients are known by their code-names of Fracto and Diffuso. Both of them are very perishable; consignments of Fracto and Diffuso are delivered to Shalmirane every day and must be used on the day of their receipt – they cannot be stored at all.

From these ingredients, four different types of paint are manufactured, called Fulminate, Trathonate, Suborcate and Mathinate. Denote the production (in litres) of Fulminate as X_1, of Trathonate as X_2, of Suborcate as X_3 and of Mathinate as X_4. The following data then indicates the standard time required in the distillation process and the standard raw material input per litre produced for each type of paint:

Requires	Input of Fracto	Input of Diffuso	Distillation time required
	l	*l*	*hr*
1 *l* of X_1	12	10	0.5
1 *l* of X_2	15	12	0.6
1 *l* of X_3	16	13	0.7
1 *l* of X_4	25	20	2.0

Shalmirane carries out planning once per month only; it does not revise its plans during a month though it may adapt its actual production to changing circumstances. It bases its plans for February 1989 upon the presumption that during the month it can buy no more than 3 600 litres of Fracto and 2 900 litres of Diffuso, equal quantities being available in each fortnight of the month. It also assumes that distillation will be carried on over a working week of 40 hours – that is, for 160 hours over the month as a whole. Shalmirane's plan assumes a cost for Fracto of £5 per litre and for Diffuso of £7 per litre, together with a variable cost for the distilling process of £80 per hour.

The Ministry of Defence is the sole customer for Shalmirane's output. It buys radar-resistant paint from a number of specialists like Shalmirane, and is therefore content to leave to Shalmirane's discretion what mix of types of paints shall be produced in any given month. The Ministry's position is that it will buy all the paint Shalmirane produces; in planning for February 1989, Shalmirane uses the Ministry's prices of £207 per litre for Fulminate, £251 for Trathonate, £271 per litre for Suborcate and £500 per litre for Mathinate.

The events which actually took place in February 1989 turned out to differ from Shalmirane's plan in the following four respects:

1. Planned maintenance of the distillation process had not been carried out properly in January.
   As a result, it turned out that throughout February every litre of Mathinate produced required 25 litres of Diffuso instead of the planned 20 litres.
   This was the only one of the four variances from the February plan which Shalmirane's management considered to lie within their control.
2. From the beginning of February, it was obvious that the standard which stated that 13 litres of Diffuso were required per litre of Suborcate produced had been set too loosely.
   In fact, only 12.5 litres of Diffuso were required per litre of Suborcate.
3. The union to which the distillation operatives at Shalmirane belonged had always insisted that distillation operatives should not work more than a 40-hour week, in order to implement a job sharing scheme.
   However, Shalmirane succeeded in the middle of February 1989 in negotiating a new shift system with the union.

This system was implemented immediately, and had the effect of making it possible to run the distillation process for up to 60 hours per week at the higher variable cost of £85 per hour.

4. Shalmirane Ltd is actually a subsidiary of a much larger parent company, Hibushi Corporation.

   Shalmirane decides on a day-to-day basis how much Fracto and Diffuso it needs, but the payments for its purchases are made by Hibushi.

   At the beginning of February, Hibushi and the supplier of Fracto were in dispute about Hibushi's slowness in paying its bills; the Fracto supplier consequently refused to make any deliveries at all to Shalmirane during February.

   The Ministry of Defence, when faced with the possibility that no paint at all would be supplied in February, agreed to provide a substitute from their own stocks; this took the form of a highly classified substance called Varilum, sold by the Ministry at £6 per litre.

   The amounts of Varilum required to produce any of the paints are exactly the same as the amounts of Fracto, and Varilum and Fracto are both equally perishable; however, while the Ministry could make available 2 000 litres of Varilum in the first half of February, in the second half it could make only 1 600 litres available.

   In the first half of February, Shalmirane produced 120 litres of Fulminate and 10 litres of Mathinate, to earn a contribution of £3 150.

   In the second half of February, Shalmirane again produced 120 litres of Fulminate but only 6 litres of Mathinate, to earn a contribution of £2 730.

For the first and second halves of February separately, **you are required**:

1. To use *ex post* budgeting in computing the forecast variance and the opportunity cost variance, breaking each of these down into:

   (a) The portion of the variance attributable to volume and mix changes

   (b) The portion of the variance attributable to price and efficiency changes.

2. To indicate how, with unchanged actual performance by Shalmirane, the variances for February would change if Varilum
   was *not* perishable.

Assume that for security reasons Varilum was supplied by the
Ministry of Defence on a 'sale or return' basis, in the sense that any
Varilum left unused at the end of February (when Fracto again
became available) had to be returned to the Ministry.

Input–Output Analysis and Linear Programming

Kerruish Tracers

Kerruish Tracers is engaged in the manufacture of radioactive dyes, which when injected intravenously can be used for medical diagnosis. Two dyes are currently produced, called Cadmium Red and Strontium Blue. Cadmium Red gives rise to a by-product called cadmium chlorate, and Strontium Blue to a by-product called strontium nitrate; both of these by-products are used elsewhere in production. There are five production processes in all, and the flow of product through them is fairly complex. It may be depicted by the diagram in Figure 7A.1.

Each of the processes produces a single product; the output of Process I is called Product I, and so on (thus calling Cadmium Red Product IV and Strontium Blue Product V). Using the interrelationships shown in Figure 7A.1, the amount of each product used up to produce a unit of each of Products I – V may be tabulated as below. For Products I, IV and V a unit of output is 1 litre, and for Products II and III a unit of output is 1 kilogram. Hence this table shows (for example) that each litre of Product IV manufactured requires 0.22 litres of Product I and 0.37 kilograms of Product III.

FIGURE 7A.1
Kerruish Tracers – Product Flow

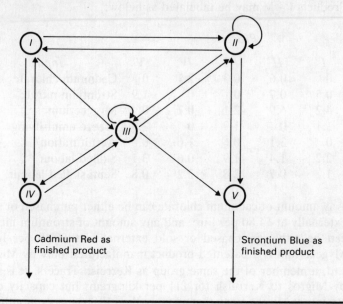

Cadmium Red as finished product

Strontium Blue as finished product

Processes

I	II	III	IV	V	Products
0	0.67	0.31	0.22	0	I
0.17	0.06	0.46	0	0.16	II
0	0.19	0.07	0.37	0.91	III
0.04	0	0.11	0	0	IV
0	0.09	0	0	0	V

As well as using internally-supplied products, the processes use inputs of materials, labour and machine time. Of the three materials required, two of them (cadmium chlorate and strontium nitrate) have the amount of their input measured in litres, and one (mygecerium) has the amount of its input measured in kilograms. Two types of machines are employed, one to perform freeze emulsifying and the other acculturation; inputs from both of these are measured in machine hours. The two grades of labour are skilled and semi-skilled; their inputs are measured in hours. The amounts of each input consumed in producing a unit of each of Products I – V may be tabulated as below:

Processes

I	II	III	IV	V	Input
0	0.6	0.3	−2.1	0	Cadmium chlorate
0.5	0.7	0	0	−1.9	Strontium nitrate
4.2	6.9	2.1	0.7	0	Mygecerium
1.1	0	1.9	0	2.3	Freeze emulsifying
0	3.1	0.6	1.6	0	Acculturation
2.2	1.4	1.9	0.6	3.1	Skilled labour
1.7	0.7	2.8	2.2	0.8	Semi-skilled labour

Any amount of cadmium chlorate can be either purchased or sold externally at £4.80 per litre, and any amount of strontium nitrate can be either purchased or sold externally at £6.40 per litre. Mygecerium is a patented product manufactured only by Migros Ltd, a member of the same group as Kerruish Tracers. It is sold by Migros to Kerruish for £11 per kilogram, but capacity constraints at Migros mean that no more than 10 000 kg per month can be shipped to Kerruish. In the month of June 1989, the maximum number of machine and labour hours available within various categories are as follows:

	Hr available
Freeze emulsifying machines	3 400
Acculturation machines	3 700
Skilled labour	5 200
Semi-skilled labour	5 900

Kerruish does not regard labour as a variable cost, since it offers its workers a guaranteed working week, and therefore pays them the same rate whether they are working or not. For June 1989, the wages bill will amount of £56 000 whatever output Kerruish produces. However, there is a significant variable cost associated with machine operation, since both the freeze emulsifying and the acculturation machines consume considerable amounts of electricity. The variable cost of operation of a freeze emulsifying machine is £6.60 per hour in June 1989, while the variable cost of operating an acculturation machine is £8.10 per hour.

The management of Kerruish have set a price of £190 per litre for Cadmium Red and of £395 per litre for Strontium Blue. They believe that they can sell all they can produce of either product at these prices. But in order to fulfil contracts with their most important customer, the National Health Service, Kerruish must produce not less than 350 litres of Cadmium Red and 275 litres of Strontium Blue during June, 1989.

You are required:

1. To advise Kerruish Tracers as to the output of Cadmium Red and Strontium Blue that it should budget to produce during June 1989, and as to the budgeted contribution and the budgeted profit to which this output will give rise.
2. To take the optimum mix and to work out from it:
   (a) The number of units of Products I – V that will need to be manufactured during June 1989
   (b) The amount of each of the inputs that will be used up during June, including the net amounts of cadmium chlorate and strontium nitrate bought or sold.

Input–Output Analysis and Linear Programming

7B

with Purchasable Intermediate Products and Joint Final Products

Raistrick Ltd

Raistrick Ltd is a division of Genco PLC, and is concerned with the manufacture of products for the brewing industry. Specifically, it manufactures as joint products a very concentrated yeast additive called Pirco and an enzyme called Urquase. This manufacturing activity involves three processes, numbered I – III. Processes I and II each give rise to a single product (Products I and II respectively). Process III is the final process, from which both Pirco and Urquase emerge, manufacture taking place in the fixed ratio of 0.8 kilograms of Urquase produced for every kilogram of Pirco. The chemical processes involved are heavily dependent upon the use of catalysts, and the flow of product through them can be depicted as in Figure 7B.1.

The amount of each product used up to produce a kilogram of Pirco and 0.8 kilograms of Urquase together may be tabulated as below, with the unit of output of Product I represented by one litre and the unit of output of Product II represented by one kilogram.

FIGURE 7B.1
Raistrick Ltd – Product Flow

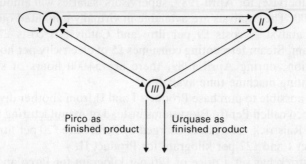

	Processes		
I	*II*	*III*	*Products*
0.05	0.4	0.3	Product I
0.1	0.03	0.5	Product II
0.02	0.04	0	Pirco
0.06	0.03	0	Urquase

All three processes take place in steam fermenting machines, and
each process requires the use of two non-recoverable catalysts.
Since the processes are potentially toxic, they require constant
supervision. Each process therefore requires inputs of labour, as
well as using up machine time and catalytic inputs. Catalyst A has
the amount of its input measured in litres, while Catalyst B has its
input measured in kilograms, and inputs of labour and machine
time are measured in hours. The amount of each of the inputs
required to produce a unit of output from each of the processes
may be tabulated as below:

	Processes		
I	*II*	*III*	*Input*
0.19	0.06	0.13	Catalyst A
0.04	0.12	0.17	Catalyst B
0.8	1.3	1.5	Supervision
0.7	1.1	2.1	Steam fermenting time

In April 1989, there are 44 000 hours of supervisory labour time available. Supervisors are salaried staff who are paid the same amount per month irrespective of the volume of production that they supervise; for April 1989, supervisors' salaries will amount to £215 600. The catalysts are available in virtually unlimited quantities; Catalyst A costs £9 per litre and Catalyst B costs £7 per kilogram. Steam fermenting consumes £5 of electricity per hour of operation; during April 1989, there are 54 000 hours of steam fermenting machine time available.

It is possible to purchase Products I and II from another division of Genco called Pentre Biosystems instead of manufacturing them within Raistrick. The prices charged by Pentre are £20 per litre for Product I and £22 per kilogram for Product II.

Raistrick has set a price of £26 per kilogram for Pirco and £17 per kilogram for Urquase. They feel that at these prices they can sell up to a maximum of 18 000 kilograms of Pirco during April. They hold no finished product stocks at the beginning of that month.

You are required to advise Raistrick as to:

1. The number of kilograms of Pirco and Urquase it should budget to produce during April 1989, and as to the budgeted contribution and the budgeted profit to which this output will give rise.
2. The number of units of Products I and II that will need to be manufactured during April.
3. The number of units of Products I and II that will need to be purchased from Pentre Biosystems during April.
4. The amount of each of the inputs that will be used up during April.

Use of Information Theory to Isolate Substantial Variances

8

Department of Transportation Analytical Offices

The Department of Transportation maintains three Analytical Offices, which perform tasks such as checking the lead content of petrol and applying gas chromatography to samples of heavy vehicle exhaust fumes. By virtue of the nature of their work, all three offices incur substantial energy costs, and the Department is anxious to monitor these closely. The three offices are widely dispersed across the country (at Scunthorpe, Bath and Dundee) and vary quite considerably in size. This range of variation rather complicates the analysis of energy costs. However, the Department wishes to undertake a close analysis of actual against budgeted costs for the most recent quarter in respect of the three energy sources which the offices use. The cost figures concerned are as follows:

	Budgeted costs			
	Scunthorpe £	Bath £	Dundee £	Total £
Gas	78 944	27 222	91 382	197 548
Electricity	42 081	51 082	9 261	102 424
Solid Fuel	16 479	12 908	51 008	80 395
	137 504	91 212	151 651	380 367

Actual costs

	Scunthorpe £	Bath £	Dundee £	Total £
Gas	84 917	26 028	95 410	206 355
Electricity	38 656	58 714	12 440	109 810
Solid Fuel	18 811	14 799	55 356	88 966
	142 384	99 541	163 206	405 131

The main interest of the Department of Transportation lies in predicting the breakdown of energy costs for budgeting purposes, rather than in trying to control them directly. While the Department's staff encourage the offices in energy saving, they know that office energy costs are mainly determined by the volume and mix of work that the offices undertake, and that this is in turn largely governed by statutory considerations.

Given this background, **you are required** to advise the Department on changes in the pattern of energy consumption as between one office and another, and as between one energy source and another.

The Single-period Cost Variance Investigation Decision

9

Star Chemical Company

The trimetheldrin diffraction process at Star Chemical Company is run from Monday to Friday, then shut down at the weekend. Quantity variances are reported weekly, and they are very often unfavourable for this process. But the standard costing system is far from perfect, and will generate unfavourable quantity variances whether or not the process is out of control. A study of these variances over a number of weeks has shown that they give rise to two normal distributions (according to whether the process is in or out of control) as follows:

	When the process is in control	When the process is out of control
	£	£
Mean unfavourable variance	9 000	10 500
Standard deviation of unfavourable variances	3 500	1 000

On Friday evenings, as the diffraction process shuts down, an opportunity arises to drain some of the liquid trimetheldrin out, and put it through an automatic chemical analyser. Once trimetheldrin has been drained out, it cannot be returned to the diffraction process for fear of contamination, and has to be thrown away. Consequently, the cost of analysing the trimetheldrin

231

depends on how much is drained out. Two possible volumes of liquid can be removed, called a 'partial drain' and a 'full drain'. A partial drain costs £200 in lost trimetheldrin, and a full drain costs £700. However, the volume of liquid removed in a partial drain is insufficient to enable the chemical analyser to detect with certainty a situation where the diffraction process is out of control; if it is, there is only a 0.4 probability that a partial drain will enable the analyser to find this out. By contrast, a full drain will always enable the analyser to detect an out of control process. If the process is found to be out of control, maintenance staff have to work a special Saturday morning shift to detect and correct the faults; this costs £150 in extra overtime payments.

Because the diffraction process is not absolutely air-tight, small chemical changes take place in the trimetheldrin as it stands over the weekend. The effect of these changes on the process tends to be adverse; if the process is in control at the beginning of the weekend there is a 0.35 probability that it will be out of control when the weekend is over. Less often, the effect of the changes can be favourable; if the process is out of control at the beginning of the weekend there is a 0.15 probability that it will be back in control by the time the weekend finishes.

During Friday 14 July, the Process Controller for trimetheldrin diffraction observes several small indications which suggest to him that the process might be out of control, and he comes to attach a probability of 0.25 to this state of affairs. A computer-generated costing report then tells him that there was an unfavourable quantity variance of £9 600 on trimetheldrin diffraction for the week which has just ended. This information serves to reassure the Process Controller, and he consequently decides not to ask for either a partial or a full drain of trimetheldrin. The diffraction process is restarted on Monday 17 July, and runs for another week, giving rise to an adverse quantity variance of £9 300, reported on Friday 21 July.

You are required:

1. To comment upon the Process Controller's decision not to drain off any of the trimetheldrin on Friday 14 July.
2. To advise the Process Controller on whether he should give instructions for a partial drain, a full drain or no drain at all on Friday 21 July.

3. To indicate to the Process Controller how your advice in 2 above would change if the facts in the question were altered in the following two respects simultaneously:

   (a) If it were discovered that the opening of valves required for a partial drain caused air to enter the process and contaminate the trimetheldrin remaining within it, so that the available options became restricted to a full drain or none at all

   (b) If the unfavourable quantity variance reported on Friday 21 July was £12 800.

4. To compute the expected cost of the optimal decision rule in 3 above, and to compare this against the expected cost of the best one-sided decision rule.

The Multi-period Cost Variance Investigation Decision

10

Mansfield Pressings

Mansfield Pressings is a small company specialising in metal stampings. They have one large stamping machine, which is in operation almost continuously, on a three-shift basis. Its electricity consumption depends to a considerable extent on whether the alignment rods (which hold the die in place when it is pressed on to the metal) are bent or not. There are, however, a number of other influences on the machine's electricity usage, notably the condition of the metal being pressed and the shape and complexity of the die being employed.

Because the electricity costs incurred in stamping constitute a significant proportion of Mansfield Pressings' total costs, they are monitored very carefully. An automatic metering/costing system has been installed, which produces a print-out at the end of each 8-hour shift stating what the cost of electricity consumed on that shift has been. If the Works Manager feels that the cost shown is excessive, he can order that the alignment rods be checked for straightness. This involves stopping the machine only briefly, but the Works Manager estimates that the production lost even in this short period diminishes contribution earned by about £40. If the alignment rods are found to be bent, they have to be replaced, involving a slightly longer stoppage losing a further £15 of contribution as a result of lost production. In addition, an outlay of £30 is required for a replacement set of rods.

The first thing that the operatives do when they come on shift is to change the die on the stamping machine. This is necessary because dies become worn out after they have been used for a shift, and have to be thrown away. The die is never changed during the course of a shift – the interruption of production involved would be prohibitively expensive. This fact is relevant to the question, because the only occasion upon which alignment rods can become twisted is when the die is being changed. Consequently, the stamping machine is in one or other of two states ('rods twisted' or 'rods not twisted') throughout the course of a shift. From long experience, the Works Manager estimates that the alignment rods will become twisted about once every four times that the die is changed. He has also developed the following probability distributions for the electricity cost per shift associated with the two possible states of the rods:

Rods not twisted		*Rods twisted*	
Cost per shift £	*Probability*	*Cost per shift* £	*Probability*
300–350	0.05	400–450	0.05
350–400	0.30	450–500	0.05
400–450	0.25	500–550	0.15
450–500	0.20	550–600	0.25
500–550	0.15	600–650	0.35
550–600	0.05	650–700	0.15

You are required to find the rule governing decisions to investigate, which serves to minimise the long-term expected cost per shift associated with running the metal stamping machine.

You are also required to compare the minimum long-term expected cost under uncertainty with the long-term cost of running the metal stamping machine under conditions of certainty.

Stochastic Cost–Volume–Profit Analysis and Decision Theory

11

Bulk Powder Producers Ltd

Bulk Powder Producers Ltd (BPP) have decided to enter the market for ink powder, although they do not currently possess the type of grinding machine required to produce it. BPP is a division of a much larger company, and Head Office have told them that they must lease rather than purchase the new grinding machine owing to a capital shortage. Two types of ink grinding machine are available for leasing; Type A machines require lease payments of £50 000 per annum while Type B machines require lease payments of £80 000 per annum. However, Type A machines grind ink powder at a variable cost of £0.50 per kilogram while Type B machines grind ink powder at a variable cost of £0.30 per kilogram. BPP has 400 customers, and on the basis of their demand for staining powders other than inks it is possible for the executives of BPP to say that there is an even chance that their demand for ink powder will lie within the range from 250–550 kilograms per customer per annum. In view of the wide margin of uncertainty involved, BPP have sent out a salesman to obtain firm orders for a year's supply of ink powder from a sample of customers. The salesman visited four customers, and the orders he obtained were for a mean amount of 357 kilograms with a standard deviation of 104 kilograms.

An opportunity then arose for the same salesman to visit a further sample of three customers, at a cost of £125 per customer.

You are required to answer the following questions:

1. On the basis of the first sample of four customers *only*, should BPP lease a Type A machine or a Type B machine?
2. Is the expected net gain from sampling associated with the second sample of three customers such that it would be worthwhile undertaking this second sample?

In answering 2 above, you are to assume that BPP's previous experience suggests that the standard deviation of powder sales per annum for a given type of powder as between customers is approximately 120 kilograms, and that the population of customers can be regarded as sufficiently large for it to be possible to ignore any non-independence of customers sampled.

Stochastic Cost–Volume–Profit Analysis: Satisficing with Short Product Lives

12

Bridgegate Foods

Bridgegate Foods is a wholesale provision merchant specialising in supplying hotels and restaurants in the Torbay area. It is considering whether or not to lease some deep freeze equipment with the complex ventilation and temperature control facilities required for the storage of oysters. Market research in local hotels and restaurants has suggested that they would demand on average a total of 200 dozen oysters per week, but that the standard deviation of their demand would be 80 dozen. Bridgegate's experience in the wholesaling of other shellfish suggests to them that they can interpret their market research as saying that they would face a normal distribution for dozens of oysters demanded, with a mean of 200 and a standard deviation of 80, at the price of £9 per dozen that they would propose to charge.

The chief complication in wholesaling oysters arises from their infrequency of supply, taken together with their extreme perishability. Bridgegate's shellfish supplier says that it has oysters available only once per week, when a consignment arrives by truck from the East Coast. Even with specialised deep freeze equipment, oysters can be kept fit for human consumption for a maximum of only 1 week. Oysters remaining unsold to hotels and restaurants at the end of a week could readily be sold to a specialist

Torbay firm of fishing bait manufacturers called Lacaisse Ltd. However, Lacaisse would be willing to pay only £1.50 per dozen for oysters for bait, while Bridgegate's supplier would charge it £4.50 per dozen.

If Bridgegate were to decide to stock oysters, then it would become the only source of supply for them to Torbay hotels and restaurants. None of these establishments have any facilities for storing oysters, even briefly, and so they would have to order their needs from Bridgegate every day. They appreciate that Bridgegate might be unable to fulfil their orders if it had exhausted the supply of oysters it had received for a particular week, and would therefore put a 'subject to availability' note against the entry for oysters on their menus.

Bridgegate are none the less certain that frustrated orders for oysters would give rise to annoyance arising from the frequent unavailability of an item on the menu, and that this annoyance on the part of diners would be reflected in ill-will toward Bridgegate by hoteliers and restaurateurs. They feel that each dozen oysters for which an order is frustrated by unavailability would cost them £2 in terms of the present value of contribution on future orders lost as a result of the ill-will generated through frustration.

Vincentos Ltd are the commercial refrigerator merchants who would lease the oyster freezing equipment to Bridgegate. The leasing arrangement would cost Bridgegate £500 per week, and would cover an 8-week 'trial' period in the first instance. Only one model of oyster freezing equipment is available, with a maximum capacity of 300 dozen oysters.

By reference to the above facts, and taking all profit figures net of the notional costs of ill-will arising from inability to meet Bridgegate's customers' orders, **you are required:**

1. To compute the average profit per week that Bridgegate could expect to earn if they ordered the profit-maximising volume of oysters each week from their shellfish supplier.
2. To specify the probability of at least breaking even in any given week in which the profit-maximising volume of oysters had been ordered.
3. To find the volume of oysters that should be ordered each week in order to maximise the probability of breaking even in any given week.

If Bridgegate's management were to specify that the stocking of oysters would only be regarded as a 'success' if it broke even or better in at least 6 weeks within the 8-week trial period, what would the maximum probability of 'success' be?

4. To indicate how the volume of oysters that should be ordered each week in order to maximise the probability of breaking even would vary in response to an announcement by Vincentos Ltd of a £50 per week increase in the cost of leasing.

Stochastic Cost–Volume–Profit Analysis: Choice Among Combinations of Products

13

Galpen Cleansing Products

Galpen Cleansing Products has pioneered the use of a silicon gel, called Rythalax, as a base for products used in cleaning delicate optical lenses. It has developed and test-marketed four Rythalax-based products, with varying strengths and drying properties. Rynatrol and Rhysomo are low-strength products, the former being more suited for application when air temperatures are below 15° C and the latter being more appropriate when air temperatures rise above this level. Ryndym and Rhyelka are higher-strength products, and again the former is better for temperatures below 15° C, the latter for higher temperatures.

All four products have been sold through specialist outlets nationwide over a 20-week period. The experience of supplying these outlets has made it clear to Galpen's management that they cannot rely on having enough Rythalax available to support the sale of all four products indefinitely, and that one of these products will have to be dropped. They have also noticed the existence of negative correlations between sales levels of the high-temperature and low-temperature versions of each strength of product. That is, sales of Rynatrol and Rhysomo are negatively correlated, as are sales of Ryndym and Rhyelka. This is because the products within these pairs are substitutes; when the weather favours the sales of one of the products within a pair, it does so at the expense of the other.

For brevity, Rynatrol may be designated as product X_1, Rhysomo as product X_2, Ryndym as product X_3 and Rhyelka as product X_4. Using this terminology, the data from the test-marketing on demand and cost for the four products may be summarised as follows, with demand expressed as the number of quarter-litre packs sold per week.

Product	Mean demand	Variance of demand	Price per pack	Variable cost per pack	Fixed cost outlay per week
			£	£	£
X_1	850	102 400	15.70	9.40	5 600
X_2	730	93 025	17.20	10.50	4 400
X_3	640	119 025	20.00	12.90	4 000
X_4	580	136 900	22.40	14.60	3 600

Correlation coefficients among the four products over the 20-week test-marketing period have been observed to be as follows:

$$r_{12} = -0.4; \; r_{13} = 0.7; \; r_{14} = 0.3$$
$$r_{23} = 0.4; \; r_{24} = 0.6; \; r_{34} = -0.5$$

You are required to answer the following questions:

1. If Galpen's management are primarily concerned to minimise the probability of failing to break even on Rythalax-based products, which of the four products would you advise them to drop on the basis of the test-marketing data?
   It may be assumed here that sales volume for each product is a normally distributed random variable.

2. Given the decision that has been taken on which product to drop, what are the 90 per cent confidence limits on the probability of at least breaking even with the remaining three products?

Short-term Investment of Cash Balances

14

Maselia Ltd

Maselia Ltd is a building contractor. At the end of May 1989, it has just received a progress payment of £25000 from a client, and wants to invest this money in a way that will maximise its expected net return. It can opt only for short-term investments, however, because the money will soon be required to meet payments to a sub-contractor. These payments will be made at the month-ends 1, 2, 3 and 4 months hence, but the amounts due at each of these times will depend upon the progress that the sub-contractor has made with his work. The management of Maselia Ltd do not feel that they can predict the progress that will be made with a great deal of confidence, because it will be strongly influenced by the effect of differing weather conditions upon the state of the building site. However, they do feel able to draw up a probability tree specifying fifteen possible sequences of payments to the sub-contractor over the coming 4 months, and associating probabilities with each of these sequences. The probability tree is given in Figure 14.1; on it, May is referred to as month 0, June as month 1, July as month 2, August as month 3 and September as month 4. Each sequence of payments is labelled with a number.

Maselia's management are looking at the possibility of lending out some or all of the £25000 by purchasing fixed-term securities. These securities are issued with maturities of 1 month, 2 months, 3 months or 4 months. The market for reselling fixed-term securities before their maturity date is an active one, so that transactions of

FIGURE 14.1
Maselia Ltd – Probability Tree

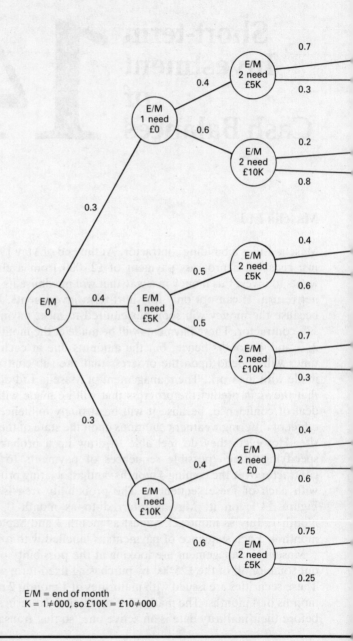

E/M = end of month
K = 1≠000, so £10K = £10≠000

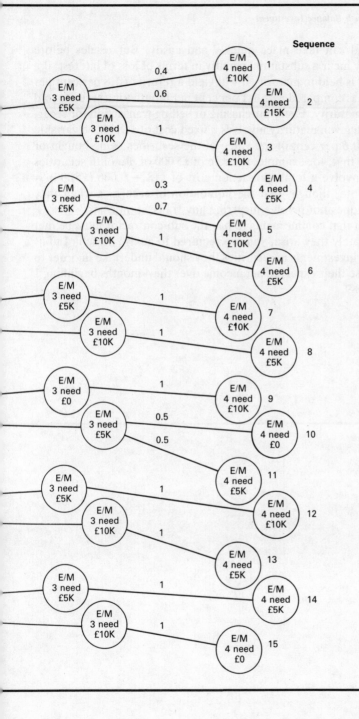

Sequence

E/M 3 need £5K	0.4	E/M 4 need £10K	1
	0.6	E/M 4 need £15K	2
E/M 3 need £10K	1	E/M 4 need £10K	3
E/M 3 need £5K	0.3	E/M 4 need £5K	4
	0.7	E/M 4 need £10K	5
E/M 3 need £10K	1	E/M 4 need £5K	6
E/M 3 need £5K	1	E/M 4 need £10K	7
E/M 3 need £10K	1	E/M 4 need £5K	8
E/M 3 need £0	1	E/M 4 need £10K	9
E/M 3 need £5K	0.5	E/M 4 need £0	10
	0.5	E/M 4 need £5K	11
E/M 3 need £5K	1	E/M 4 need £10K	12
E/M 3 need £10K	1	E/M 4 need £5K	13
E/M 3 need £5K	1	E/M 4 need £5K	14
E/M 3 need £10K	1	E/M 4 need £0	15

this kind can take place quickly and easily. But resales before maturity incur a substantial penalty in terms of loss of interest; if a security is held to maturity it will yield a return of 1.8 per cent per month, as compared with 1.1 per cent per month for a security sold before maturity. Every purchasing or selling transaction for securities of a given maturity involves a fixed cost of £18 plus a variable cost of 0.6 per cent of the value of the securities being bought or sold (so that, for example, the sale of £5000 of n-month securities would involve a total transaction cost of £18 + 0.006 (£5000) = £48). Note, though, that the liquidation of securities when they mature does not involve incurring any transaction costs.

Given that commitments to pay the sub-contractor must be met immediately they arise, **you are required** to advise Maselia Ltd as to what investments in securities they should undertake in order to maximise their expected net income over the 4 months beginning 1 June 1989.

Payments Netting in Multinational Cash Management

15

Thornend Communication Systems PLC

Thornend Communication Systems (TCS) is a multinational enterprise of medium size with head offices in London, and operating subsidiaries in the United Kingdom, the United States, France, Germany and Sweden. It specialises in the manufacture of telephone switchgear, and there is a great deal of trade between the subsidiaries as switchgear components made in one country are assembled together in another. At 31 March 1989, all the debts owed by subsidiaries in one country to subsidiaries in another were translated into pound sterling terms by reference to the exchange rates then prevailing. In units of £10 000, the debts at 31 March appeared as follows:

			Paying companies			
Receiving companies	UK	USA	France	Germany	Sweden	Total
UK	–	41	16	9	31	97
USA	52	–	18	23	47	140
France	27	50	–	8	16	101
Germany	12	29	6	–	22	69
Sweden	22	11	18	34	–	85
Total	113	131	58	74	116	492

The transaction costs involved in transferring foreign exchange as between the five countries in which TCS has subsidiaries were also computed as on 31 March 1989. Expressed as a proportion of the sterling value transferred, they were as follows:

Transfer between	and	Cost as proportion of £ value transferred
UK	USA	0.006
UK	France	0.009
UK	Germany	0.008
UK	Sweden	0.012
USA	France	0.010
USA	Germany	0.009
USA	Sweden	0.013
France	Germany	0.007
France	Sweden	0.011
Germany	Sweden	0.013

It is assumed in drawing up the above table that transaction costs do not vary with the direction of transfer of funds between two countries.

You are required, on the basis of the above facts, to advise TCS as to the payments netting scheme they should adopt in order to settle the outstanding debts among the subsidiaries with a minimum level of transaction costs.

The Learning Curve and Financial Planning 16

Claygill Holdings

Claygill Holdings manufacture capital equipment for the pottery industry. They have recently pioneered one of the first applications of ultrasound technology to this industry, in the form of an Automatic Inspection Facility (AIF). The AIF detects the pattern of sound waves thrown back in an echo from contact with china or porcelain; the presence of a flaw causes a false 'ring' which is recorded on the AIF and enables the piece concerned to be rejected. A few prototypes of the AIF have been manufactured on a temporary production line, which has since been dismantled. The cumulative average number of labour hours spent per AIF produced on this line (y) has been regressed against the number of AIF units produced to date (x) to produce an equation of the following form:

$$\ln y = 6.69 - 0.1203 \ln x$$

The management team concerned with the AIF want to use this learning curve to predict the consequences of choosing to manufacture the AIF on either one or two production lines. Whichever alternative is chosen, it will involve problems sufficiently different from those encountered on the temporary production line for learning to be considered to have started 'from scratch', that is, from the $x = 1$ position on the above learning curve.

Each direct labour hour spent on AIF production involves Claygill in a cash outflow of £4.50; there are 110 000 labour hours available per annum, and the supply of the skilled labour required cannot be expanded in the short term. The contribution before deducting costs of direct labour arising from selling an AIF is estimated to be £3 000. Claygill's marketing staff do not anticipate any difficulty in selling all the AIF units that can be produced over the first 2 years.

The choice as to whether to concentrate all the direct labour on one production line, or to split the labour hours available equally over two lines, has some implications for the level of fixed costs. A single production line would impose more pressure upon the maintenance function that would arise from the less rapid pace of production to be found where two lines run simultaneously. Consequently, adoption of the single-line alternative would involve a cash outflow on fixed costs of £280 000 per annum, while the corresponding cash outflow per annum for the two-line alternative would be only £250 000.

There is a dispute currently going on at Claygill Holdings about the technology of AIF manufacture, and this has implications for estimates of the extent of learning that is possible. One school of thought contends that since the technology concerned is at the frontiers of knowledge, there is no reason why average labour hours per unit should not follow the learning curve downward throughout the first 2 years of AIF production. Another school argues that enough is known about the manufacturing techniques for it to be clear that an AIF can never be produced in less than 400 labour hours; once this level of efficiency has been achieved, further learning will be all but impossible.

You are required to answer the following questions; in answering 1 and 2 below produce separate solutions for *each* of the two schools of thought:

1. What is the break-even level of output in the first year:
    (a) For a single production line?
    (b) For two production lines?
2. If the learning experience proceeds exactly as each school of thought anticipates, what will be the levels of output and of profit in the first year and in the second year of production:
    (a) With a single production line?
    (b) With two production lines?

3. Assume that learning will continue throughout the first and second years.
   What then will be the effect upon output from a single production line in each of the first and second years if there has at the same time been *both* a 2 per cent overestimate of the learning rate *and* a 10 per cent underestimate of the initial assembly time?

Joint Product Decisions

17

Kwisant Oils

Kwisant Oils is a division of Dunan PLC. Its business involves the manufacture of light oils which, when sprayed on to the surface of bodies of water, act to inhibit evaporation. These are used, for example, in desalination works where fresh water is extracted from seawater under desert conditions. The light oils are all derived from a standard mixture of substances called Teilu mixture. This is a product of chemical processes carried out within Kwisant Oils at a cost of £0.70 per litre of mixture produced. The Teilu mixture settles into two layers, with roughly the same volume of liquid in each layer. From the upper, lighter layer, a substance called Baxin is obtained; 5 litres of this layer are sufficient to produce 4 litres of Baxin, at a further processing cost of £0.85 per litre. Baxin serves as a cheap but relatively inefficient evaporation inhibitor, and is sold as a final product to some of Kwisant's less demanding customers.

From the lower, heavier layer of Teilu mixture, a substance called Haderol may be synthesised. 5 litres of this layer give rise to 4 litres of Haderol, with a cost of synthesis of £0.55 per litre produced. Haderol is not a final product, though it may be sold without further processing to Celos Ltd, another division of Dunan, which uses it for a purpose completely unrelated to the work of Kwisant's products. The senior management of Dunan have fixed a transfer price of £1.80 per litre of Haderol sold to Celos; Kwisant is not under any obligation to sell any Haderol to

Celos, but knows that Celos will purchase all the Haderol offered for sale to them at this price.

The Haderol which is not sold to Celos is placed for a brief period in a centrifuge, which breaks it down into three products. For every 4 litres of Haderol placed in the centrifuge, 0.5 litres of a waste product called 'skim' is produced; this is thrown away. The remaining 3.5 litres are composed of 2 litres of 'black' Haderol and 1.5 litres of 'white' Haderol. Because the centrifuge is run for so short a time, the costs of operating it can be taken as negligble for practical purposes. The 2 litres of 'black' Haderol can be refined into 2 litres of a final product called Gholak, at a further processing cost of £1.30 per litre, while the 1.5 litres of 'white' Haderol can also be refined, to produce 1.5 litres of a final product called Seitsol, at a further processing cost of £1.40 per litre.

The production processes outlined in the previous three paragraphs are shown in diagrammatic form in Figure 17.1. In Figure 17.1 the way in which 10 litres of Teilu mixture goes to make each of the products is illustrated.

The demand conditions prevailing in the markets for Baxin, Gholak and Seitsol differ greatly, though all three markets are characterised both by imperfect competition and by the impossibility of practising price discrimination, so that extra sales can be obtained only by reducing the price per litre at which a product is sold to *all* customers. Baxin is a low-performance product with a wide range of available substitutes, so that its sales are very price-sensitive. Gholak also competes with a number of substitutes, though the competition it faces is much less fierce than that facing Baxin. Seitsol is at the other extreme, having a number of unusual performance properties, such that demand for it is rather insensitive to variations in its price. Kwisant's management do not object to the treatment of the demand functions for these three products as being roughly linear, and have derived the following estimates of sales (in litres per week) at alternative selling prices:

Baxin		Gholak		Seitsol	
Price per l £	*Sales level*	*Price per l* £	*Sales level*	*Price per l* £	*Sales level*
2.75	2 300	4.00	1 100	4.50	1 200
2.25	3 600	3.00	1 800	3.50	1 400

FIGURE 17.1
Kwisant Oils – Products/Costs from 10 l. Teilu

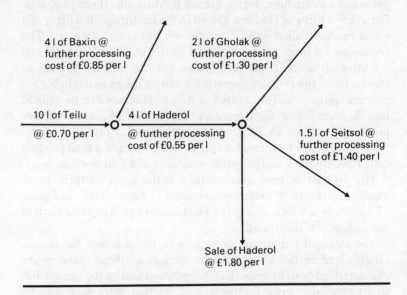

4 l of Baxin @ further processing cost of £0.85 per l

2 l of Gholak @ further processing cost of £1.30 per l

10 l of Teilu @ £0.70 per l

4 l of Haderol @ further processing cost of £0.55 per l

1.5 l of Seitsol @ further processing cost of £1.40 per l

Sale of Haderol @ £1.80 per l

1. Using the above data, **you are required** to advise Kwisant Oils as to what its weekly production and sales levels should be for Baxin, Gholak and Seitsol, and as to the price per litre it should charge for each of these three products.

   Your advice should also cover the question of whether any Haderol should be sold to Celos Ltd, and if so how much should be sold.

2. How would your advice to Kwisant vary if you were told that the maximum amount of Teilu mixture that could be made available in any given week was restricted to 4 000 litres?

Part III
Analysis of
Problems For
Self-study

Standard Costing and Matrix Algebra

1

Arconate Ltd

1. The first step is to calculate the price variances for materials purchased, by taking the quantity bought and multiplying it by the excess of the actual unit price paid over the standard unit price. This computation may be tabulated as follows, with negative numbers in brackets and the letters U and F respectively to denote unfavourable and favourable variances:

January price variances for materials

Chemical	Amount purchased	Actual less standard unit price	Price variance
	Kg	*£*	*£*
Hexachlorophene	3 750	0.20	750 U
Paradichlorosol	2 750	0.30	825 U
Bentonite	10 000	(0.10)	1 000 F
Carbon trimorphate	2 500	0.45	1 125 U
Ethyl acetate	6 000	(0.15)	900 F
Total price variance			800 U

The quantity variances for materials are given by multiplying the excess of the quantity actually used over the standard quantity for 107 batches by the standard unit price. This computation appears as follows, with the same conventions as in the table above:

January quantity variances for materials

Chemical	Actual less standard quantity used	Standard unit price	Quantity variance
	Kg	*£*	*£*
Hexachlorophene	(50)	4.50	225 *F*
Paradichlorosol	225	3.00	675 *U*
Bentonite	1 215	0.80	972 *U*
	l		
Carbon trimorphate	60	2.50	150 *U*
Ethyl acetate	(50)	1.25	62.5 *F*
Total quantity variance			1 509.5 *U*

The quantity (efficiency), rate of pay and mixed variances for labour may be calculated using the following terminology. Let:

P represent the standard hourly rate of pay for a category of labour

ΔP represent the excess of the actual hourly rate over the standard

Q represent the standard hours which should be worked by a category of labour to produce 107 batches

ΔQ represent the excess of the actual hours worked over the standard

Then matrices relating to the three categories of labour may be subjected to a partitioned multiplication as follows:

$$\begin{array}{c} P \\ \Delta P \end{array} \left[\begin{array}{c|c|c} 4.20 & 3.15 & 2.80 \\ 0.30 & 0.60 & 0.60 \end{array}\right] \begin{array}{cc} Q & \Delta Q \end{array} \left[\begin{array}{c|c} 1\,926 & 326 \\ \hline 2\,782 & 122 \\ \hline 3\,317 & -248 \end{array}\right]$$

$$= \begin{bmatrix} 8\,089.2 & 1\,369.2 \\ 577.8 & 97.8 \end{bmatrix} + \begin{bmatrix} 8\,763.3 & -384.3 \\ 1\,669.2 & -73.2 \end{bmatrix} + \begin{bmatrix} 9\,287.6 & -694.4 \\ 1\,990.2 & -148.8 \end{bmatrix}$$

Tabulating these matrices gives rise to:

Labour category	Actual cost	Efficiency variance	Rate of pay variance	Mixed variance	Standard cost
Grade	£	£	£	£	£
A	10 134	−1 369.2U −	577.8U −	97.8U	= 8 089.2
B	9 975	+ 384.3F −	1 669.2U +	73.2F	= 8 763.3
C	10 434.6	+ 694.4F −	1 990.2U +	148.8F	= 9 287.6

2. As a matter of terminology, the inputs require to be numbered 1–8 in the order in which they appear in the problem's tabulation of the composition of inputs. Hence (for example) ethyl acetate is input 5. Then inputs 1–3 form the ammoniate mix, inputs 4 and 5 the oxidising mix and inputs 6–8 the labour mix; input substitution is possible within each of these mixes, but not between one mix and another. The first step is to calculate the standard proportions within their mix represented by each of the three inputs to the ammoniate mix, the two inputs to the oxidising mix and the three inputs to the labour mix. Let:

SM_i represent the standard proportion for the ith input

Using total quantities per 100 kilogram batch of output in numerator and denominator gives rise to:

$SM_1 = 25/(25+25+75) = 0.2$; $SM_2 = 0.2$; $SM_3 = 0.6$
$SM_4 = 20/(20+50) = 0.2857$; $SM_5 = 0.7143$
$SM_6 = 18/(18+26+31) = 0.24$; $SM_7 = 0.3467$; $SM_8 = 0.4133$

Next it is necessary to derive, for each input i, the quantity Q_{2i}, representing the amount of that input which should have been consumed if the standard proportions had been adhered to over the total quantity of that mix's inputs actually consumed. This quantity has the subscript 2 because it is an element within the second row of the quantity matrix Q below. For the eight inputs, the Q_{2i} values are as follows:

$Q_{21} = (2\,625 + 2\,900 + 9\,240)\,(0.2) = 2\,953; Q_{22} = 2\,953; Q_{23} = 8\,859$

$Q_{24} = (2\,200 + 5\,300)\,(0.2857) = 2\,142.75; Q_{25} = 5\,357.25$

$Q_{26} = (2\,252 + 2\,660 + 3\,069)\,(0.24) = 1\,915.44;$

$Q_{27} = 2\,767.01; Q_{28} = 3\,298.55$

The Q matrix is postmultiplied by a unit standard price matrix P, in which the non-zero entries are in three blocks, reflecting the separation of the ammoniate mix, the oxidising mix and the labour mix. This matrix multiplication serves to value the elements within Q at standard cost, in a new 3×3 matrix R. It proceeds as below:

$$Q = \begin{bmatrix} 2\,675 & 2\,675 & 8\,025 & 2\,140 & 5\,350 & 1\,926 & 2\,782 & 3\,317 \\ 2\,953 & 2\,953 & 8\,859 & 2\,142.75 & 5\,357.25 & 1\,915.44 & 2\,767.01 & 3\,298.55 \\ 2\,625 & 2\,900 & 9\,240 & 2\,200 & 5\,300 & 2\,252 & 2\,660 & 3\,069 \end{bmatrix}$$

$$P = \begin{bmatrix} 4.50 & 0 & 0 \\ 3.00 & 0 & 0 \\ 0.80 & 0 & 0 \\ 0 & 2.50 & 0 \\ 0 & 1.25 & 0 \\ 0 & 0 & 4.20 \\ 0 & 0 & 3.15 \\ 0 & 0 & 2.80 \end{bmatrix}$$

$$R = \begin{bmatrix} R_{11} = 26\,482.5 & R_{12} = 12\,037.5 & R_{13} = 26\,140.1 \\ R_{21} = 29\,234.7 & R_{22} = 12\,053.44 & R_{23} = 25\,996.87 \\ R_{31} = 27\,904.5 & R_{32} = 12\,125 & R_{33} = 26\,430.6 \end{bmatrix}$$

The mix and yield variances may now be computed as follows:

£

Mix variance for ammoniate group	$= R_{31} - R_{21} =$	1 330.2F
Yield variance for ammoniate group	$= R_{21} - R_{11} =$	2 752.2U
Mix variance for oxidising group	$= R_{32} - R_{22} =$	71.56U
Yield variance for oxidising group	$= R_{22} - R_{12} =$	15.94U
Mix variance for labour	$= R_{33} - R_{23} =$	433.73U
Yield variance for labour	$= R_{23} - R_{13} =$	143.23F

Attention may be focused on the ammoniate group, where the mix and yield variances are relatively large. In interpreting them, it is helpful to calculate the actual proportions within the ammoniate mix represented by each of the three inputs to that mix. Representing these actual proportions by AM_1, AM_2, and AM_3, computation shows that

$$AM_1 = (2\,625)/(2\,625+2\,900+9\,240) = 0.178; AM_2 = 0.196;$$
$$AM_3 = 0.626$$

Comparing these with the standard proportions $SM_1 = 0.2$, $SM_2 = 0.2$, $SM_3 = 0.6$ reveals the substitution of relatively cheap bentonite for relatively expensive hexachlorophene which has taken place. This substitution has given rise to a favourable mix variance for ammoniates more than offset by an unfavourable yield variance twice the size. The attempt to substitute a cheap for an expensive ingredient has proved unprofitable, and should be discontinued.

Stochastic Process Costing 2

Kleeford Distilled Compounds

1. The partitioned stochastic matrix P for this question may be represented as follows:

$$P = \left[\begin{array}{ccc:cc} 0.10 & 0.78 & 0 & 0 & 0.12 \\ 0.14 & 0.11 & 0.69 & 0 & 0.06 \\ 0.09 & 0 & 0 & 0.83 & 0.08 \\ \hdashline 0 & 0 & 0 & 1 & 0 \\ 0 & 0 & 0 & 0 & 1 \end{array}\right]$$

The fundamental matrix F is given by $F = (I - Q)^{-1}$, where I for this problem is a 3×3 identity matrix. Carrying out the computation yields:

$$F = \left[\begin{array}{ccc} 1.383 & 1.212 & 0.837 \\ 0.314 & 1.399 & 0.965 \\ 0.125 & 0.109 & 1.075 \end{array}\right]$$

It is now necessary to define a row vector k containing the new elements started into production each transfer period; in this problem, the transfer period is a week. The 1×3 vector k appears as follows:

$$k = [23\,500 \quad 3\,900 \quad 0]$$

The average steady-state in-process inventories are given by postmultiplying the k vector by the fundamental matrix. Representing these inventories by a 1×3 row vector v gives:

$$v = [33\,725 \quad 33\,938 \quad 23\,433]$$

This vector indicates that, during a working week, an average of 33 725 litres are undergoing Stage 1 distillation, while an average of 33 938 litres are undergoing Stage 2 distillation and an average of 23 433 litres are undergoing Stage 3.

The first step in working out the upper bonds on the standard deviations of these figures is to convert the elements within k into proportions, giving rise to a new 1×3 row vector g. This is as follows:

$$g = [0.8577 \quad 0.1423 \quad 0]$$

The calculations then proceed as below:

$$I - Q_{sq} = \begin{bmatrix} 1 & 0 & 0 \\ 0 & 1 & 0 \\ 0 & 0 & 1 \end{bmatrix} - \begin{bmatrix} 0.01 & 0.6084 & 0 \\ 0.0196 & 0.0121 & 0.4761 \\ 0.0081 & 0 & 0 \end{bmatrix}$$

$$= \begin{bmatrix} 0.99 & -0.6084 & 0 \\ -0.0196 & 0.9879 & -0.4761 \\ -0.0081 & 0 & 1 \end{bmatrix}$$

$$(I - Q_{sq})^{-1} = \begin{bmatrix} 1.025 & 0.631 & 0.301 \\ 0.024 & 1.027 & 0.489 \\ 0.008 & 0.005 & 1.002 \end{bmatrix}$$

$$g_{sq} = [0.7356 \quad 0.02025 \quad 0]$$

$$g_{sq}(I - Q_{sq})^{-1} = [0.7545 \quad 0.4850 \quad 0.2313]$$
$$gF = [1.2309 \quad 1.2386 \quad 0.8552]$$
$$ka = 27\,400$$
$$ka\,[gF - g_{sq}\,(I - Q_{sq})^{-1}] = 27\,400\,[0.4764 \quad 0.7536 \quad 0.6239]$$
$$\text{Var. } (v) \leqq [13\,053 \quad 20\,649 \quad 17\,095]$$
$$\text{Sd } (v) \leqq [114.2 \quad 143.7 \quad 130.7]$$

The upper limits on the standard deviations of the steady-state in-process inventories are respectively 114.2 litres, 143.7 litres and 130.7 litres for Stages 1, 2 and 3.

2. The expected outputs of synthetic lemon oil and of wash, grouts and fallings thrown away per week are given by the 1×2 row vector y, where:

$$y = \begin{bmatrix} 33\,725 & 33\,938 & 23\,433 \end{bmatrix} \begin{bmatrix} 0 & 0.12 \\ 0 & 0.06 \\ 0.83 & 0.08 \end{bmatrix}$$

$$= \begin{bmatrix} 19\,449 & 7\,958 \end{bmatrix}$$

There will be an average output of 19 449 litres of synthetic lemon oil per week, and 7 958 litres per week will on average be thrown away as either wash, grouts or fallings. The sum of these two figures corresponds to the 27 400 litres entering the production of synthetic lemon oil per week, apart from a small rounding error.

3. The expected number of units of activity for each of Stages 1–3 are given by the elements within row vector v. Using these, the expected variable cost per working week may be calculated as follows:

Stage	Expected no. of units of activity	Variable cost per unit	Expected variable cost per week
		£	£
1	33 725	1.90	64 077
2	33 938	2.75	93 329
3	23 433	2.20	51 553
	Total expected cost		208 959

4. The 3×2 matrix B gives in each row the probability that a litre started respectively in each of Stages 1–3 will either turn out as good product or be thrown away at some stage. It is obtained by postmultiplying the fundamental matrix F by the submatrix R. The calculation is as follows:

$$B = \begin{bmatrix} 1.383 & 1.212 & 0.837 \\ 0.314 & 1.399 & 0.965 \\ 0.125 & 0.109 & 1.075 \end{bmatrix} \begin{bmatrix} 0 & 0.12 \\ 0 & 0.06 \\ 0.83 & 0.08 \end{bmatrix}$$

$$= \begin{bmatrix} 0.695 & 0.305 \\ 0.801 & 0.199 \\ 0.892 & 0.108 \end{bmatrix}$$

Having calculated B, it is possible to proceed to compute the upper limits on the standard deviations of good and defective production levels as follows:

$$g_{sq}(I-Q_{sq})^{-1}R_{sq} = [0.7545 \quad 0.4850 \quad 0.2313] \begin{bmatrix} 0 & 0.0144 \\ 0 & 0.0036 \\ 0.6889 & 0.0064 \end{bmatrix}$$

$$= [0.1593 \quad 0.0141]$$

$$gB = [0.8577 \quad 0.1423 \quad 0] \begin{bmatrix} 0.695 & 0.305 \\ 0.801 & 0.199 \\ 0.892 & 0.108 \end{bmatrix}$$

$$= [0.7101 \quad 0.2899]$$

$$\text{Var.}(y) \leqq 27\,400 \quad [0.5508 \quad 0.2758]$$

$$\leqq \qquad\qquad [15\,902 \quad 7\,557]$$

$$\text{Sd}\,(y) \leqq \qquad\qquad [122.8 \quad 86.9]$$

The standard deviation of the output of synthetic lemon oil per working week is 122.8 litres, and the standard deviation of the amount of product thrown away is 86.9 litres.

5. To obtain a litre of good output from Stage 1 of distillation, it is necessary to start $1/0.695 = 1.4388$ litres into Stage 1. The increase in production per working week that is required is $21\,000 - 19\,449 = 1\,551$ litres. To achieve this, with a constant supply of citric essence, would necessitate starting an extra $1.4388 \times 1\,551 = 2\,232$ litres into Stage 1, to give a total input of $25\,732$ litres per week of feed oil.

As a check on the above calculation, note that if:

$$k = [25\,732 \quad 3\,900 \quad 0]$$

$$\text{Then } v = [36\,812 \quad 36\,643 \quad 25\,301]$$

$$\text{and } y = [21\,000 \quad 8\,640]$$

Credit Management and Markov Chains: Partial Balance Aging Method

3

Langdale Ltd

1. Represent the actual partial balance age structure of debts at the end of month j as I_j, and within I_j refer to the kth element as $i_{j,k}$ where $k = P,B,3,4,5,6,7$ corresponds respectively to states $P,B,0,1,2,3,4$. Here states 0–4 refer to the five states of a debt from 'less than 1 month old' (state 0) to 'over 4 months old' (state 4). Refer to October as month $j = 1$, November as $j = 2$ and December as $j = 3$. Then the transition probabilities of payment t_{kP} are as follows for $k = 3\ldots5$ and $j = 1\ldots3$.

k	Col.1 $i_{1,k}$		Col.2 $i_{2,k+1}$		Col.3 Paid	$t_{kP}=$ Col.3/Col.1
3	511 401	–	79 261	=	432 140	0.845
4	94 853	–	55 212	=	39 641	0.418
5	53 711	–	12 471	=	41 240	0.768
	$i_{2,k}$		$i_{3,k+1}$			
3	662 666	–	103 722	=	558 944	0.844
4	79 261	–	43 685	=	35 576	0.449
5	55 212	–	42 433	=	12 779	0.231

The transition probabilities are thus as follows:

November: $t_{3P} = 0.845$; $t_{4P} = 0.418$; $t_{5P} = 0.768$
$t_{34} = 1-0.845 = 0.155$. Similarly, $t_{45} = 0.582$
and $t_{56} = 0.232$

December: $t_{3P} = 0.844$; $t_{4P} = 0.449$; $t_{5P} = 0.231$
$t_{34} = 1-0.844 = 0.156$. Similarly, $t_{45} = 0.551$
and $t_{56} = 0.769$

For $k = 6$, the transition probability of payment in both November and December is estimated at $t_{6P} = 0.35$, so that $t_{67} = 0.65$.

The first step toward finding the transition probabilities for $k = 7$ is to find the amount paid from state 4 in a given month j. This is given by the following formula:

$$\text{Paid from 4 in } j = i_{j,7} + t_{67}i_{j,6} - i_{j+1,7} - i_{j+1,B}$$

Applying this formula yields:

Paid from 4 in November $= 78\,854 + (0.65)\ (26\,108) - 61\,854 - 19\,901 = £14\,069$

Paid from 4 in December $= 61\,854 + (0.65)\ (12\,471) - 50\,730 - 14\,108 = £5\,122$

Expressing these figures as proportions of the state 4 balances at the beginning of the month concerned gives for November $t_{7P} = 0.178$ and for December $t_{7P} = 0.083$.

The transition probability for bad debts t_{7B} is given by $t_{7B} = i_{j+1,B}/i_{j,7}$. For November, $t_{7B} = 0.252$ and for December $t_{7B} = 0.228$. Since $t_{77} = 1-(t_{7P} + t_{7B})$, for November $t_{77} = 0.570$ and for December $t_{77} = 0.689$.

From the above data, the partitioned transition matrix for October/November is:

	P	B	0	1	2	3	4
P	1	0	0	0	0	0	0
B	0	1	0	0	0	0	0
0	0.845	0	0	0.155	0	0	0
1	0.418	0	0	0	0.582	0	0
2	0.768	0	0	0	0	0.232	0
3	0.350	0	0	0	0	0	0.650
4	0.178	0.252	0	0	0	0	0.570

Call the above matrix T_N.

Also from the above data, the partitioned transition matrix for November/December is:

$$
\begin{array}{c|cc|ccccc}
 & p & B & 0 & 1 & 2 & 3 & 4 \\
P & 1 & 0 & 0 & 0 & 0 & 0 & 0 \\
B & 0 & 1 & 0 & 0 & 0 & 0 & 0 \\
\hline
0 & 0.844 & 0 & 0 & 0.156 & 0 & 0 & 0 \\
1 & 0.449 & 0 & 0 & 0 & 0.551 & 0 & 0 \\
2 & 0.231 & 0 & 0 & 0 & 0 & 0.769 & 0 \\
3 & 0.350 & 0 & 0 & 0 & 0 & 0 & 0.650 \\
4 & 0.083 & 0.228 & 0 & 0 & 0 & 0 & 0.689
\end{array}
$$

Call the above matrix T_D.

Denoting the 'average' (exponentially smoothed) matrix for January as $\bar{A}_J$, then:

$$\bar{A}_J = \alpha\, T_D + (1-\alpha)T_N$$

With $\alpha = 0.8$, $\bar{A}_J = 0.8T_D + 0.2T_N$

Performing this calculation gives rise to a matrix $\bar{A}_J$ as follows:

$$
\begin{array}{c|cc|ccccc}
 & p & B & 0 & 1 & 2 & 3 & 4 \\
P & 1 & 0 & 0 & 0 & 0 & 0 & 0 \\
B & 0 & 1 & 0 & 0 & 0 & 0 & 0 \\
\hline
0 & 0.8442 & 0 & 0 & 0.1558 & 0 & 0 & 0 \\
1 & 0.4428 & 0 & 0 & 0 & 0.5572 & 0 & 0 \\
2 & 0.3384 & 0 & 0 & 0 & 0 & 0.6616 & 0 \\
3 & 0.3500 & 0 & 0 & 0 & 0 & 0 & 0.6500 \\
4 & 0.1020 & 0.2328 & 0 & 0 & 0 & 0 & 0.6652
\end{array}
$$

It is next necessary to premultiply $\bar{A}_J$ by the vector I_3 showing the partial balance age structure of debts at the end of December. This multiplication gives rise to the vector E_4 showing the estimated aging of debtor balances in January 1990, including payments and bad debts. It proceeds as follows:

$I_3 = [0 \quad 0 \quad 672\,390 \quad 103\,722 \quad 43\,685 \quad 42\,433 \quad 50\,730]$
$I_3\,\bar{A}_J = E_4 = [648\,369 \quad 11\,810 \quad 0 \quad 104\,758 \quad 57\,794 \quad 28\,902 \quad 61\,327]$

The forecast cash receipts for January 1990 are given by $e_{4,1} =$ £648 369.

2. In forecasting the cash receipts for February 1990, the first step is to insert the forecast credit sales figure for January 1990 into the E_4 vector in place of $e_{4,3}$. If $e_{4,1}$ and $e_{4,2}$ are both set equal to zero, the E_4 vector so modified represents the estimated partial balance age structure of debts at the end of January, and may thus be labelled I_4. It appears as:

$$I_4 = [0 \quad 0 \quad 492\,000 \quad 104\,758 \quad 57\,794 \quad 28\,902 \quad 61\,327]$$

It remains only to multiply these balances by the latest estimates (within $\bar{A}_J$) of the transition probabilities of payment from the various debtor states $t_{3P} \ldots t_{7P}$. Hence the estimated February 1990 cash receipts are given by:

$$\text{Receipts} = (492\,000)\,(0.8442) + \ldots + (61\,327)\,(0.102)$$
$$= £497\,662$$

Credit Management and Markov Chains: Modified Total Balance Aging Method

4

Firenza Associates

1. It is first necessary to establish some terminology. Call the end of May 1989 time t, and call the end of June 1989 time $t + 1$. In each case, refer to the month just completed as age category 1, so that for time t May 1989 is age category 1 and for time $t + 1$ June 1989 is age category 1. The account data for May and June may then be laid out as follows, with all figures in thousands of pounds:

Account no.	Balance at t Partial balance aging			Total amount	Total balance aging
	Age 1	Age 2	Age 3		
1	10	–	–	10	1
2	9	2	–	11	2
3	–	–	7	7	3
4	5	6	3	14	3
5	6	11	–	17	2
6	13	15	2	30	3
7	–	8	16	24	3
8	7	4	–	11	2
9	–	–	12	12	3
10	16	–	4	20	3
11	–	10	–	10	2
12	7	14	5	26	3

Account no.	Balance at $t+1$			Total amount	Total balance aging
	Partial balance aging				
	Age 1	Age 2	Age 3		
1	14	4	–	18	2
2	–	9	–	9	2
3	5	–	–	5	1
4	–	–	–	–	–
5	7	6	11	24	3
6	–	13	–	13	2
7	9	–	24	33	3
8	3	7	–	10	2
9	–	–	12	12	Bad
10	12	16	–	28	2
11	13	–	–	13	1
12	5	–	–	5	1

Summing the amounts in each total balance age category at time t shows there to be a total of £10 000 in age category 1, £49 000 in age category 2 and £133 000 in age category 3. Two extra categories now require to be defined, category 0 relating to 'amount paid' and category 4 relating to 'amount declared bad debt'. A modified total balance aging table may then be set up for each of the twelve accounts as follows:

From age category	Account no.	To category					B values
		0	4	1	2	3	
1	1	6	–	–	4	–	$B_{10} = 6$; $B_{12} = 4$
2	2	2	–	–	9	–	$B_{20} = 2$; $B_{22} = 9$
	5	–	–	–	–	17	$B_{23} = 17$
	8	4	–	–	7	–	$B_{20} = 4$; $B_{22} = 7$
	11	10	–	–	–	–	$B_{20} = 10$
3	3	7	–	–	–	–	$B_{30} = 7$
	4	14	–	–	–	–	$B_{30} = 14$
	6	17	–	–	13	–	$B_{30} = 17$; $B_{32} = 13$
	7	–	–	–	–	24	$B_{33} = 24$
	9	–	12	–	–	–	$B_{34} = 12$
	10	4	–	–	16	–	$B_{30} = 4$; $B_{32} = 16$
	12	26	–	–	–	–	$B_{30} = 26$

Having aggregated numbers within each of the B_{jk} values, the R and Q submatrices within the partitioned stochastic matrix P are obtained by dividing each B_{jk} value by the total balance in its age category. This process is illustrated by the B matrix below:

$$
\begin{array}{c}
 \\
1 \\
2 \\
3
\end{array}
\begin{array}{cccccc}
0 & 4 & 1 & 2 & 3 & \\
\left[\begin{array}{ccccc}
6 & 0 & 0 & 4 & 0 \\
16 & 0 & 0 & 16 & 17 \\
68 & 12 & 0 & 29 & 24
\end{array}\right] &
\begin{array}{c}
\div\ 10 \\
\div\ 49 \\
\div\ 133
\end{array}
\end{array}
$$

Evaluating out the R and Q submatrices, and combining them with the I and φ submatrices gives rise to the stochastic matrix P below:

$$
P =
\begin{array}{c}
 \\
0 \\
4 \\
1 \\
2 \\
3
\end{array}
\begin{array}{c}
\begin{array}{ccccc}
0 & 4 & 1 & 2 & 3
\end{array} \\
\left[\begin{array}{ccccc}
1 & 0 & 0 & 0 & 0 \\
0 & 1 & 0 & 0 & 0 \\
\hline
0.6 & 0 & 0 & 0.4 & 0 \\
0.3265 & 0 & 0 & 0.3265 & 0.3470 \\
0.5113 & 0.0902 & 0 & 0.2180 & 0.1805
\end{array}\right]
\end{array}
$$

The fundamental matrix is given by $F = (I-Q)^{-1}$, where I is an identity matrix of the same 3×3 dimensions as Q. Computation yields:

$$
F =
\begin{bmatrix}
1 & 0.688 & 0.291 \\
0 & 1.721 & 0.729 \\
0 & 0.458 & 1.414
\end{bmatrix}
$$

Postmultiplying F by R, which is the submatrix within the bottom left-hand section of P, yields:

$$
FR =
\begin{bmatrix}
0.9734 & 0.0262 \\
0.9346 & 0.0658 \\
0.8725 & 0.1275
\end{bmatrix}
$$

Let k represent the vector of balances owed to Firenza Associates at the end of June, so that

$$
k = [68\,000 \quad 55\,000 \quad 35\,000]
$$

Postmultiplying k by FR gives rise to:

$$kFR = [148\,135 \qquad 9\,865]$$

The expected value of receipts from the £158 000 owed at the end of June is thus £148 135, and the expected value of bad debts is £9 865.

2. The first step is to convert the k vector into a probability vector c, which appears as follows:

$$c \quad = [0.4304 \quad 0.3481 \quad 0.2215]$$

The variance of expected value for receipts and bad debts is given by V, where $V = kg\,[cFR - (cFR)_{sq}]$ and g is a column unit vector with three elements. By computation:

$$
\begin{aligned}
cFR &= [0.9375 \quad 0.0625] \\
V &= 158\,000\,[0.0586 \quad 0.0586] \\
&= [9\,259 \quad 9\,259]
\end{aligned}
$$

The variance for receipts and bad debts is thus £9 259, giving rise to a standard deviation for the value of bad debts of £96.22. Hence this part of the problem resolves itself into asking what value of a normal distribution with a mean of 9 865 and a standard deviation of 96.22 is such that 99 per cent of the area under that distribution lies to the left of the value concerned. Since 99 per cent of the area under a normal distribution lies to the left of a point 2.3267 standard deviations to the right of the mean, the answer is that if 9 865 + 2.3267 (96.22) = £10 089 is allowed for bad debts there will then only be a 0.01 probability that actual bad debts will exceed the amount allowed for them.

3. Let the discount rate per month be v, so that $v = 0.015$ here. Then define $d = 1/(1+v) = 0.9852$, and let the present value vector for receipts and bad debts be y_{pv}, where $y_{pv} = k(I - dQ)^{-1}R$.

By computation:

$$
(I - dQ)^{-1} =
\begin{bmatrix}
1 & 0.669 & 0.278 \\
0 & 1.698 & 0.706 \\
0 & 0.444 & 1.401
\end{bmatrix}
$$

$$k(I - dQ)^{-1}R = [145\,810 \quad 9\,631]$$

The present value of the £148 135 that was forecast to be collected from the amount owed at the end of June is £145 810, at a rate of discount of 1½ per cent per month. Similarly, the present value of the expected bad debt loss is £9 631.

4. Let the vector p represent the amount of new debt entering each age category per month, so that here:

$$p = [65\,000 \quad 0 \quad 0]$$

Then the vector representing debtor balances in the steady state is given by k_{ss}, this being obtained through the postmultiplication of p by the fundamental matrix F. Evaluation yields:

$$k_{ss} = [65\,000 \quad 44\,720 \quad 18\,915]$$

By summing the elements within k_{ss}, it appears that Firenza Associates can expect to have an investment in debtors of £128 635 in the steady state, with an acquisition rate for new debts of £65 000 per month.

Linear Programming and Decisions on Internal v. External Purchases of Services

5

Remosense PLC

The first step toward solving this problem involves computing the 1989 variable operating costs per unit of service provided for each of departments $S_1 - S_4$. These work out as follows:

Telephones (S_1) cost £2.80 per hour of service provided (abbreviated to a 'phone-hr')
Telex (S_2) costs £1.90 per hour of service provided (abbreviated to a 'telex-hr')
Document transmission (S_3) costs £0.40 per facsimile page provided (abbreviated to a 'fax-p')
Electronic data transfer (S_4) costs £0.60 per metre of computer printout provided (abbreviated to a 'print-m')

Next, it is necessary to divide through the output figure for each service department by the figures for inputs from other service departments required to produce that output. This gives rise to technological coefficients as follows:

To produce	*Requires*		
1 phone-hr in S_1	0.016 telex-hr from S_2	0.0833 fax-p from S_3	0.0705 print-m from S_4
1 telex-hr in S_2	0.1448 phone-hr from S_1	0.3724 fax-p from S_3	0.4172 print-m from S_4
1 fax-p in S_3	0.0304 phone-hr from S_1	0.0607 telex-hr from S_2	0.0921 print-m from S_4
1 print-m in S_4	0.014 phone-hr from S_1	0.0434 telex-hr from S_2	0.1039 fax-p from S_3

The objective is to minimise the total amount spent per year on the four service departments and on the services (if any) supplied by Transferincorp. Let:

X_1–X_4 represent the volume of services respectively produced by each of the departments S_1–S_4

X_5 represent the no. of metres of computer printout bought from Transferincorp

X_6 represent the no. of facsimile pages of document transmission bought from Transferincorp

Then the problem may be formulated as follows:

Minimise $C = 2.8X_1 + 1.9X_2 + 0.4X_3 + 0.6X_4 + 0.75X_5 + 0.55X_6$

Subject to:

$$X_1 - 0.1448X_2 - 0.0304X_3 - 0.014X_4 = 230\,000$$
$$- 0.016X_1 + X_2 - 0.0607X_3 - 0.0434X_4 = 195\,000$$
$$- 0.0833X_1 - 0.3724X_2 + X_3 - 0.1039X_4 + X_6 = 820\,000$$
$$- 0.0705X_1 - 0.4172X_2 - 0.0921X_3 + X_4 + X_5 = 408\,000$$

The solution to this problem is that the minimum cost of £1 988 752 per annum for the four services together is obtained with volume figures for each of them as follows:

$X_1 = 258\,836$; $X_2 = 199\,141$; $X_3 = 0$; $X_4 = 0$; $X_5 = 509\,330$; $X_6 = 915\,721$

It is immediately apparent that the optimal solution involves buying both of the services offered by Transferincorp, despite the fact that their charge per unit of service is considerably in excess of the variable cost per unit of service within departments S_3 and S_4. The reason for this is that ceasing to operate departments S_3 and S_4 will result in Remosense being able to run departments S_1 and S_2 at lower levels of output, because they will no longer need to supply support services to S_3 and S_4. The consequent reduction in cost will more than offset the higher direct costs of providing document transmission and electronic data transfer from outside. It is necessary to take into account the indirect cost savings associated with a reduced need to supply services from S_1 to S_2 as well as the direct cost savings arising from the elimination of any need to supply services from S_1 and S_2 on the one hand to S_3 and S_4 on the other. Reference may also be made to the fact that in order to supply these services, S_1 and S_2 had in turn to consume services from S_3 and S_4, which need vanishes if outside purchase of services is adopted.

The solution to the Remosense problem specifies a dual real variable value of -0.181 associated with the supply of services by department S_3, and a dual real variable value of -0.072 associated with the supply of services by department S_4. These two figures indicate the amounts by which the variable costs per unit for the services supplied by each of S_3 and S_4 would have to be reduced before X_3 and X_4 entered into the optimal solution, respectively displacing X_6 and X_5. That is, if the variable cost per unit of X_3 were reduced from £0.4 to a figure just below (£0.4 − £0.181) = £0.219, then with all other variables held constant X_3 would just enter into the optimal solution, displacing X_6. Similarly, if the variable cost per unit of X_4 were reduced to just below (£0.6 − £0.072) = £0.528, then with all other variables (including unit cost of X_3) held constant, X_4 would just enter into the optimal solution, displacing X_5.

The fundamental reason why the provision of services by department S_3 is economic only if its variable cost per unit is almost halved lies in its heavy consumption of telephone and telex services per service unit produced. This may be compared with the much lighter use of telephone and telex by department S_4. The provision of its services could be made economic if it could achieve as little as a 12 per cent cut in their unit cost.

Linear Programming, Opportunity Losses and *ex post* Budgeting

6

Shalmirane Ltd

1. The issues in Shalmirane Ltd revolve around the constrained maximisation of contribution using a linear programming approach. With this approach, the *ex ante* problem for February 1989 may be formulated as follows:

Maximise $37X_1 + 44X_2 + 44X_3 + 75X_4$

This maximisation is subject to the following constraints:

$$12X_1 + 15X_2 + 16X_3 + 25X_4 \leqq 3\,600 \qquad (1.1)$$
$$10X_1 + 12X_2 + 13X_3 + 20X_4 \leqq 2\,900 \qquad (1.2)$$
$$0.5X_1 + 0.6X_2 + 0.7X_3 + 2X_4 \leqq 160 \qquad (1.3)$$

The optimum solution is $X_1^a = 260$; $X_2^a = 0$, $X_3^a = 0$, $X_4^a = 15$, for a contribution of £10 745. Since output is divisible into parts of a litre, the *ex ante* solution for both the first half and the second half of February is seen to involve producing 130 litres of Fulminate and 7.5 litres of Mathinate, to earn a contribution of £5 372.50 in each half. The wording of the problem rules out the creation of a new *ex ante* plan for the second half of February on the basis of additional information obtained in the first half of the month. If such a new plan were created, it would give rise to variances for the second half of February differing from those presented here.

Paragraphs 2 and 4 of the narrative of February's events concern changes affecting the first half of the month. Taking these changes into account enables the *ex post* problem for the first half of February to be formulated as follows:

$$\text{Maximise } 25X_1 + 29X_2 + 31.5X_3 + 50X_4$$

This maximisation is subject to the following constraints:

$$12X_1 + 15X_2 + 16X_3 + 25X_4 \leqq 2\,000 \qquad (2.1)$$
$$10X_1 + 12X_2 + 12.5X_3 + 20X_4 \leqq 1\,450 \qquad (2.2)$$
$$0.5X_1 + 0.6X_2 + 0.7X_3 + 2X_4 \leqq 80 \qquad (2.3)$$

The optimum solution to this problem is $X_1^p = 20$, $X_2^p = 0$, $X_3^p = 100$, $X_4^p = 0$, for a contribution of £3\,650.

In the second half of February, paragraph 3. within the narrative of events affects the *ex post* problem, as does the restriction of supply of Varilum mentioned at the end of paragraph 4 of the narrative. The combined effect of these two further changes is to give rise to an *ex post* problem for the second half of February which may be formulated as follows:

$$\text{Maximise } 22.5X_1 + 26X_2 + 28X_3 + 40X_4$$

This maximisation is subject to the following constraints:

$$12X_1 + 15X_2 + 16X_3 + 25X_4 \leqq 1\,600 \qquad (3.1)$$
$$10X_1 + 12X_2 + 12.5X_3 + 20X_4 \leqq 1\,450 \qquad (3.2)$$
$$0.5X_1 + 0.6X_2 + 0.7X_3 + 2X_4 \leqq 120 \qquad (3.3)$$

The optimum solution to this problem is $X_1^p = 133.33$, $X_2^p = 0$, $X_3^p = 0$, $X_4^p = 0$, to earn a contribution of £3\,000.

The data for *ex post* variance analysis in February 1989 may be laid out as follows:

First half of February		*Second half of February*	
C^pX^a	$25(130)+50(7.5) = 3\,625$	$22.5(130)+40(7.5)$	$= 3\,225$
C^pX^p	$25(20 + 31.5(100) = 3\,650$	$22.5(133.33)$	$= 3\,000$
C^aX^a	$37(130)+75(7.5) = 5\,372.5$	$37(130) + 75(7.5)$	$= 5\,372.5$
C^pX^o	$25(120)+50(10) = 3\,500$	$22.5(120)+40(6)$	$= 2\,940$
C^oX^o	$25(120)+15(10) = 3\,150$	$22.5(120)+5(6)$	$= 2\,730$

Working through the *ex post* variance analysis for February yields the following results, with F denoting a favourable variance and U an unfavourable one:

First half of February	£
Volume and mix forecast variance	25.0F
Price and efficiency forecast variance	1747.5U
Volume and mix opportunity cost variance	150.0U
Price and efficiency opportunity cost variance	350.0U
Total variance	2222.5U

Second half of February	£
Volume and mix forecast variance	225.0U
Price and efficiency forecast variance	2147.5U
Volume and mix opportunity cost variance	60.0U
Price and efficiency opportunity cost variance	210.0U
Total variance	2642.5U

The sum of the total variances for the first and second halves of February is £4865U, which is equal to the excess of the contribution in the *ex ante* plan for February (£10745) over the actual contribution for February (£5880).

2. The effect of being able to store Varilum within the month of February is to make it necessary to formulate the Varilum constraints in a different way. There has to be a constraint (4.1) spanning both halves of February, to reflect the fact that any Varilum left unused at the end of the first half can be held to augment the stock in the second half. A separate constraint (4.2) is required for the first half of February, to reflect the fact that Varilum supplied in the second half cannot be transferred

backwards in time to augment the first half's supplies. However, the stipulation that Varilum is supplied on a 'sale or return' basis within February avoids the further complication of having to value the closing inventory.

The constraint spanning both halves of February creates an interdependence between the solutions for each half, so that the linear programming problem must be formulated for both halves of the month simultaneously. To formulate this problem, take X_1 as denoting the production of Fulminate during the first half of February and X_5 as denoting Fulminate production during the second half. Create an identical distinction of meaning between X_2 and X_6, between X_3 and X_7 and between X_4 and X_8. Then the *ex post* problem may be stated as follows:

Maximise $25X_1 + 29X_2 + 31.5X_3 + 50X_4 + 22.5X_5 + 26X_6$
$+ 28X_7 + 40X_8$

This maximisation is subject to the following constraints:

$$12X_1+15X_2+16X_3+25X_4+12X_5+15X_6+16X_7+25X_8 \leqq 3\,600 \tag{4.1}$$

$$12X_1+15X_2+16X_3+25X_4 \leqq 2\,000 \tag{4.2}$$

$$10X_1+12X_2+12.5X_3+20X_4 \leqq 1\,450 \tag{4.3}$$

$$10X_5+12X_6+12.5X_7+20X_8 \leqq 1450 \tag{4.4}$$

$$0.5X_1+0.6X_2+0.7X_3+2X_4 \leqq 80 \tag{4.5}$$

$$0.5X_5+0.6X_6+0.7X_7+2X_8 \leqq 120 \tag{4.6}$$

The optimum solution to this problem is $X_1^p = 20$, $X_2^p = 0$, $X_3^p = 100$, $X_4^p = 0$, $X_5^p = 145$, $X_6^p = 0$, $X_7^p = 0$, $X_8^p = 0$. This solution gives rise to a contribution of £6 912.50, which is £262.50 higher than the sum of the *ex post* contributions for the first and second halves of February taken separately. The variances for the first half of February are the same whether or not Varilum is considered as storeable, because the optimum solution is the same. The extra £262.50 of contribution arises from the production in the second half of 11.67 extra litres of Fulminate at a contribution of £22.50 per litre. This extra production is made possible because the optimum solution for the first half leaves 160 litres of Varilum unused from that half's supply; this extra stock entering the second half supports the production of 11.67 more litres of Fulminate, thus consuming 140 out of the 160 litres available. The remaining 20 litres of Varilum cannot be used, because a production level of 145 litres of Fulminate serves to exhaust completely the 1 450 litres of Diffuso available in the second half of February.

Producing 145 litres of Fulminate in the second half of February changes $C^p X^p$ for the second half to a value of $C^p X^p = £3\,262.50$, and in doing so alters the variances to the following new values:

Second half of February	£
Volume and mix forecast variance	37.5F
Price and efficiency forecast variance	2 147.5U
Volume and mix opportunity cost variance	322.5U
Price and efficiency opportunity cost variance	210.0U
Total variance	2 642.5U

The total variance for the second half of February is unchanged from its previous value, because $C^p X^p$ cancels out within it. But the volume and mix forecast variance has changed sign, and the volume and mix opportunity cost variance is £262.50 larger, reflecting the increased opportunity loss which has arisen from actual performance being unchanged while the maximum amount of contribution attainable has increased.

The change in the optimum contribution arising from the storability of Varilum illustrates the difficulty of defining the period over which the optimising model is said to stretch in *ex post* budgeting. Once Varilum is said to be storable, the 2-week optimisation model gives misleading results, and even the validity of the 4-week model depends upon the rather contrived 'sale or return' assumption.

Input–Output Analysis and Linear Programming

7A

Kerruish Tracers

1. Let q^o_{ij} represent the number of units of Product i ($i = 1 \ldots 5$) produced by a unit of activity within Process j ($j = 1 \ldots 5$). Since each of the five processes produces a single product, the matrix of output coefficients q^o must be an identity matrix of order five, as shown below:

$$
q^o =
\begin{bmatrix}
1 & 0 & 0 & 0 & 0 \\
0 & 1 & 0 & 0 & 0 \\
0 & 0 & 1 & 0 & 0 \\
0 & 0 & 0 & 1 & 0 \\
0 & 0 & 0 & 0 & 1
\end{bmatrix}
$$

Let q^i_{ij} represent the number of units of Product i used by each unit of activity within Process j. Then from the problem the matrix of input coefficients q^i is as follows:

$$
q^i =
\begin{bmatrix}
0 & 0.67 & 0.31 & 0.22 & 0 \\
0.17 & 0.06 & 0.46 & 0 & 0.16 \\
0 & 0.19 & 0.07 & 0.37 & 0.91 \\
0.04 & 0 & 0.11 & 0 & 0 \\
0 & 0.09 & 0 & 0 & 0
\end{bmatrix}
$$

283

The net input–output coefficient $q_{ij} = q_{ij}^o - q_{ij}^i$. The matrix of input–output coefficients q is given by:

$$q = \begin{bmatrix} 1 & -0.67 & -0.31 & -0.22 & 0 \\ -0.17 & 0.94 & -0.46 & 0 & -0.16 \\ 0 & -0.19 & 0.93 & -0.37 & -0.91 \\ -0.04 & 0 & -0.11 & 1 & 0 \\ 0 & -0.09 & 0 & 0 & 1 \end{bmatrix}$$

The external inputs entering Kerruish Tracers number seven in all, being made up of three materials, two types of machines and two grades of labour. Let:

d_{kj} represent the number of units of input k ($k = 1 \ldots 7$) required by one unit of activity of Process j ($j = 1 \ldots 5$)

v_k represent the variable cost of input k

Then, from the data in the problem, a matrix d can be drawn up covering all d_{kj}, together with a column vector v covering all v_k. These appear as follows:

$$d = \begin{bmatrix} 0 & 0.6 & 0.3 & -2.1 & 0 \\ 0.5 & 0.7 & 0 & 0 & -1.9 \\ 4.2 & 6.9 & 2.1 & 0.7 & 0 \\ 1.1 & 0 & 1.9 & 0 & 2.3 \\ 0 & 3.1 & 0.6 & 1.6 & 0 \\ 2.2 & 1.4 & 1.9 & 0.6 & 3.1 \\ 1.7 & 0.7 & 2.8 & 2.2 & 0.8 \end{bmatrix} \quad v = \begin{bmatrix} 4.8 \\ 6.4 \\ 11 \\ 6.6 \\ 8.1 \\ 0 \\ 0 \end{bmatrix}$$

Within the v vector, the elements $v_6 = 0$, $v_7 = 0$ arise from the policy of treating labour as a fixed cost in the short term.

The gross internal coefficient matrix q' is the inverse of the input–output coefficient matrix q. Performing this inversion gives rise to:

$$q' = \begin{bmatrix} 1.233 & 1.213 & 1.091 & 0.675 & 1.187 \\ 0.279 & 1.549 & 0.906 & 0.397 & 1.072 \\ 0.106 & 0.494 & 1.420 & 0.549 & 1.371 \\ 0.061 & 0.103 & 0.200 & 1.087 & 0.198 \\ 0.025 & 0.139 & 0.082 & 0.036 & 1.096 \end{bmatrix}$$

The d' matrix, representing the external input requirements per unit of net production, is given by postmultiplying the d matrix by the gross internal coefficient matrix q'. Carrying out this computation yields:

$$
d' = \begin{bmatrix}
0.0711 & 0.8613 & 0.5496 & -1.8798 & 0.6387 \\
0.7643 & 1.4267 & 1.0239 & 0.5470 & -0.7385 \\
7.3690 & 16.8922 & 13.9556 & 7.4881 & 15.3999 \\
1.6152 & 2.5926 & 4.0867 & 1.8684 & 6.4314 \\
1.0261 & 5.2631 & 3.9806 & 3.2993 & 4.4626 \\
3.4187 & 6.2685 & 6.7408 & 3.8477 & 10.2335 \\
2.7424 & 4.8674 & 6.9705 & 5.3828 & 7.9195
\end{bmatrix}
$$

The process of costing out these physical requirements for external inputs begins by transposing the 7×1 column vector v into a 1×7 row vector v^T, so that:

$$v^T = [4.8 \quad 6.4 \quad 11 \quad 6.6 \quad 8.1 \quad 0 \quad 0]$$

Postmultiplying v^T by d' serves to convert the matrix of physical inputs per unit of net output into a row vector of variable costs per unit of net output. Calling this row vector c^T, it shows from left to right the unit variable costs for each of Products I–V, as below:

$$c^T = [105.26 \quad 258.82 \quad 221.92 \quad 115.90 \quad 246.33]$$

In formulating the objective function for the linear programming problem, it is first necessary to establish some terminology, as follows. Let:

X_1 represent the June 1989 output of Cadmium Red (in litres)

X_2 represent the June 1989 output of Strontium Blue (in litres)

From the c^T vector, the variable cost per litre of net output of Cadmium Red is £115.90; per litre of net output of Strontium Blue it is £246.33. With selling prices of £190 per litre and £395 per litre for the Red and Blue products respectively, the contribution-maximising objective function for Kerruish is as follows:

Maximise $74.1X_1 + 148.67X_2$

For the external inputs which are in constrained supply, it is possible to read from the d' matrix the amounts required to produce a litre of net product of Cadmium Red and of Strontium Blue. Working down the fourth and fifth columns of the d' matrix from the third row, this gives rise to the following five constraints:

$$7.4881X_1 + 15.3999X_2 \leqq 10\,000 \qquad (1)$$
$$1.8684X_1 + 6.4314X_2 \leqq 3\,400 \qquad (2)$$
$$3.2993X_1 + 4.4626X_2 \leqq 3\,700 \qquad (3)$$
$$3.8477X_1 + 10.2335X_2 \leqq 5\,200 \qquad (4)$$
$$5.3828X_1 + 7.9195X_2 \leqq 5\,900 \qquad (5)$$

Of these constraints, (1) relates to the supply of mygecerium, (2) and (3) respectively to the supply of machine time for freeze emulsifying and acculturation and (4) and (5) respectively, to the supply of skilled and semi-skilled labour hours. Finally, there are the two contractual commitment constraints:

$$X_1 \geqq 350 \qquad (6)$$
$$X_2 \geqq 275 \qquad (7)$$

The solution to this linear programming problem involves the manufacture for sale of 620 litres of Cadmium Red and 275 litres of Strontium Blue, from which a budgeted contribution of £86 830 would be earned in April 1989. After deducting the fixed labour cost of £56 000, a budgeted profit of £30 830 would remain, though this figure does not allow for any revenue from sales of by-products, a topic discussed below.

2. (a) The next task is to find the gross ouputs of Products I–V required to enable the optimal net outputs just calculated to be produced for sale.

Let $\bar{Q}^T$ denote the row vector of optimal net outputs of Products I–V, so that:

$$\bar{Q}^T = [0 \quad 0 \quad 0 \quad 620 \quad 275]$$

Then the gross output required is given by postmultiplying q' by $\hat{Q}$ to give (with transposition) the following 1×5 row vector $\hat{Q}^T$:

$$\hat{Q}^T = [744.925 \quad 540.94 \quad 717.405 \quad 728.39 \quad 323.72]$$

This vector shows, from left to right, the required levels of gross output of Products I–V.

(b) The vector of external input requirements is obtained by postmultiplying the d matrix by $\hat{Q}$ to give rise to a 8×1 column vector $\bar{D}$. This appears as follows:

$$\bar{D} = \begin{bmatrix} -989.83 \\ 136.05 \\ 8\,877.59 \\ 2\,927.04 \\ 3\,272.78 \\ 5\,199.79 \\ 5\,515.20 \end{bmatrix}$$

The first element in the $\bar{D}$ vector is negative, indicating that 989.93 litres of *net* output of cadmium chlorate will be produced, and thus be available for sale. All the remaining elements in the $\bar{D}$ vector are positive, and show the amount of each input which needs to be purchased or used up. For example, the $\bar{D}_{61}$ element shows that 5\,200 hours of skilled labour will be used up (subject to rounding error) and that skilled labour supply is therefore a binding constraint.

The total variable cost of the optimum output is given by postmultiplying c^T by $\hat{Q}$, to yield a figure of £139\,598.75. When this is subtracted from the sales revenue from Cadmium Red and Strontium Blue, a contribution figure of £86\,824.33 is obtained, which agrees with that from the linear programming solution, apart from rounding errors. However, this figure does not allow for the revenue from the sales of the by-product, cadmium chlorate, which when 989.83 litres is sold at £4.80 per litre yields £4\,751.18. This raises the total budgeted contribution for June 1989 to a final figure of £91\,581.18, and raises the budgeted profit correspondingly to £35\,581.18.

Input–Output Analysis and Linear Programming 7B with Purchasable Intermediate Products and Joint Final Products

Raistrick Ltd

1. Process III in Raistrick Ltd gives rise to two joint products, manufactured in the fixed ratio of 0.8 kilograms of Urquase to 1 kilogram of Pirco. Since this is the last of the three processes, the other two of which each produce a single product, the output coefficients, input coefficients and net input–output coefficients may be represented in 4×3 matrix form, as follows:

$$q^o = \begin{bmatrix} 1 & 0 & 0 \\ 0 & 1 & 0 \\ 0 & 0 & 1 \\ 0 & 0 & 0.8 \end{bmatrix}$$

$$q^i = \begin{bmatrix} 0.05 & 0.4 & 0.3 \\ 0.1 & 0.03 & 0.5 \\ 0.02 & 0.04 & 0 \\ 0.06 & 0.03 & 0 \end{bmatrix}$$

$$q = \begin{bmatrix} 0.95 & -0.4 & -0.3 \\ -0.1 & 0.97 & -0.5 \\ -0.02 & -0.04 & 1 \\ -0.06 & -0.03 & 0.8 \end{bmatrix}$$

Let p_i represent the selling price of product i, giving rise to a 1×4 row vector p^T where:

$$p^T = [0 \quad 0 \quad 26 \quad 17]$$

Let $\tilde{c}_i$ represent the unit cost of intermediate product i purchased externally, so that here:

$$\tilde{c}^T = [20 \quad 22 \quad 0 \quad 0]$$

From the question, the matrix of units of external input per unit of activity d and the column vector of variable costs per unit of external input v are as follows:

$$d = \begin{bmatrix} 0.19 & 0.06 & 0.13 \\ 0.04 & 0.12 & 0.17 \\ 0.8 & 1.3 & 1.5 \\ 0.7 & 1.1 & 2.1 \end{bmatrix} \qquad v = \begin{bmatrix} 9 \\ 7 \\ 0 \\ 5 \end{bmatrix}$$

Let $\tilde{Q}_i$ represent the optimal quantity of intermediate product i to be purchased externally

Let Q_i represent the optimal net output of product i, each value of Q_i constituting an element within the column vector $\tilde{Q}$

Transposing $\breve{Q}$ for convenience, and bearing in mind that Raistrick does not sell either of Products I or II, the vector of optimal net outputs appears as follows:

$$\breve{Q}^T = [0 \quad 0 \quad Q_3 \quad Q_4]$$

Let $\hat{Q}_i$ represent the optimal activity level at which to run process i, being that level giving rise to a gross volume of output sufficient to sustain the optimal net output $\breve{Q}$

Then the first set of constraints enforces the equality of the net output of any product with the amount of that product sold *less* the amount purchased externally. The general form of this type of constraint is:

$$q\hat{Q} - \breve{Q} + \tilde{Q} = 0$$

Inserting the net input–output coefficient values in this general constraint form yields the following four constraints for this problem:

$$
\begin{align}
0.95\hat{Q}_1 - 0.4\hat{Q}_2 - 0.3\hat{Q}_3 + \tilde{Q}_1 &= 0 \tag{1} \\
-0.1\hat{Q}_1 + 0.97\hat{Q}_2 - 0.5\hat{Q}_3 + \tilde{Q}_2 &= 0 \tag{2} \\
-0.02\hat{Q}_1 - 0.04\hat{Q}_2 + \hat{Q}_3 - Q_3 &= 0 \tag{3} \\
-0.06\hat{Q}_1 - 0.03\hat{Q}_2 + 0.8\hat{Q}_3 - Q_4 &= 0 \tag{4}
\end{align}
$$

Let D_k represent the number of units of external input k required to produce the optimal net outputs of Products III and IV, and let $\breve{D}$ represent the column vector of these input requirements. Hence, in this problem, with transposition:

$$\breve{D}^T = [D_1 \ldots D_4]$$

The second set of constraints equates the total quantity of external inputs required by production $d\hat{Q}$ with the quantity of external inputs purchased, as given by $\breve{D}$. It is convenient to represent this type of constraint in the following form:

$$d\hat{Q} - \breve{D} = 0$$

Taking figures from the d matrix for this problem enables the formulation of constraints as below:

$$0.19\hat{Q}_1 + 0.06\hat{Q}_2 + 0.13\hat{Q}_3 - D_1 = 0 \tag{5}$$
$$0.04\hat{Q}_1 + 0.12\hat{Q}_2 + 0.17\hat{Q}_3 - D_2 = 0 \tag{6}$$
$$0.8\hat{Q}_1 + 1.3\hat{Q}_2 + 1.5\hat{Q}_3 - D_3 = 0 \tag{7}$$
$$0.7\hat{Q}_1 + 1.1\hat{Q}_2 + 2.1\hat{Q}_3 - D_4 = 0 \tag{8}$$

The next set of constraints confines the total quantity of each external input used to an amount within the total quantity available. In this problem, the external inputs subject to restricted supply are hours of supervision and hours of steam fermenting time. The constraints involved are as follows:

$$D_3 \leqq 44\,000 \tag{9}$$
$$D_4 \leqq 54\,000 \tag{10}$$

The final constraint specifies the maximum quantity of Pirco (and therefore of Urquase) that may be sold during April 1989. This constraint is as follows:

$$Q_3 \leqq 18\,000 \tag{11}$$

In this mode of analysis, the objective function takes the general form specified below:

Maximise $p^T \tilde{Q} - (\tilde{c}^T \tilde{Q} + v^T \bar{D})$

Inserting the relevant values for this problem enables the formulation of an objective function as follows:

Maximise $26Q_3 + 17Q_4 - 20\tilde{Q}_1 - 22\tilde{Q}_2 - 9D_1 - 7D_2 - 5D_4$

Maximising this function subject to constraints (1) – (11) above gives rise to a contribution for April 1989 of £300 962, obtained with the following values:

$$\hat{Q}_1 = 8\,825 \qquad D_1 = 4\,504$$
$$\hat{Q}_2 = 7\,114 \qquad D_2 = 4\,345$$
$$\hat{Q}_3 = 18\,461 \qquad D_3 = 44\,000$$
$$Q_3 = 18\,000 \qquad D_4 = 52\,771$$
$$Q_4 = 14\,026$$
$$\tilde{Q}_2 = 3\,212$$

The optimal output for April 1989 is seen to be 18 000 kilo-grams of Pirco (Q_3) and 14 026 kilograms of Urquase (Q_4), yielding a budgeted profit (after deducting the fixed cost of labour) of £85 362. From the above solution values, the answers to the three remaining parts of the problem may be read off as described below.

2. Process I should be run at a level producing 8 825 litres of Product I during April, and Process II should be run at a level producing 7 114 kilograms of Product II. Process III should be run at a level of 18 461 units of activity, thus producing 18 461 litres of Pirco and 14 769 litres of Urquase. The excess of this level of operation of Process III over the level of sales of finished products is accounted for by the need to feed some of the Pirco and Urquase back to Processes I and II.

3. The optimal solution involves purchasing 3 212 kilograms of Product II from Pentre Biosystems, to supplement the amount produced in Process II. No Product I, however, should be purchased from this source, as $\tilde{Q}_1$ does not enter into the optimal solution.

4. The inputs required to support the optimal production schedule in April are 4 504 litres of Catalyst A, 4 345 kilograms of Catalyst B, 44 000 hours of supervision and 52 771 hours of steam fermenting time. Sensitivity analysis on the binding constraints shows that an increase of 1 hour in the supervisory time available in April would increase contribution by £5.60 over the range from 44 000 – 48 345 hours. (The only other binding constraint is the one on the amount of Pirco that could be sold, where a change of 1 kilogram would change contribution by £3.02 over the range from 16 771 – 70 771 kilograms sold during April.)

Use of Information Theory to Isolate Substantial Variances

8

Department of Transportation Analytical Offices

It is initially necessary to establish some notation. Let:

p_{ij} represent the budgeted expenditure on energy source i by office j as a proportion of total budgeted expenditure

q_{ij} represent the actual expenditure on energy source i by office j as a proportion of total actual expenditure

X represent the classification of expenditure by energy source, so that gas is labelled as source X_1, electricity as source X_2 and solid fuel as source X_3

Y represent the classification of expenditure by office location, so that Scunthorpe is labelled as office Y_1, Bath as office Y_2 and Dundee as office Y_3

With this notation, the computations for budgeted and actual proportions appear as follows:

	Y_1	Y_2	Y_3	Total
X_1	$p_{11} = 0.2076$	$p_{12} = 0.0716$	$p_{13} = 0.2402$	$p_{10} = 0.5194$
X_2	$p_{11} = 0.1106$	$p_{22} = 0.1343$	$p_{23} = 0.0244$	$p_{20} = 0.2693$
X_3	$p_{31} = 0.0433$	$p_{32} = 0.0339$	$p_{33} = 0.1341$	$p_{30} = 0.2113$
Total	$p_{01} = 0.3615$	$p_{02} = 0.2398$	$p_{03} = 0.3987$	1

	Y_1	Y_2	Y_3	*Total*
X_1	$q_{11} = 0.2096$	$q_{12} = 0.0643$	$q_{13} = 0.2355$	$q_{10} = 0.5094$
X_2	$q_{21} = 0.0954$	$q_{22} = 0.1449$	$q_{23} = 0.0307$	$q_{20} = 0.2710$
X_3	$q_{31} = 0.0464$	$q_{32} = 0.0365$	$q_{33} = 0.1367$	$q_{30} = 0.2196$
Total	$q_{01} = 0.3514$	$q_{02} = 0.2457$	$q_{03} = 0.4029$	1

Consider equations (8.4) – (8.10) inclusive from the analysis of the Heversham Horticulture problem. Applying these equations to this problem, in which there are $m = 3$ energy sources and $n = 3$ offices, gives rise to computations as below. All the figures in these computations are in units of 10^{-4} nits:

$$I(X, Y) = \sum_{i=1}^{3} \sum_{j=1}^{3} q_{ij} \ln(q_{ij}/p_{ij}) = 29.49$$

$$I(Y|X_1) = \sum_{j=1}^{3} (q_{1j}/q_{10}) \ln[(q_{1j}/q_{10})/(p_{1j}/p_{10})] = 6.84$$

$$I(Y|X_2) = \sum_{j=1}^{3} (q_{2j}/q_{20}) \ln[(q_{2j}/q_{20})/(p_{2j}/p_{20})] = 83.69$$

$$I(Y|X_3) = \sum_{j=1}^{3} (q_{3j}/q_{30}) \ln[(q_{3j}/q_{30})/(p_{3j}/p_{30})] = 3.23$$

$$I(Y|X) = \sum_{i=1}^{3} q_{i0} \, I(Y|X_i) = 26.88$$

$$I(X) = \sum_{i=1}^{3} q_{i0} \ln(q_{i0}/p_{i0}) = 2.61$$

As a computational check, note that $I(Y|X) = I(X, Y) - I(X)$.

$$I(X|Y_1) = \sum_{i=1}^{3} (q_{i1}/q_{01}) \ln[(q_{i1}/q_{01})/(p_{i1}/p_{01})] = 30.62$$

$$I(X|Y_2) = \sum_{i=1}^{3} (q_{i2}/q_{02}) \ln[(q_{i2}/q_{02})/(p_{i2}/p_{02})] = 33.48$$

$$I(X|Y_3) = \sum_{i=1}^{3} (q_{i3}/q_{03}) \ln [(q_{i3}/q_{03})/(p_{i3}/p_{03})] = 20.24$$

$$I(X|Y) = \sum_{j=1}^{3} q_{0j} \, I(X|Y_j) = 27.14$$

$$I(Y) = \sum_{j=1}^{3} q_{0j} \ln(q_{0j}/p_{0j}) = 2.35$$

As a computational check, note that $I(X|Y) = I(X,Y) - I(Y)$.

A feature of interest in the overall interpretation of these results is the relatively small value of $I(X,Y)$ in comparison with the corresponding value in the Heversham Horticulture problem. This indicates that budgeted energy costs, by office and by source of energy, served overall as relatively good predictors of actual costs – the contrast here being between the volatility of sales elements in the Heversham problem and the comparative stability of recurrent cost elements here.

The other major overall feature is that $I(Y|X)$ is very close to $I(X|Y)$, while $I(X)$ is very close to $I(Y)$. On the first of these points, $I(Y|X)$ measures the quality of the forecast contained in the budget as to how the cost of a given energy source would be distributed over the three offices. The quality of this forecast was much the same as the quality of the budget's forecast as to how the energy costs incurred in a given office would be spread over the three energy sources, the latter being measured by $I(X|Y)$.

On the second point, the closeness of $I(X)$ and $I(Y)$ indicates that the prediction in the budget as to the proportion of total energy costs that would be accounted for by each source of energy was similar in accuracy to the prediction as to the proportion of total energy costs that would be accounted for by each office. The accuracy of the former prediction is measured by $I(X)$, and that of the latter prediction by $I(Y)$.

At the level of the individual information expectations, the high value associated with $I(Y|X_2)$ stands out sharply. This indicates that the actual distribution of electricity costs across offices deviated from the one anticipated in the budget. Looking at the comparison of the actual against the budgeted energy source mix of costs for each individual office makes it clear where the issue is located. $I(X|Y_1)$ and $I(X|Y_2)$ are comparable, and both are markedly larger than $I(X|Y_3)$. It is in the proportion of total electricity costs accounted for by the Scunthorpe and Bath offices that the variation from forecast has arisen, and this anomaly may warrant further study.

The Single-period Cost Variance Investigation Decision

9

Star Chemical Company

1. In dealing with this problem it is first necessary to establish some terminology. Let:

S_1 represent the situation in which the process is in control

S_2 represent the situation in which the process is out of control

a_1 represent the act of ordering a full drain

a_2 represent the act of ordering a partial drain

a_3 represent the act of ordering no drain at all

From the data in the problem, the break-even probability $f_a(S_2)$ as between a_1 and a_2 is given by:

$$f_a(S_2) = \frac{700 - 200}{1\,500(1-0.4)+150(0.4-1)}$$

$$= 0.617$$

The break-even probability $f_b(S_2)$ as between a_2 and a_3 is given by:

$$f_b(S_2) = \frac{200}{(1\,500-150)(0.4)}$$

$$= 0.370$$

The prior probabilities are given by $f_0(S_1) = 0.75$ and $f_0(S_2) = 0.25$. These probabilities require revision by reference to an observed quantity variance of $x = 9\,600$ for week $n = 1$, ending on Friday 14 July. Using Bayes' Theorem, the calculation appears as follows:

$$f_1(S_1|x) =$$

$$\frac{\left(\dfrac{1}{3\,500}\right)f_u\left(\dfrac{9\,600-9\,000}{3\,500}\right)(0.75)}{\left(\dfrac{1}{3\,500}\right)f_u\left(\dfrac{9\,600-9\,000}{3\,500}\right)(0.75)+\left(\dfrac{1}{1\,000}\right)f_u\left(\dfrac{9\,600-10\,500}{1\,000}\right)(0.25)}$$

$$= 0.558$$

Hence $f_1(S_2|x) = 0.442$. Since $f_1(S_2|x) > f_b(S_2)$, expected cost would have been minimised if the Process Controller had authorised a partial drain rather than continuing to operate the process for a further week with no drain at all.

2. Postmultiplying the vector $[f_1(S_1|x)\ f_1(S_2|x)]$ by the matrix of transition probabilities from one state to another over the weekend results in the following calculation:

$$[0.558 \quad 0.422]\begin{bmatrix} 0.65 & 0.35 \\ 0.15 & 0.85 \end{bmatrix} = [0.429 \quad 0.571]$$

Thus $f_1'(S_1) = 0.429$ and $f_1'(S_2) = 0.571$. These probabilities act as the prior probabilities for week $n = 2$, beginning on Monday 17 July, and require revision by reference to the observed quantity variance of $x = 9\,300$ for that week. The calculations are as follows:

$$f_2(S_1|x) =$$

$$\frac{\left(\dfrac{1}{3\,500}\right)f_u\left(\dfrac{9\,300-9\,000}{3\,500}\right)(0.429)}{\left(\dfrac{1}{3\,500}\right)f_u\left(\dfrac{9\,300-9\,000}{3\,500}\right)(0.429)+\left(\dfrac{1}{1\,000}\right)f_u\left(\dfrac{9\,300-10\,500}{1\,000}\right)(0.571)}$$

$$= 0.305$$

Hence $f_2(S_2|x) = 0.695$. This probability is considerably in excess of $f_a(S_2)$, indicating that, to minimise expected cost, the Process Controller should issue instructions for a full drain to be carried out on the morning of Saturday 22 July.

There is no inconsistency in recommending that a partial drain should have been carried out after an observed quantity variance of $x = 9600$ in the first week, while at the same time asserting that a full drain should be carried out after a smaller quantity variance of $x = 9300$ in the second week. It is the cumulative effect of two quantity variances lying above the in-control mean of $x = 9000$ that have led to the later recommendation for a full drain, taken together with the fact that state changes as between the first and second weeks were more likely to take the process out of control than back into control.

3. Change (a) here reduces the problem to a simpler two-action, two-state form, for which the quadratic equation approach of Capettini and Collins can be adopted. If the act 'order full drain' remains act a_1, while the act 'do nothing' is relabelled a_2, then the Capettini and Collins rule can be stated as follows:

'Do a_1 if $ax^2 + bx + c > 0$; otherwise do a_2'

In applying this rule, a, b and c are computed as below:

$$a = \left(\frac{1}{2}\right)\left[\frac{1}{(3\,500)^2} - \frac{1}{(1\,000)^2}\right] = -4.592 \times 10^{-7}$$

$$b = -\left[\frac{9\,000}{(3\,500)^2} - \frac{10\,500}{(1\,000)^2}\right] = 0.009765$$

$$c = \log_e\left[\left(\frac{1\,500-150-700}{700}\right)\left(\frac{0.571}{0.429}\right)\left(\frac{3\,500}{1\,000}\right)\right] +$$

$$\left(\frac{1}{2}\right)\left[\frac{(9\,000)^2}{(3\,500)^2} - \frac{(10\,500)^2}{(1\,000)^2}\right]$$

$$= -50.35$$

The solution to the quadratic equation $ax^2 + bx + c = 0$ with a, b and c as above is $x = 10\,632.6 \pm 1\,845.6$, which can be expressed as:

$$x = 8\,787 \text{ or } 12\,478.2$$

Within the range $8\,787 \leqq x \leqq 12\,478.2$, $ax^2 + bx + c > 0$.

From this, the Capettini–Collins decision rule for week $n = 2$ (ending on Friday 21 July) may be expressed as follows:

'Carry out a full drain if the adverse quantity variance lies between £8\,787 and £12\,478.2; do not drain any of the trimetheldrin at the end of the week if the adverse quantity variance lies outside this range'

Hence an unfavourable quantity variance of £12\,800 should not cause any trimetheldrin to be drained.

4. The above decision rule is a two-sided one, in that the Process Controller has two cost observations for which he would be indifferent as between a full drain and none at all. Representing expected cost for a rule in week $n = 2$ as EC_2 (rule) gives for this rule:

EC_2 $(a_1$ if $8\,787 \leqq x \leqq 12\,478.2) = (0.429)$ (700) (Prob. of $8\,787 \leqq x \leqq 12\,478.2$ if $\bar{x} = 9\,000$, $s = 3\,500)$ + $(0.571)[(850)$(Prob. of $8\,787 \leqq x \leqq 12\,478.2$ if $\bar{x} = 10\,500, s = 1\,000)+(1\,500)(1-$Prob. of $8\,787 \leqq x \leqq 12\,478.2$ if $\bar{x} = 10\,500$, $s = 1\,000)]$

$EC_2(a_1$ if $8\,787 \leqq x \leqq 12\,478.2) = (0.429)(700)(0.364) + (0.571)[850(0.933) + (1\,500)(0.067)]$

$EC_2(a_1$ if $8\,787 \leqq x \leqq 12\,478.2) = 619.50$

This expected cost of £619.50 needs to be compared with the expected cost of the best one-sided decision rule. Here it is act a_2 which has a disjoint region, between £8\,787 and £12\,478.20. If this region is treated as having no upper boundary, so that there is no cost level above which act a_2 (do not investigate) comes to be preferred, then the best one-sided rule can be derived as $EC_2(a_1$ if $x \geqq 8787)$. Expected cost for this rule is given by:

EC_2 $(a_1$ if $x \geqq 8787) = (0.429)(700)$(Prob. of $x \geqq 8787$ if $\bar{x} = 9000$, $s = 3500$) $+ (0.571)[(850)$(Prob. of $x \geqq 8787$ if $\bar{x} = 10500$, $s = 1000$) $+ (1500$(Prob. of $x < 8787$ if $\bar{x} = 10500$, $s = 1000)]$

EC_2 $(a_1$ if $x \geqq 8787) = (0.429)(700)(0.524) + (0.571)[850(0.957) + (1500)(0.043)]$
$EC_2(a_1$ if $x \geqq 8787) = 658.31$

The excess of this expected cost of £658.31 over the expected cost of £619.50 associated with the optimal decision rule represents the expected cost of ignoring the disjoint region; here it is £38.81.

In this case, the disjoint region arises because when the process is running properly it is subject to all kinds of large random cost variations, but when it is out of control its cost falls into a more predictable pattern, dominated perhaps by the technical problem which has caused the process to go out of control. Very high readings of cost tend to be associated with the widely-fluctuating cost observations which arise when the process is in control, rather than with the more narrowly-varying observations which arise from an out of control process.

The
Multi-period
Cost Variance
Investigation
Decision

10

Mansfield Pressings

The first step in solving this problem is to discretise the in control and out of control distributions. This produces the following:

Process in control (Rods not bent)		Process out of control (Rods bent)	
Cost £	Probability	Cost £	Probability
325	0.05	425	0.05
375	0.30	475	0.05
425	0.25	525	0.15
475	0.20	575	0.25
525	0.15	625	0.35
575	0.05	675	0.15

Denoting the in control state as state 1 and the out of control state as state 2, the means for the two distributions are $\mu_1 = 437.5$ and $\mu_2 = 587.5$, so that $\Delta\mu = 150$. From the data in the problem, the cost of investigation $I = 40$, and the cost of correction $K = 15+30 = 45$. With $g = 0.75$, the parameters a and b can be computed as follows:

$$a = (1 - 0.75)(45) + 40 - (0.75)(150) = -61.25$$
$$b = (0.75)(40) = 30$$

A table may now be drawn up as below:

Control limit	$F_2(x)$	$\pi_1(x)$	Max $F_1(x)$	$C(x)$
$x < 425$	0	1	0.35	515.75
$x < 475$	0.05	0.987	0.60	509.28
$x < 525$	0.10	0.973	0.80	504.55
$x < 575$	0.25	0.923	0.95	504.66
$x < 625$	0.50	0.8	1	514.50

The cost-minimising decision rule turns out to be one of 'investigate if the electricity cost recorded for a shift is equal to or greater than £525', although the substitution of £575 for £525 would increase the long-term expected cost per shift by only £0.11. The optimal solution is clearly not very sensitive to small changes in the parameters of the problem.

A policy of 'never checking the alignment rods' would have a long-term expected cost per shift of £587.50, while one of 'checking the rods after every shift' would have a cost of £526.25. Finally, the long-term cost per shift of running the metal stamping machine under conditions of certainty is £496.25.

Stochastic Cost–Volume–Profit Analysis and Decision Theory

11

Bulk Powder Producers Ltd

1. Some initial terminology may be set out as below. Let:

a_1 represent the act of leasing the Type A machine

a_2 represent the act of leasing the Type B machine

S represent the average sales of ink powder, in kilograms per customer per annum

Cost functions for a_1 and a_2 (in pounds per annum) may be drawn up as follows:

$$C(a_1,S) = 50\,000 + (0.5)(400)S$$
$$C(a_2,S) = 80\,000 + (0.3)(400)S$$

The break-even point for S as between a_1 and a_2 is given by S_b, where $S_b = 30\,000/[400(0.5 - 0.3)] = 375$ kilograms per customer per annum.

A normal prior distribution for demand is specified in the problem, with 50 per cent of its area lying between levels of 250 and 550 kilograms per customer per annum. From the symmetry of the normal distribution, this implies a prior mean $E_0(\mu) = 400$. Representing the standard deviation of the prior distribution by σ_0 and standardising gives rise to the following equation, which exploits the property that 25 per cent of the area under a standardised normal distribution lies to the right of $z = 0.675$:

$$(550 - 400)/\sigma_0 = 0.675, \text{ hence } \sigma_0 = 222.2$$

From the sample of four customers, the result obtained has been one of mean sales per customer $\bar{x} = 357$, with a standard deviation $s = 104$. The standard error of the sample mean is given by $\sigma_{\bar{x}} = 104/\sqrt{4} = 52$. There is no need for a finite population correction here, since the sample represents only 1 per cent of the population from which it was drawn.

The analysis is thus seen to involve the revision of a normal prior distribution with mean $E_0(\mu) = 400$ and standard deviation $\sigma_0 = 222.2$ by reference to sample findings giving an estimate of mean sales $\bar{x} = 357$ subject to a standard error $\sigma_{\bar{x}} = 52$. Let:

$E_1(\mu)$ represent the mean of the posterior distribution
σ_1 represent the standard deviation of the posterior distribution

The computations then proceed as follows:

$$E_1(\mu) = \frac{(400)(52^2) + (357)(222.2^2)}{(222.2^2) + (52^2)} = 359.2$$

$$\sigma_1 = \sqrt{\frac{(222.2^2)(52^2)}{(222.2^2) + (52^2)}} = 50.6$$

Since $E_1(\mu) < S_b$, on the basis of the information supplied by the sample of four customers, the Type A machine should be leased. However, there is a non-negligible probability that this decision may prove to be wrong. The probability concerned is given by the area under a standardised normal distribution to the right of $z = (375 - 359.2)/50.6 = 0.31$. From tables, this area is 0.377, so that the probability that a decision to lease a Type A machine may prove to be wrong exceeds 1 in 3. This result supplies a hint that further sampling may prove to be desirable.

2. The estimated variance of the population is given by $\sigma^2 = 120^2$ $= 14\,400$. Denoting the reduction in variance due to a sample of size n by σ^{*2}, then for $n = 3$ the computation proceeds as follows:

$$\sigma^{*2} = \frac{(3)(50.6^4)}{14\,400+(3)(50.6^2)} \text{ hence } \sigma^* = 29.8$$

It is necessary next to define a standardised variable D^*, where:

$$D^* = \left| \frac{S_b - E_1(\mu)}{\sigma^*} \right| = 0.53$$

The opportunity loss function is given by $0.2(400)(S - S_b)$ for $S > S_b$ and by $0.2(400)(S_b - S)$ for $S_b > S$, so that the rate of change of the opportunity loss function with respect to S is seen to be 80.

It is thus possible to derive the expected value of sample information (EVSI) for $n = 3$ as EVSI $= (80)(29.8)(0.1887) =$ £449.80. The cost of sampling is given by $(3)(£125) = £375$. Subtracting this cost from the EVSI gives rise to an expected net gain from sampling three more customers of £74.80. Undertaking the further sampling of three customers would thus seem to be justified. In practice, the problem's dichotomy between sampling exactly three more customers and not sampling further at all would represent an artificial simplification, and the expected net gain from sampling would be computed for a range of sample sizes around $n = 3$.

Stochastic Cost–Volume– Profit Analysis: 12 Satisficing with Short Product Lives

Bridgegate Foods

1. The initial step is to define symbols as follows: Let:

c	represent the contribution margin per dozen oysters sold to hotels and restaurants
h	represent the loss per dozen oysters sold for fish bait
s	represent the contribution lost per dozen oysters which are ordered but cannot be supplied
μ	represent the mean weekly demand (in dozens of oysters)
σ	represent the standard deviation of weekly demand
F	represent the cost per week of leasing oyster freezing equipment
$P(D \geqq X)$	represent the probability that demand will not fall below X dozen oysters in any given week

Then, from the data in the problem:

$c = £4.5; h = £3; s = £2$
$\mu = 200; \sigma = 80; F = 500$

The profit-maximising size of weekly order for oysters X^* is such that $P(D \geqq X^*) = 3/9.5 = 0.316$. From tables of the inverse normal function, it may be seen that an area of 0.316 under the standardised normal distribution lies to the right of a value of $z = 0.479$. X^* thus lies 0.479 standard deviations (of 80) to the right of the mean (of 200). That is:

$$X^* = 200 + (80)(0.479) = 238 \text{ dozen oysters}$$

Since the freezing equipment will never contain oysters derived from 2 weeks' orders at the same time, it is plain that its capacity of 300 dozen oysters is ample. The expected profit per week is given by $E(Z)$, where:

$$E(Z) = (6.5)(238) - (9.5)[(238 - 200)\Phi(0.479) + 80f_N (0.479)] - (2)(200) - 500$$

Here, $\Phi(0.479)$ represents the probability that a standard normal random variable is less than $z = 0.479$, and $f_N (0.479)$ represents the value of the standard normal probability density function at $z = 0.479$. Evaluation of this expression gives $E(Z) = 130$, so that the average profit per week obtainable from ordering the profit-maximising volume of oysters is seen to be £130.

2. A target of 'at least breaking even' can alternatively be expressed as one of 'earning a minimum acceptable contribution Y_t which is equal to the level of fixed costs F'. Hence in this case $Y_t = 500$. Let:

D_U and D_L represent (respectively) the largest and smallest demands for oysters in a week which are consistent with breaking even in that week

Then

$$D_U = \frac{(4.5+2)(238) - 500}{2} = 523$$

$$D_L = \frac{(3)(238) + 500}{(4.5 + 3)} = 162$$

The probability of at least breaking even in a week in which X^* = 238 dozen oysters have been ordered may be written as $P_{238}[Z \geqq 0]$, where:

$$P_{238}[Z \geqq 0] \quad = \Phi\left(\frac{523-200}{80}\right) - \Phi\left(\frac{162-200}{80}\right)$$

$$= 1 - 0.317 = 0.683$$

When the profit-maximising size of orders for oysters is made, Bridgegate's trade in oysters will at least break even (net of costs of ill-will) slightly more often than 2 weeks out of 3.

3. The size of weekly order X^{**} for which P_X^{**} $(Z \geqq 0)$ is maximised is given by:

$$X^{**} = \frac{(1\,409.18) + \sqrt{(1\,409.18)^2 - (10.4025)(157\,928)}}{10.4025}$$

$$= 192 \text{ dozen oysters per week}$$

For this size of order, the probability of at least breaking even in a given week is obtained from:

$$P_{192}[Z \geqq 0] \quad = \Phi\left(\frac{374 - 200}{80}\right) - \Phi\left(\frac{143.5 - 200}{80}\right)$$

$$= 0.985 - 0.240 = 0.745$$

The effect of setting out to maximise the probability of at least breaking even has been to raise the frequency of its occurrence from roughly 2 weeks out of 3 to roughly 3 weeks out of 4. This satisficing strategy has an expected profit $E(Z)$ given by:

$$\begin{aligned} E(Z) &= (4.5+2)(192)-(4.5+2+3)[(192-200) \\ &\quad (0.4602)+(80)(0.397]-(2)(200)-500 \\ &= 81.25 \end{aligned}$$

The expected weekly cost of adopting the satisficing approach here rather than a profit-maximising one is thus given by £130−£81.25 = £48.75.

When the probability of at least breaking even is maximised, this probability is 0.745. Hence the maximum probability of at least breaking even in 6 or more of the 8 weeks in the 'trial period' can be obtained by answering the following question:

'What is the probability of obtaining six or more successes in eight trials of a Bernouilli process with a probability of success of 0.745?'

Denoting the above probability as P_s, by the binomial theorem:

$$P_s = 8C6(0.745)^6 (0.255)^2 + 8C7(0.745)^7 (0.255) + (0.745)^8$$
$$= 0.6661$$

Given the way in which Bridgegate's management propose to judge the 'success' of the oyster stocking policy, the best order quantity that can be adopted gives this policy two chances in three of meeting their 'success' criterion.

4. To answer this question, it is necessary to recalculate X^{**} with $F = 550$ instead of $F = 500$. Doing this gives $X^{**} = 199$ dozen oysters per week, an increase of seven dozen oysters over the quantity per week to be ordered when $F = 500$. Here again, an increase in fixed cost, in diminishing corporate wealth, causes increasingly risk-averse managers to be willing to bear greater risk. As the quantity ordered increases, so the probability distribution for profit in a week becomes more widely spread and less peaked.

Stochastic Cost–Volume–Profit Analysis: Choice Among Combinations of Products

13

Galpen Cleansing Products

1. Given that Galpen's management have decided that one of the Rythalax-based products designated $X_1 \ldots X_4$ will have to be dropped, there are four alternative strategies open to them. These may be described and labelled as being:

To make	Which call Strategy
X_1, X_2 and X_3 only	A
X_1, X_2 and X_4 only	B
X_1, X_3 and X_4 only	C
X_2, X_3 and X_4 only	D

To establish some terminology, let:

$\hat{\mu}_i$ represent the (sample) mean demand for product X_i

$\hat{\sigma}_i$ represent the (sample) standard deviation of demand for product X_i

$\hat{\sigma}_{ij}$ represent the variance of demand for product X_i if $i = j$

$\hat{\sigma}_{ij}$ represent the covariance of demand between products X_i and X_j if $i \neq j$

The variance-covariance matrix for the four products then appears as follows:

	X_1	X_2	X_3	X_4
X_1	$\hat{\sigma}_{11} = 102\,400$	$\hat{\sigma}_{12} = -39\,040$	$\hat{\sigma}_{13} = 77\,280$	$\hat{\sigma}_{14} = 35\,520$
X_2	$\hat{\sigma}_{21} = -39\,040$	$\hat{\sigma}_{22} = 93\,025$	$\hat{\sigma}_{23} = 42\,090$	$\hat{\sigma}_{24} = 67\,710$
X_3	$\hat{\sigma}_{31} = 77\,280$	$\hat{\sigma}_{32} = 42\,090$	$\hat{\sigma}_{33} = 119\,025$	$\hat{\sigma}_{34} = -63\,825$
X_4	$\hat{\sigma}_{41} = 35\,520$	$\hat{\sigma}_{42} = 67\,710$	$\hat{\sigma}_{43} = -63\,825$	$\hat{\sigma}_{44} = 136\,900$

Some necessary additional terminology is as follows. Let:

c_i — represent the contribution margin per pack for product X_i

f_i — represent the fixed cost outlay per week for product X_i

$E(\hat{Y}_X)$ — represent the estimated mean of the probability density function for profit associated with a given Strategy X

$V(\hat{Y}_X)$ — represent the estimated variance of the probability density function for profit associated with a given Strategy X

Computation yields the following values for the mean and standard deviation of profit associated with each of Strategies A–D, listed in alphabetical order:

$E(\hat{Y}_A) = £790;$ $\sqrt{V(\hat{Y}_A)} = £4675.7$
$E(\hat{Y}_B) = £1\,170;$ $\sqrt{V(\hat{Y}_B)} = £4882.8$
$E(\hat{Y}_C) = £1\,223;$ $\sqrt{V(\hat{Y}_C)} = £4661.4$
$E(\hat{Y}_D) = £1\,959;$ $\sqrt{V(\hat{Y}_D)} = £4745.2$

In general terms, the probability of at least breaking even associated with a given Strategy X is obtained as $P(Y_X \geqq 0)$, where:

$$P(Y_X \geqq 0) = 1 - P\left[z < \frac{0 - E(\hat{Y}_X)}{\sqrt{V(\hat{Y}_X)}} \right]$$

Point estimates of this probability for each of Strategies A–D are listed below:

Strategy	Point estimate of probability
A	$P(Y_A \geqq 0) = 0.57$
B	$P(Y_B \geqq 0) = 0.59$
C	$P(Y_C \geqq 0) = 0.60$
D	$P(Y_D \geqq 0) = 0.66$

While these probabilities are sufficiently close together for the choice of strategy to be swayed by non-quantitative considerations, as they stand they indicate a clear (if small) preference for Strategy D. This strategy will, therefore, be the focus of the next section.

2. The 90 per cent confidence limits around the expected profit $E(Y_D)$ of Strategy D are given by:

$$1959 - t_{19} \sqrt{\frac{(4\,745.2)^2}{20}} < E(Y_D) < 1959$$

$$+ \, t_{19} \sqrt{\frac{(4\,745.2)^2}{20}}$$

Here t_{19} represents the t-value for 19 degrees of freedom which corresponds to an area of 0.10 in both tails of the t-distribution combined. Carrying out the computation gives 90 per cent confidence limits for $E(Y_D)$ of:

$$£124.43 < E(Y_D) < £3\,793.57$$

The 90 per cent confidence limits around the standard deviation of profits from Strategy D are given by:

$$\frac{4\,745.2\sqrt{19}}{\sqrt{\chi^2_{19,0.95}}} < \sqrt{V(Y_D)} < \frac{4\,734.2\sqrt{19}}{\sqrt{\chi^2_{19,0.05}}}$$

Here, $\chi^2_{19,0.95}$ represents the value of the chi-squared distribution such that the area in the right tail is 0.05 and $\chi^2_{19,0.05}$ represents the value of the chi-squared distribution such that the area in the left tail is 0.05. Carrying out the computation gives 90 per cent confidence limits for $\sqrt{V(Y_D)}$ of:

$$£3\,767.56 < \sqrt{V(Y_D)} < £6\,501.91$$

The probability $P(Y_D \geq 0)$ must lie within the limits imposed by the application of the following:

(a) The upper bound on the 90 per cent confidence interval for $E(Y_D)$, together with the lower bound on the 90 per cent confidence interval for $\sqrt{V(Y_D)}$

(b) The lower bound on the 90 per cent confidence interval for $E(Y_D)$, together with the upper bound on the 90 per cent confidence interval for $\sqrt{V(Y_D)}$

In numerical terms, this appears as below:

$$1-P\left(z<\frac{0-3\,793.57}{3\,767.56}\right)\geq P(Y_D>0)\geq 1-P\left(z<\frac{0-124.43}{6\,501.91}\right)$$

Computation yields $0.84 \geq P(Y_D > 0) \geq 0.51$. To say that 'Strategy D is the safest strategy, and in respect of it there is a 90 per cent certainty that the probability of breaking even does not exceed four chances in five nor is it less than 50–50', seems a fairly weak assertion. Yet it is based on a moderately lengthy sampling period of 20 weeks. This is an example of the (probably quite common) situation in which statistical techniques can do no more than throw a modest amount of light on the issues involved; the rest is up to management.

Short-term Investment of Cash Balances

14

Maselia Ltd

The first step in dealing with this problem is to draw up a table of the cumulative cash demand A_{jt} associated with $t = 1 \ldots 4$ for each branch $j = 1 \ldots 15$ of the probability tree. This is done below:

Cumulative cash demand A_{jt} for cash sequence j in month t

Cash sequence	Month				Probability of Sequence $j(p_j)$
	$t = 1$	$t = 2$	$t = 3$	$t = 4$	
	£K	£K	£K	£K	
$j = 1$	0	5	10	20	0.0336
$j = 2$	0	5	10	25	0.0504
$j = 3$	0	5	15	25	0.0360
$j = 4$	0	10	15	20	0.0108
$j = 5$	0	10	15	25	0.0252
$j = 6$	0	10	20	25	0.1440
$j = 7$	5	10	15	25	0.0800
$j = 8$	5	10	20	25	0.1200
$j = 9$	5	15	15	25	0.1400
$j = 10$	5	15	20	20	0.0300
$j = 11$	5	15	20	25	0.0300
$j = 12$	10	10	15	25	0.0480
$j = 13$	10	10	20	25	0.0720
$j = 14$	10	15	20	25	0.1350
$j = 15$	10	15	25	25	0.0450

1

Next, it is necessary to tabulate, for the jth cash sequence, the month τ_{jk} as representing the first month in which cash layer k is used up. This tabulation is shown below, for five cash layers, each of £5 000.

Values of τ_{jk} for cash sequence j and cash layer k

Cash Sequence	k = 1	k = 2	Cash layer k = 3	k = 4	k = 5
j = 1	2	3	4	4	–
j = 2	2	3	4	4	4
j = 3	2	3	3	4	4
j = 4	2	2	3	4	–
j = 5	2	2	3	4	4
j = 6	2	2	3	3	4
j = 7	1	2	3	4	4
j = 8	1	2	3	3	4
j = 9	1	2	2	4	4
j = 10	1	2	2	3	–
j = 11	1	2	2	3	4
j = 12	1	1	3	4	4
j = 13	1	1	3	3	4
j = 14	1	1	2	3	4
j = 15	1	1	2	3	3

From this data, the sets Ω_{kt} can be built up, each set representing that group of cash sequences in which cash layer k is first used up at the end of month t. This is done below, with the symbol ϕ being used to indicate the existence of an empty set.

Sequences in Ω_{kt}

Cash layer	Month t=1	t=2	t=3	t=4
k=1	[7 ... 15]	[1 ... 6]	φ	φ
k=2	[12 ... 15]	[4 ... 11]	[1 ... 3]	φ
k=3	φ	[9,10,11,14,15]	[3,4,5,6,7,8,12,13]	[1,2]
k=4	φ	φ	[6,8,10,11,13,14,15]	[1...5,7,9,12]
k=5	φ	φ	[15]	[2,3,5...9,11...14]

Letting π_{kt} represent the probability that the kth layer of cash will be used up in month t, a tabulation of the values of π_{kt} at $t = 0$ can be drawn up as follows:

Values of π_{kt} at $t=0$

Cash layer	Month			
	$t=1$	$t=2$	$t=3$	$t=4$
$k = 1$	0.7	0.3	0	0
$k = 2$	0.3	0.58	0.12	0
$k = 3$	0	0.38	0.536	0.084
$k = 4$	0	0	0.576	0.424
$k = 5$	0	0	0.045	0.8806

The return on a 1-month security in this problem is certain, and for a single cash layer it amounts to $5\,000(0.018) - [(0.006)(5\,000)+18] = $ £42. Each cash layer has its own planning horizon; for $k = 1$ it is $n = 2$, for $k = 2$ it is $n = 3$ and for $k = 3,4,5$ it is $n = 4$. Expected returns net of transaction costs now have to be worked out, for the available patterns of investment and reinvestment in securities of differing maturities, up to the planning horizon for each cash layer. Representing the expected net return from investing cash layer k at the end of month t in a security maturing after m_t months as $r_{kt}(m_t)$, tabulations appear as follows:

Values of $r_{kt}(m_t)$ for cash layer $k = 1$

Time of investment	Duration of security to maturity m_t (months)		
	0	1	2
$t = 0$	0	42	10.9
$t = 1$	0	12.6	
$t = 2$	0		

Values of $r_{kt}(m_t)$ for cash layer $k = 2$

Time of investment	Duration of security to maturity m_t (months)			
	0	1	2	3
$t = 0$	0	42	80.1	22.46
$t = 1$	0	29.4	-7.94	
$t = 2$	0	5.04		
$t = 3$	0			

Values of $r_{kt}(m_t)$ for cash layer $k = 3$

Time of investment	Duration of security to maturity m_t (months)				
	0	1	2	3	4
$t = 0$	0	42	132	143	68.51
$t = 1$	0	42	66.26	10.57	
$t = 2$	0	26.04	−10.89		
$t = 3$	0	3.53			
$t = 4$	0				

Values of $r_{kt}(m_t)$ for cash layer $k = 4$

Time of investment	Duration of security to maturity m_t (months)				
	0	1	2	3	4
$t = 0$	0	42	132	222	172.03
$t = 1$	0	42	132	102.19	
$t = 2$	0	42	32.35		
$t = 3$	0	17.81			
$t = 4$	0				

Values of $r_{kt}(m_t)$ for cash layer $k = 5$

Time of investment	Duration of security to maturity m_t (months)				
	0	1	2	3	4
$t = 0$	0	42	132	222	301.06
$t = 1$	0	42	132	212.64	
$t = 2$	0	42	124.22		
$t = 3$	0	40.11			
$t = 4$	0				

The final step in this analysis involves using dynamic programming to specify the optimal investment policy. This policy must cover the period up to the planning horizon for each layer. The horizon is located at $n = 2$ months for cash layer $k = 1$, at $n = 3$ months for cash layer $k = 2$, and at $n = 4$ months for cash layers $k = 3,4,5$. The dynamic programming involves the backward solution of a recurrence relation for f_t, as representing the maximum expected net return from investing a given cash layer between the end of month t and the planning horizon for that layer. This process of backward solution gives rise to the following computations:

Cash layer k = 1

$$f_2 = 0$$
$$f_1 = \text{Max.} \, [\{r_1(0) + f_2\}, \, m_1 = 1 \, \{r_1(m_1) + f_{1+m_1}\}]$$
$$f_1 = \text{Max.} \, [(0+0), \, (12.6+0)] = 12.6, \text{ where } m_1 = 1$$

$$f_0 = \text{Max.} \, [\{r_0(0) + f_1\}, \, m_0 = \underset{\text{Max.}}{1,2} \, \{r_0(m_0 + f_{m_0})\}]$$

$$= \text{Max.} \, [(0+12.6), \, \text{Max.} \, \{(42+12.6), \, (10.9+0)\}] = 54.6,$$
where $m_0 = 1$

Cash layer k = 2

$$f_3 = 0$$
$$f_2 = \text{Max.} \, [\{r_2(0) + f_3\}, \, m_2 = 1 \, \{r_2(m_2) + f_{2+m_2}\}]$$
$$= \text{Max.} \, [(0+0), \, (5.04)] = 5.04, \text{ where } m_2 = 1$$

$$f_1 = \text{Max.} \, [\{r_1(0) + f_2\}, \, m_1 = \underset{\text{Max.}}{1,2} \, \{r_1(m_1) + f_{1+m_1}\}]$$

$$= \text{Max.} \, [(0+5.04), \, \text{Max.} \, \{(29.4+5.04), \, (-7.94+0)\}]$$
$$= 34.44, \text{ where } m_1 = 1$$

$$f_0 = \text{Max.} \, [\{r_0(0) + f_1\}, \, m_0 = \underset{\text{Max.}}{1,2,3} \, \{r_0(m_0) + f_{m_0}\}]$$

$$= \text{Max.} \, [(0+34.44), \, \text{Max.} \, \{(42+34.44), \, (80.1+5.04),$$
$$(22.46+0)\}]$$
$$= 85.14, \text{ where } m_0 = 2$$

Cash layer k = 3

$$f_4 = 0$$

$f_3 = \text{Max.} [\{r_3(0) + f_4\}, m_3 = 1 \{r_3(m_3) + f_{3+m_3}\}]$

$f_3 = \text{Max.} [(0+0), (3.53+0)] = 3.53$, where $m_3 = 1$

$f_2 = \text{Max.} [\{r_2(0) + f_3\}, m_2 = \underset{\text{Max.}}{1,2} \{r_2(m_2) + f_{2+m_2}\}]$

$f_2 = \text{Max.} [(0+3.53), \text{Max.} \{(26.04+3.53), (-10.89+0)\}]$
$= 29.57$, where $m_2 = 1$

$f_1 = \text{Max.} [\{r_1(0) + f_2\}, m_1 = \underset{\text{Max.}}{1,2,3} \{r_1(m_1) + f_{1+m_1}\}]$

$= \text{Max.} [(0+29.57), \text{Max.} \{(42+29.57), (66.26+3.53),$
$(10.57+0)\}]$
$= 71.57$, where $m_1 = 1$

$f_0 = \text{Max.} [\{r_0(0) + f_1\}, m_0 = \underset{\text{Max.}}{1,2,3,4} \{r_0(m_0) + f_{m_0}\}]$

$= \text{Max.}[(0+71.57), \text{Max.} \{(42+71.57), (132+29.57),$
$(143+3.53), (68.51+0)\}]$
$= 161.57$, where $m_0 = 2$

Cash layer k = 4

$$f_4 = 0$$

$f_3 \quad = \text{Max.} [(0+0), (17.81 + 0)] = 17.81$, where $m_3 = 1$

$f_2 \quad = \text{Max.}[(0+17.81), \text{Max.}\{(42+17.81), (32.35+0)\}] =$
$\quad\quad 59.81$, where $m_2 = 1$

$f_1 \quad = \text{Max.} [(0+59.81), \text{Max.}\{(42+59.81), (132+17.81),$
$\quad\quad (102.19+0)\}]$
$\quad\quad = 149.81$, where $m_1 = 2$

$f_0 \quad = \text{Max.} [(0+149.81), \text{Max.}\{(42+149.81), (132+59.81),$
$\quad\quad (222+17.81), (172.03+0)\}] = 239.81$, where $m_0 = 3$

Cash layer k = 5

$$f_4 = 0$$

f_3 = Max.[(0+0), (40.11 + 0)] = 40.11, where $m_3 = 1$

f_2 = Max.[(0+40.11), Max. {(42+40.11), (124.22+0)}]
  = 124.22, where $m_2 = 2$

f_1 = Max.[(0+124.22), Max.{(42+124.22), (132+40.11), (212.64+0)}]
  = 212.64, where $m_1 = 3$

f_0 = Max.[(0+212.64), Max.{(42+212.64), (132+124.22), (222+40.11), (301.06+0)}]
  = 301.06, where $m_0 = 4$

Overall optimal plan

From the above computations, the overall optimal short-term investment programme may be built up as follows:

Invest £5 000 (layer $k = 1$) in 1-month securities at time $t = 0$
If this layer is not required to meet payments at $t = 1$, it should be reinvested in 1-month securities.

Invest £10 000 (layers $k = 2$ and $k = 3$) in 2-month securities at time $t = 0$.
If layer $k = 2$ is not required to meet payments at either $t = 1$ or $t = 2$, it should be reinvested at $t = 2$ in 1-month securities. If layer $k = 3$ is not required to meet payments at $t = 2$, it should be reinvested in 1-month securities, and an identical further reinvestment should take place if layer $k = 3$ is not required to meet payments at $t = 3$.

Invest £5 000 (layer $k = 4$) in 3-month securities at time $t = 0$
If this layer is not required for payments at $t = 3$, it should be reinvested in 1-month securities.

Finally, invest £5 000 (layer $k = 5$) in 4-month securities at time $t = 0$.

The aggregate expected net return for all five layers, ignoring any cost savings arising from investing or disinvesting more than one cash layer in securities of a given maturity at the same time, is £842.18.

A cost saving equal to the fixed transaction cost of £18 is made every time two cash layers are invested or disinvested in securities of a given maturity. The following are the cases where this can happen within the optimal strategy, together with their probabilities of occurrence and the expected cost savings arising from these probabilities.

Transaction	*Probability of occurrence*	*Expected cost savings*
		£
Layers $k = 2$ and $k = 3$ invested in 2-month securities at $t = 0$	1	18.0
Layers $k = 2$ and $k = 3$ invested in 1-month securities at $t = 2$	(0.12)(0.62)=0.0744	1.34
Layers $k = 3$ and $k = 4$ invested in 1-month securities at $t = 3$	(0.084)(0.424)=0.0356	0.64
Expected cost savings		19.98

When these expected cost savings are added to the total expected net return (computed without regard to these savings) a final figure for the expected value of the optimal investment policy is obtained as £862.16.

Payments Netting in Multinational Cash Management

15

Thornend Communication Systems PLC

The first step here is to classify the subsidiaries according to their net indebtedness positions. For subsidiary i, the net inflow or outflow of cash consequent upon overall debt settlement is given by f_i. The classification of subsidiaries by their f_i values – and the a_i and b_i values which follow from them – can be done in a way leading to the following tabulation:

Subsidiary	No.	f_i value	
UK	$i = j = 1$	16	$a_1 = 16$
Germany	$i = j = 2$	5	$a_2 = 5$
Sweden	$i = j = 3$	31	$a_3 = 31$
USA	$i = j = 4$	−9	$b_4 = 9$
France	$i = j = 5$	−43	$b_5 = 43$

It is then convenient to rewrite the table of transaction costs in terms of the i and j values, as follows:

Transfer between	*and*	*Costs as proportion of £ value transferred*
$i = 1$	$j = 2$	0.008
$i = 1$	$j = 3$	0.012
$i = 1$	$j = 4$	0.006
$i = 1$	$j = 5$	0.009
$i = 2$	$j = 3$	0.013
$i = 2$	$j = 4$	0.009
$i = 2$	$j = 5$	0.007
$i = 3$	$j = 4$	0.013
$i = 3$	$j = 5$	0.011
$i = 4$	$j = 5$	0.010

From the above data, $m = 3$ and $n = 5$. Hence the general form of the constraints is:

$$\sum_{\substack{j=1 \\ j \neq i}}^{5} x_{ij} = a_i \qquad i = 1 \ldots 3$$

$$\sum_{\substack{i=1 \\ i \neq j}}^{5} x_{ij} = b_j \qquad j = 4,5$$

In detail, the constraints are as follows:

$$x_{12} + x_{13} + x_{14} + x_{15} = 16 \qquad (1)$$
$$x_{21} + x_{23} + x_{24} + x_{25} = 5 \qquad (2)$$
$$x_{31} + x_{32} + x_{34} + x_{35} = 31 \qquad (3)$$
$$x_{14} + x_{24} + x_{34} + x_{54} = 9 \qquad (4)$$
$$x_{15} + x_{25} + x_{35} + x_{45} = 43 \qquad (5)$$

The general form of the objective function is:

$$\text{Minimise} \sum_{i=1}^{3} \sum_{\substack{j=1 \\ j \neq i}}^{5} c_{ij}\, x_{ij} + \sum_{i=4}^{5} \sum_{\substack{j=4 \\ i \neq j}}^{5} c_{ij}\, x_{ij}$$

When written out in full, letting the total transaction cost incurred be C, the objective function appears as:

$$\text{Minimise } C = 0.008x_{12} + 0.012x_{13} + 0.006x_{14} + 0.009x_{15} +$$
$$0.008x_{21} + 0.013x_{23} + 0.009x_{24} + 0.007x_{25} + 0.012x_{31} +$$
$$0.013x_{32} + 0.013x_{34} + 0.011x_{35} + 0.010x_{54} + 0.010x_{45}$$

Solving this linear programming problem gives the following result:

$$x_{14} = 9; \ x_{15} = 7; \ x_{25} = 5; \ x_{35} = 31; \ C = 0.493$$

The payments netting scheme to which this gives rise involves transfers of funds as below, with all amounts in sterling equivalents:

1. The United Kingdom transfers £90 000 worth of funds to the United States.
2. The United Kingdom transfers £70 000 worth of funds to France.
3. Germany transfers £50 000 worth of funds to France.
4. Sweden transfers £310 000 worth of funds to France.

This solution involves transferring a total of £520 000 worth of funds, as compared with the £4 920 000 worth that would be transferred in the absence of any netting procedure. The total transactions cost of this solution is £4 930; even a complete bilateral netting solution would involve a total cost of £13 310.

As a matter of interest, the best that can be done with bilateral netting only is to produce a solution as follows:

$$x_{14} = 11; \ x_{15} = 11; \ x_{12} = 3; \ x_{31} = 9; \ x_{45} = 32$$
$$x_{42} = 6; \ x_{34} = 36; \ x_{25} = 2; \ x_{53} = 2; \ x_{23} = 12$$

Trying to work from a diagram of the best bilateral netting in order to find the best multilateral netting by eye is an unwieldy approach here. The bilateral netting diagram contains ten arrows connecting five nodes, and it is easy to miss an opportunity for netting in the face of its complexity. The linear programming approach, which has the additional advantage of taking differing unit transfer costs into account, is to be preferred even though only five countries are involved. With more countries, multilateral netting without linear programming swiftly becomes infeasible.

The Learning Curve and Financial Planning

16

Claygill Holdings

The data on cumulative average numbers of hours spent and on cumulative output has been subjected to a logarithmic transformation in order to turn a curvilinear relation into a log-linear form. For the purpose of further calculation, it is necessary to take antilogarithms, giving:

$$y = 804.3x^{-0.1203}$$

This is the usual formulation of the learning curve, here with $a = 804.3$ and $b = -0.1203$ so that $b + 1 = 0.8797$. The learning rate R is given by solving $\ln R = b \ln 2$, so that here $R = 0.92$. This is equivalent to saying that the regression on the data from the temporary production line has identified the presence of a 92 per cent learning curve. Before accepting this finding in practice, it would be prudent to compute the 95 per cent confidence interval for the value of b in the regression; insufficient data is given for this purpose in the problem.

Denoting by f_1 the cash outlay on fixed costs per annum associated with a single production line, and by f_2 the corresponding outlay for two production lines, the other parameters relevant to finding break-even levels in the first year may be written as follows:

$$p = 3\,000; c = 4.5; f_1 = 280\,000; f_2 = 250\,000$$

1. In approaching this part of the problem, the assumption will first be made that learning continues throughout the 2 years. If this is the case, then for one-line working the break-even level in the first year is given by that value of x which satisfies the equation:

$$3\,000x - 3\,619.35x^{0.8797} - 280\,000 = 0$$

i.e. $x = 247$ AIF units

For two-line working, the break-even level in the first year is given by that value of x which satisfies the equation:

$$3\,000x - (2)(3\,619.35)(0.5^{0.8797})x^{\,0.8797} - 250\,000 = 0$$

i.e. $x = 255$ AIF units

Although running two lines instead of one reduces the outlay on fixed costs by £30 000 in the first year, the break-even point is still higher for two lines than it is for one line. This is because the fixed cost advantage of two lines is just slightly outweighed by the disadvantage arising from the slower progress of two lines down their learning curves relative to the progress of one faster line down its learning curve.

The other case which requires consideration is that in which the learning effect ceases once a level of efficiency has been reached at which an AIF is produced in 400 labour hours. Here, the first step is to find the level of output x_s at which learning effects are exhausted. For an individual production line, this level is given by a cumulative production of:

$$x_s = [400/\{(804.3)(0.8797)\}]^{1/-0.1203} = 115 \text{ AIF units}$$

For one-line working, learning effects are thus exhausted after 115 AIF units have been produced, and for two-line working these effects are exhausted after 115 units have been produced on each line, that is after a cumulative production of 230 units. For both the one-line and two-line cases, the break-even levels already calculated lie above the levels of output at which learning is exhausted. Consequently, both of these break-even levels will be raised by revising the assumption made from the continuous learning one to one of a limit constraining the learning effect. Break-even levels with the 'constrained learning' assumption may be recalculated as below:

For one-line working, it is first necessary to compute the total number of labour hours T_s required to exhaust the learning effect.

This is given by:

$$T_s = (804.3)(115^{0.8797}) = 52\,265 \text{ hr}$$

The break-even level is then given by that value of x which satisfies the equation:

$$x = \frac{(4.5)(52\,265) - (4.5)(400)(115) + 280\,000}{3\,000 - (4.5)(400)}$$

$$= 257 \text{ AIF units}$$

For two-line working, the number of labour hours required to exhaust the learning effect must be exactly double the number required for one-line working. Consequently, the break-even level is given by that value of x which satisfies the equation:

$$x = \frac{(4.5)(2)(52\,265) - (4.5)(2)(400)(115) + 250\,000}{3\,000 - (4.5)(400)}$$

$$= 255 \text{ AIF units}$$

With two-line working, the effect of the constraint on learning arises only after the break-even level has been almost reached, and thus has a negligible effect on this level (raising it only by 0.2 of a unit). However, with one-line working, the effect of the constraint on learning is felt at a relatively low level of output, and since no further learning is experienced beyond this level, the break-even value is raised quite sharply.

2. The first case which will be considered is that in which learning continues throughout the first 2 years. For this case, the calculations are as follows:

One production line: first year

Output x_1 is given by:

$$x_1 = \left(\frac{110\,000}{804.3}\right)^{1/0.8797} = 268 \text{ AIF units}$$

Profit π_1 is given by:

$$\pi_1 = (3\,000)(268) - (4.5)(804.3)(268^{0.8797}) - 280\,000$$
$$= £28\,937$$

One produc.ion line: second year

Output x_2 is given by:

$$x_2 = \left(\frac{220\,000}{804.3}\right)^{1/0.8797} - 268$$

$$= 321 \text{ AIF units}$$

Profit π_2 is given by the cumulative profit on the first 2 years of output together *less* the profit on the first year (already calculated). That is,

$$\pi_2 = (3\,000)(589) - (4.5)(804.3)(589^{0.8797}) - 560\,000 - 28\,937$$
$$= £188\,369$$

Two production lines: first year

Output x_1 is given by:

$$x_1 = (2)\left(\frac{55\,000}{804.3}\right)^{1/0.8797} = 244 \text{ AIF units}$$

Profit π_1 is given by:

$$\pi_1 = (3\,000)(244) - (2)(4.5)(804.3)(0.5^{0.8797})(244^{0.8797}) - 250\,000$$
$$= -£13\,493, \text{ that is a loss of } £13\,493$$

Two production lines: second year

Output x_2 is given by:

$$x_2 = (2)\left(\frac{110\,000}{804.3}\right)^{1/0.8797} - 244$$

$$= 292 \text{ AIF units}$$

Profit π_2 is given by:

$$\pi_2 = (3\,000)(536) - (2)(4.5)(804.3)(0.5^{0.8797})(536^{0.8797}) - 500\,000 + 13\,493$$
$$= £131\,354$$

If learning ceases once an efficiency level of 400 labour hours per unit produced has been achieved, then the calculations of output and profit levels will appear as follows:

One production line: first year

Output x_1 is given by:

$$x_1 = (110\,000 - 52\,265)/400 + 115$$
$$= 259 \text{ AIF units}$$

Profit π_1 is given by:

$$\pi_1 = (3\,000)(259) - (4.5)(52\,265) - (4.5)(400)(259 - 115) - 280\,000 = £2\,607$$

One production line: second year

Learning effects have been exhausted by the second year, so that output x_2 is given by:

$$x_2 = \frac{110\,000}{400} = 275 \text{ AIF units}$$

Profit π_2 is given by:

$$\pi_2 = (3\,000)(275) - (4.5)(110\,000) - 280\,000$$
$$= £50\,000$$

Two production lines: first year

Output x_1 is given by:

$$x_1 = (110\,000 - 104\,530)/400 + 230$$
$$= 244 \text{ AIF units}$$

Profit π_1 is given by:

$$\pi_1 = (3\,000)(244) - (4.5)(104\,530) - (4.5)(400)(244 - 230) -$$
$$250\,000 = -\,£13\,585 \text{ loss}$$

Two production lines: second year

Learning effects have been exhausted by the second year, so that output x_2 is given by:

$$x_2 = \frac{(2)(55\,000)}{400} = 275 \text{ AIF units}$$

Profit π_2 is given by:

$$\pi_2 = (3\,000)(275) - (4.5)(110\,000) - 250\,000$$
$$= £80\,000$$

The answer to part 2 of the problem may be summarised in terms of the following cash flows:

If learning continues over 2 years

	Year 1	Year 2
	£	£
One production line	28 937	188 369
Two production lines	−13 493	131 354

If learning stops at 400 labour hours

	Year 1	Year 2
	£	£
One production line	2 607	50 000
Two production lines	−13 585	80 000

The question of whether learning ceases, and if so at what level of efficiency, is seen to affect both the overall return from producing AIF units and the relative attractiveness of doing so on either one or two production lines.

3. Representing δ_1 as the proportional error in the learning rate and δ_2 as the proportional error in the initial assembly time gives rise, in this question, to $\delta_1 = 0.98$ and $\delta_2 = 1.1$. The revised output estimate for one-line working in the first year x_1' and the second year x_2' is:

$$x_1' = \left[\frac{110\,000}{(1.1)(804.3)} \right]^{1/[\{\ln(0.98)(0.92)/\ln 2\} + 1]}$$

$$= 290 \text{ AIF units}$$

$$x_2' = \left[\frac{220\,000}{(1.1)(804.3)} \right]^{1/[\{\ln(0.98)(0.92)/\ln 2\} + 1]} - 290$$

$$= 365 \text{ AIF units}$$

These results should be compared against those at the beginning of part 2. of the problem. It may then be seen that a relatively small fall in the learning rate R (that is, a relatively small increase in the gradient of the learning curve) more than offsets a relatively large increase in the initial assembly time.

Joint Product Decisions

Kwisant Oils

1. For each of the three products sold under imperfectly competitive conditions, the (linear) demand function may be taken to have the form $P = a - bD$, where:

P represents the price charged per litre
D represents the demand, in litres per week
b represents the gradient of the function
a represents the intercept term

Two pairs of D and P values have been estimated for each of the products facing imperfect competition. From these estimates, two simultaneous equations can be set up in order to compute the two unknowns a and b. The results obtained are as follows:

Baxin	Gholak	Seitsol
$2.75 = a - 2300b$	$4 = a - 1100b$	$4.5 = a - 1200b$
$2.25 = a - 3600b$	$3 = a - 1800b$	$3.5 = a - 1400b$
Hence: $a = 3.6346$	Hence: $a = 5.5714$	Hence: $a = 10.5$
$b = 0.000385$	$b = 0.001429$	$b = 0.005$

It is now necessary to define the terms that will be required in the analysis of this problem. Let:

P_B, P_G and P_S	represent respectively the selling prices per litre for Baxin, Gholak and Seitsol
X_B, X_G and X_S	represent respectively the volume of sales (in litres per week) for Baxin, Gholak and Seitsol
H_P	represent the number of litres per week of Haderol used in the manufacture of the final products Gholak and Seitsol
H_C	represent the number of litres per week of Haderol sold to Celos Ltd
X_T	represent the number of litres of Teilu mixture produced per week

Using this terminology, the demand functions for the three products facing imperfect competition appear as follows:

$$P_B = 3.6346 - 0.000385X_B$$
$$P_G = 5.5714 - 0.001429X_G$$
$$P_S = 10.5 - 0.005X_S$$

The revenue per week R is given by:

$$R = P_BX_B + P_GX_G + P_SX_S + 1.8H_C$$

The cost per week C is given by the number of litres of each of the intermediate and final products processed per week, multiplied by the cost of processing per litre. This is given by:

$$C = 0.7X_T + 0.85X_B + 0.55(H_P + H_C) + 1.3X_G + 1.4X_S$$

The profit function is given by $\pi = R - C$. Expanding and simplifying the expressions for R and C gives rise to the following objective function:

$$\text{Maximise } \pi = 2.7846X_B - 0.000385X_B^2 + 4.2714X_G - 0.001429X_G^2 + 9.1X_S - 0.005X_S^2 + 1.25H_C - 0.7X_T - 0.55H_P$$

This maximisation is subject to the following constraints:

$X_B - 0.4X_T \leqq 0$ (that is, the amount of Baxin produced and sold cannot exceed 40 per cent of the amount of Teilu mixture produced)

$H_C + H_P - 0.4X_T \leqq 0$ (that is, the amount of Haderol available either for sale to Celos or for the manufacture of Gholak and Seitsol cannot exceed 40 per cent of the amount of Teilu mixture produced)

$X_G - 0.5H_P \leqq 0$ (that is, the amount of Gholak sold cannot exceed 50 per cent of the amount of Haderol not sold to Celos)

$X_S - 0.375H_P \leqq 0$ (that is, the amount of Seitsol sold cannot exceed 37.5 per cent of the amount of Haderol not sold to Celos)

$X_T, X_B, X_G, X_S, H_P, H_C \geqq 0$ (non-negativity constraints)

Reformulating this problem in the Lagrangean mode enables it to be expressed as:

$$
\begin{aligned}
\text{Maximise } M = \ & 2.7846X_B - 0.000385X_B^2 + 4.2714X_G - \\
& 0.001429X_G^2 + 9.1X_S - 0.005X_S^2 + 1.25H_C \\
& - 0.7X_T - 0.55H_P - \lambda_1(X_B - 0.4X_T) - \\
& \lambda_2(H_C + H_P - 0.4X_T) - \lambda_3(X_G - 0.5H_P) \\
& - \lambda_4(X_S - 0.375H_P)
\end{aligned}
$$

The complementary slackness conditions for this problem are as follows:

$$
\begin{aligned}
& X_B\,[2.7846 - 0.00077X_B - \lambda_1] = 0 \\
& X_G\,[4.2714 - 0.002858X_G - \lambda_3] = 0 \\
& X_S\,[9.1 - 0.01X_S - \lambda_4] = 0 \\
& X_T\,[-0.7 + 0.4\lambda_1 + 0.4\lambda_2] = 0 \\
& H_P\,[-0.55 - \lambda_2 + 0.5\lambda_3 + 0.375\lambda_4] = 0 \\
& H_C\,[1.25 - \lambda_2] = 0
\end{aligned}
$$

$$\lambda_1 \left[0.4X_T - X_B \right] = 0$$
$$\lambda_2 \left[0.4X_T - H_C - H_P \right] = 0$$
$$\lambda_3 \left[0.5H_P - X_G \right] = 0$$
$$\lambda_4 \left[0.375H_P - X_S \right] = 0$$

The interior solution to these conditions is given by:

$$X_T = 7417.5; \; X_B = 2967; \; X_G = 883.7; \; X_S = 662.773$$
$$H_C = 1199.6; \; H_P = 1767.4$$
$$\lambda_1 = 0.5; \; \lambda_2 = 1.25; \; \lambda_3 = 1.7458; \; \lambda_4 = 2.4723$$

With this solution, all the four constraints hold as strict equalities, so that there are no by-products, all the products being joint. In detail, the optimum prices and production levels are as follows:

Product	Sales/Production level	Price
	(l per week)	*(£ per l)*
Baxin	2967.0	2.49
Gholak	883.7	4.31
Seitsol	662.8	7.19
Haderol (for sale to Celos)	1199.6	1.80

These price and production levels give rise to a profit of $\pi =$ £6702 per week.

The marginal revenue functions for Baxin, Gholak and Seitsol are represented respectively by MR_B, MR_G and MR_S, where:

$$MR_B = 3.6346 - 0.00077X_B$$
$$MR_G = 5.5714 - 0.002858X_G$$
$$MR_S = 10.5 - 0.01X_S$$

Denoting the separate processing costs for Baxin, Gholak and Seitsol respectively by C_B, C_G and C_S, from the question $C_B = 0.85$; $C_G = 1.3$; $C_S = 1.4$. In the optimal solution, the following relationship must hold:

Marginal revenue for a product = Allocated joint cost per unit of that product manufactured + Cost of separate processing per unit of that product manufactured

This relationship may be demonstrated for each product as follows:

$$
\begin{aligned}
&& \textit{When} \\
MR_B &= \lambda_1 + C_B = 1.35 & X_B &= 2\,967 \\
MR_G &= \lambda_3 + C_G = 3.0458 & X_G &= 883.7 \\
MR_S &= \lambda_4 + C_S = 3.872 & X_S &= 662.8
\end{aligned}
$$

As regards the Haderol sold to Celos Ltd, the marginal and average revenue are identical at £1.80, which represents the sum of the allocated joint cost $\lambda_2 = £1.25$ and the cost of synthesising Haderol, which is £0.55 per litre.

2. The effect of the restriction on the supply of Teilu mixture is to place another constraint on the solution, of the form that

$$
X_T - 4\,000 \leqq 0
$$

A new term then enters the maximand M, as follows:

$$
M = \ldots -\lambda_5(X_T - 4\,000)
$$

There is also an extra complementary slackness condition, of the form:

$$
\lambda_5 [4\,000 - X_T] = 0
$$

and the condition with X_T outside the square bracket changes to:

$$
X_T [-0.7 + 0.4\lambda_1 + 0.4\lambda_2 - \lambda_5] = 0
$$

The revised interior solution has $H_C = -167.4$, which violates the $H_C \geqq 0$ non-negativity constraint. It is therefore necessary to set $H_C = 0$, so that the $\lambda_2 = 1.25$ equation is eliminated, and the equation with λ_2 outside the square bracket becomes $0.4X_T - H_P = 0$. The solution is then:

$$
\begin{aligned}
X_T &= 4\,000; X_B = 1\,600; X_G = 800; X_S = 600; H_P = 1\,600 \\
\lambda_1 &= 1.5526; \lambda_2 = 1.605; \lambda_3 = 1.985; \lambda_4 = 3.1; \lambda_5 = 0.56304
\end{aligned}
$$

The optimum prices and production levels are:

Product	Sales/production level	Price
	(l per week)	*(£ per l)*
Baxin	1 600	3.02
Gholak	800	4.43
Seitsol	600	7.50

These price and production levels give rise to a profit of $\pi =$ £5 952 per week.

It is important to note that the interpretation of λ as the allocated cost of passing a unit of product through a joint production process ceases to be valid once there are constraints on input availability. An interpretation of the $\lambda_1 = 0.5$, $\lambda_2 = 1.25$ result in part 1. is that the £0.70 per litre cost of producing Teilu mixture can be allocated as $0.4(£0.5) = £0.20$ to Baxin and $0.4(£1.25) = £0.50$ to Haderol. It is not possible to interpret the $\lambda_1 = 1.5526$, $\lambda_2 = 1.605$ result above in this manner, because of the effect of the λ_5 term arising from the resource constraint.

Appendices

Checklist of Topics and Related Problems

1 Standard Costing and Matrix Algebra

Primary Reference	W. Franks and R. Manes, 'A Standard Cost Application of Matrix Algebra', *Accounting Review*, XLII 3 (July 1967) 516–25
Fully-worked Problem	Radium Dyestuffs Ltd
Problem for Self-study	Arconate Ltd

2 Stochastic Process Costing

Primary Reference	A. W. Corcoran and W. E. Leininger, 'Stochastic Process Costing Models', *Accounting Review*, XLVIII 1 (January 1973) 105–14
Fully-worked Problem	Ottoline Electronics
Problem for Self-study	Kleeford Distilled Compounds

3 Credit Management and Markov Chains: Partial Balance Aging Method

Primary Reference	A. W. Corcoran, 'The Use of Exponentially-Smoothed Transition Matrices to Improve Forecasting of Cash Flows from Accounts Receivable', *Management Science*, XXIV 7 (March 1978) 732–9
Fully-worked Problem	Stryford Ltd
Problem for Self-study	Langdale Ltd

4 Credit Management and Markov Chains: Modified Total Balance Aging Method

Primary References	R. M. Cyert, H. J. Davidson and G. L. Thompson, 'Estimation of the Allowance for Doubtful Accounts by Markov Chains', *Management Science*, VIII 3 (April 1962) 287–303
	J. A. M. van Keulen, J. Spronk and A. W. Corcoran, 'On the Cyert–Davidson–Thompson Doubtful Accounts Model', *Management Science*, XXVII 1 (January 1981) 108–12
Fully-worked Problem	Michelsky Ltd
Problem for Self-study	Firenza Associates

5 Linear Programming and Decisions on Internal v. External Purchases of Services

Primary Reference	K. R. Baker and R. E. Taylor, 'A Linear Programming Framework for Cost Allocation

and External Acquisition When Reciprocal Services Exist', *Accounting Review*, LIV 4 (October 1979) 784–90

Fully-worked Problem   Knockshinnock Mines Ltd
Problem for Self-study   Remosense PLC

6 Linear Programming, Opportunity Losses and *ex post* Budgeting

Primary Reference   J. S. Demski, 'An Accounting System Structured on a Linear Programming Model', *Accounting Review*, XLII 4 (October 1967) 701–12

Fully-worked Problem   Araque Perfumes Ltd
Problem for Self-study   Shalmirane Ltd

7 Input–Output Analysis and Linear Programming

Primary Reference   G. A. Feltham, 'Some Quantitative Approaches to Planning for Multiproduct Production Systems', *Accounting Review*, XLV 1 (January 1970) 11–26

Fully-worked Problems   Taumor Industries
                              Salmedge Products
Problems for Self-study   Kerruish Tracers
                              Raistrick Ltd

8 Use of Information Theory to Isolate Substantial Variances

Primary Reference   B. Lev, 'An Information Theory Analysis of Budget Variances', *Accounting Review*, XLIV 4 (October 1969) 704–10

| *Fully-worked Problem* | Heversham Horticulture Ltd |
| *Problem for Self-study* | Department of Transportation Analytical Offices |

9 The Single-period Cost Variance Investigation Decision

Primary References	R. Capettini and D. Collins, 'The Investigation of Deviations from Standard Costs in the Presence of Unequal State Variances', *Journal of Business Finance and Accounting*, V 4 (Winter 1978) 335–51
	T. R. Dyckman, 'The Investigation of Cost Variances', *Journal of Accounting Research*, VII 2 (Autumn 1969) 215–44
Fully-worked Problem	Alston Glassworks
Problem for Self-study	Star Chemical Company

10 The Multi-period Cost Variance Investigation Decision

Primary Reference	D. A. Dittman and P. Prakash, 'Cost Variance Investigation: Markovian Control of Markov Processes', *Journal of Accounting Research*, XVI 1 (Spring 1978) 14–25
Fully-worked Problem	Fitzroy Paper Products
Problem for Self-study	Mansfield Pressings

11 Stochastic Cost–Volume–Profit Analysis and Decision Theory

Primary Reference	J. E. Jarrett, 'An Approach to Cost–Volume–Profit Analysis Under Uncertainty', *Decision Sciences*, IV 3 (July 1973) 405–20
Fully-worked Problem	William Lehman Timber Ltd
Problem for Self-study	Bulk Powder Producers Ltd

12 Stochastic Cost–Volume–Profit Analysis: Satisficing with Short Product Lives

Primary Reference	B. E. Ismail and J. G. Louderback, 'Optimizing and Satisficing in Stochastic Cost–Volume–Profit Analysis', *Decision Sciences*, X 2 (April 1979) 205–17
Fully-worked Problem	Knowsley Medical Products
Problem for Self-study	Bridgegate Foods

13 Stochastic Cost–Volume–Profit Analysis:Choice Among Combinations of Products

Primary Reference	J. P. Dickinson, 'Cost–Volume–Profit Analysis Under Uncertainty', *Journal of Accounting Research*, XII 1 (Spring 1974) 182–7
Fully-worked Problem	Barrow Gurney Orchards Ltd
Problem for Self-study	Galpen Cleansing Products

14 Short-term Investment of Cash Balances

Primary References	J. C. T. Mao and C. E. Sarndal, 'Cash Management: Theory and Practice', *Journal of Business*

Finance and Accounting, V 3 (Autumn 1978) 329–38

A. Punter, 'Optimal Cash Management Under Conditions of Uncertainty', *Journal of Business Finance and Accounting*, IX 3 (Autumn 1982) 329–40

Fully-worked Problem Alvor Developments
Problem for Self-study Maselia Ltd

15 Payments Netting in Multinational Cash Management

Primary Reference A. C. Shapiro, 'Payments Netting in International Cash Management', *Journal of International Business Studies*, IX 2 (Fall 1978) 51–8

Fully-worked Problem Lintock Corporation
Problem for Self-study Thornend Communication Systems PLC

16 The Learning Curve and Financial Planning

Primary References D. W. Harvey, 'Financial Planning Information for Production Start-ups', *Accounting Review*, LI 4 (October 1976) 838–45

E. V. McIntyre, 'Cost–Volume–Profit Analysis Adjusted for Learning', *Management Science*, XXIV 2 (October 1977) 149–60

Fully-worked Problem Holt Electronics PLC
Problem for Self-study Claygill Holdings

17   Joint Product Decisions

Primary Reference   L. R. Amey, 'Joint Product Decisions: The Fixed Proportions
Case', *Journal of Business Finance and Accounting*, XI 3 (Autumn 1984) 295–300

Fully-worked Problem Cydilla Separators Ltd
Problem for Self-study Kwisant Oils

Detailed References by Topic 2

1 Standard Costing and Matrix Algebra

A. D. Bailey, 'Analysis of a Standard Cost Application of Matrix Algebra', in J. L. Livingstone (ed.), *Management Planning and Control: Mathematical Models* (New York: McGraw-Hill, 1970) 207–30.

A. W. Corcoran and W. E. Leininger, 'Isolating Accounting Variances Via Partitioned Matrices', *Accounting Review*, L 1 (January 1975) 184–8.

W. Franks and R. Manes, 'A Standard Cost Application of Matrix Algebra', *Accounting Review*, XLII 3 (July 1967) 516–25.

2 Stochastic Process Costing

A. W. Corcoran and W. E. Leininger, 'Stochastic Process Costing Models', *Accounting Review*, XLVIII 1 (January 1973) 105–14.

J. G. Kemeny and J. L. Snell, *Finite Markov Chains* (New York: Springer–Verlag, 1983) 24–68.

W. E. Leininger, *Quantitative Methods in Accounting* (New York: D. Van Nostrand Co., 1980) 302–10.

3 Credit Management and Markov Chains: Partial Balance Aging Method

A. W. Corcoran, 'The Use of Exponentially-Smoothed Transition Matrices to Improve Forecasting of Cash Flows from Accounts Receivable', *Management Science*, XXIV 7 (March 1978) 732–9.
A. W. Corcoran, *Costs: Accounting, Analysis and Control* (New York: John Wiley and Sons, 1978) 101–8.

4 Credit Management and Markov Chains: Modified Total Balance Aging Method

A. I. Barkman, 'Testing the Markov Chain Approach on Accounts Receivable', *Management Accounting (NAA)* (January 1981) 48–50.
R. M. Cyert, H. J. Davidson and G. L. Thompson, 'Estimation of the Allowance for Doubtful Accounts by Markov Chains', *Management Science*, VIII 3 (April 1962) 287–303.
J. A. M. van Kuelen, J. Spronk and A. W. Corcoran, 'On the Cyert–Davidson–Thompson Doubtful Accounts Model', *Management Science*, XXVII 1 (January 1981) 108–12.
Leininger, *Quantitative Methods*, 55–79.

5 Linear Programming and Decisions on Internal v. External Purchases of Services

K. R. Baker and R. E. Taylor, 'A Linear Programming Framework for Cost Allocation and External Acquisition When Reciprocal Services Exist', *Accounting Review*, LIV 4 (October 1979) 784–90.
R. Capettini and G. L. Salamon, 'Internal Versus External Acquisition of Services When Reciprocal Services Exist', *Accounting Review*, LII 3 (July 1977) 690–6.
Joyce T. Chen, 'Cost Allocation and External Acquisition of

Services When Self-Services Exist', *Accounting Review,* LVIII 3 (July 1983) 600–5.

R. P. Manes, S. H. Park and R. Jensen, 'Relevant Costs of Intermediate Goods and Services', *Accounting Review*, LVII 3 (July 1982) 594–606.

6 Linear Programming, Opportunity Losses and *ex post* Budgeting

L. R. Amey, 'Hindsight v. Expectations in Performance Measurement', in L. R. Amey (ed.), *Readings in Management Decision* (London: Longman, 1973) ch. 12, 258–72.

B. E. Cushing, 'Some Observations on Demski's *Ex Post* Accounting System', and J. S. Demski, 'A Reply', *Accounting Review*, XLIII 4 (October 1968) 668–74.

J. S. Demski, 'An Accounting System Structured on a Linear Programming Model', *Accounting Review*, XLII 4 (October 1967) 701–12.

V. Jaaskelainen, *Linear Programming and Budgeting* (Lund, Sweden: Studentlitteratur, 1975) 119–31.

G. L. Salamon 'Analysis of an Accounting System Structured on a Linear Programming Model', in Livingstone (ed.), *Management Planning*, 267–78.

7 Input–Output Analysis and Linear Programming

A. W. Corcoran and W. E. Leininger, 'In-Process Inventories and Multiproduct Production Systems', *Accounting Review*, XLVIII 2 (April 1973) 373–6.

G. A. Feltham, 'Some Quantitative Approaches to Planning for Multiproduct Production Systems', *Accounting Review*, XLV 1 (January 1970) 11–26.

Y. Ijiri, 'An Application of Input–Output Analysis to Some Problems in Cost Accounting', *Management Accounting (NAA)* (April 1968) 49–61.

Leininger, *Quantitative Methods*, 187–220.

8 Use of Information Theory to Isolate Substantial Variances

B. Lev, 'An Information Theory Analysis of Budget Variances', *Accounting Review*, XLIV 4 (October 1969) 704–10.

B. Lev, 'Testing a Prediction Method for Multivariate Budgets', *Journal of Accounting Research*, VII (1969), supplement entitled *Empirical Research in Accounting: Selected Studies*, 182–97.

H. Theil, 'How to Worry About Increased Expenditures', *Accounting Review*, XLIV 1 (January 1969) 27–37.

9 The Single-period Cost Variance Investigation Decision

R. Capettini and D. Collins, 'The Investigation of Deviations from Standard Costs in the Presence of Unequal State Variances', *Journal of Business Finance and Accounting*, V 4 (Winter 1978) 335–51.

T. R. Dyckman, 'The Investigation of Cost Variances', *Journal of Accounting Research*, VII 2 (Autumn 1969) 215–44.

10 The Multi-period Cost Variance Investigation Decision

D. A. Dittman and P. Prakash, 'Cost Variance Investigation: Markovian Control of Markov Processes', *Journal of Accounting Research*, XVI 1 (Spring 1978) 14–25.

D. A. Dittman and P. Prakash, 'Cost Variance Investigation: Markovian Control Versus Optimal Control', *Accounting Review*, LIV 2 (April 1979) 358–73.

R. S. Kaplan, 'Optimal Investigation Strategies with Imperfect Information', *Journal of Accounting Research*, VII 1 (Spring 1969) 32–43.

350   References

11, 12 and 13   Stochastic Cost–Volume–Profit Analysis

The papers relating to this group of topics have such close interrelationships that a separate classification by individual topic would be unhelpful. They are:

J. P. Dickinson, 'Cost–Volume–Profit Analysis Under Uncertainty', *Journal of Accounting Research*, XII 1 (Spring 1974) 182–7.
Donna A. Driscoll, W. T. Lin and P. R. Watkins, 'Cost–Volume–Profit Analysis Under Uncertainty: A Synthesis and Framework for Evaluation', *Journal of Accounting Literature*, III (Spring 1984) 85–115.
B. E. Ismail and J. G. Louderback, 'Optimizing and Satisficing in Stochastic Cost–Volume–Profit Analysis', *Decision Sciences*, X 2 (April 1979) 205–17.
J. E. Jarrett, 'An Approach to Cost–Volume–Profit Analysis Under Uncertainty', *Decision Sciences*, IV 3 (July 1973) 405–20.
G. L. Johnson and S. S. Simik, 'Multiproduct C–V–P Analysis Under Uncertainty', *Journal of Accounting Research*, IX 2 (Autumn 1971) 278–86.
H. S. Lau, 'Some Extensions of Ismail–Louderback's Stochastic CVP Model Under Optimizing and Satisficing Criteria', *Decision Sciences*, XI 3 (July 1980) 557–61.
R. E. Norland, 'Refinements in the Ismail–Louderback Stochastic CVP Model', *Decision Sciences*, XI 3 (July 1980) 562–72.

14   Short-term Investment of Cash Balances

J. C. T. Mao, *Corporate Financial Decisions* (Palo Alto, California: Pavan Publishers, 1976) 209–31.
J. C. T. Mao and C. E. Sarndal, 'Cash Management: Theory and Practice', *Journal of Business Finance and Accounting*, V 3 (Autumn 1978) 329–38.
A. Punter, 'Optimal Cash Management Under Conditions of Uncertainty', *Journal of Business Finance and Accounting*, IX 3 (Autumn 1982) 329–40.

15 Payments Netting in Multinational Cash Management

A. C. Shapiro, 'Payments Netting in International Cash Management', *Journal of International Business Studies*, IX 2 (Fall 1978) 51–8.
A. C. Shapiro, *Multinational Financial Management* (Boston, Massachusetts: Allyn and Bacon, 1982) 235–245.
D. Wood and J. Byrne, *International Business Finance* (London: Macmillan, 1981) 112–30.

16 The Learning Curve and Financial Planning

D. W. Harvey, 'Financial Planning Information for Production Start-ups', *Accounting Review*, LI 4 (October 1976) 838–45.
E. V. McIntyre, 'Cost–Volume–Profit Analysis Adjusted for Learning', *Management Science*, XXIV 2 (October 1977) 149–60.
L. E. Yelle, 'The Learning Curve: Historical Review and Comprehensive Survey', *Decision Sciences*, X 2 (April 1979) 302–28.

17 Joint Product Decisions

L. R. Amey, 'Joint Product Decisions: The Fixed Proportions Case', *Journal of Business Finance and Accounting*, XI 3 (Autumn 1984) 295–300.
D. L. Jensen, 'The Role of Cost in Pricing Joint Products: A Case of Production in Fixed Proportions', *Accounting Review*, XLIX 3 (July 1974) 465–76.
R. S. Kaplan, *Advanced Management Accounting* (Englewood Cliffs, New Jersey: Prentice-Hall, 1982) 395–409.
R. L. Weil, 'Allocating Joint Costs', *American Economic Review*, LVIII 5 Part 1 (December 1968) 1342–5.

Guides to Further Study 3

To locate expositions of other techniques related to those described in this book, reference may be made to the following surveys covering the quantitative aspects of management accounting. Taken together, these surveys provide a broad critique of this area of study. Where a comment on the content of a survey has been provided by a discussant, the discussant's contribution is not separately referenced, but the page numbers given for the survey are inclusive of those occupied by his contribution.

K. N. Bhaskar, 'Quantitative Aspects of Management Accounting', in M. Bromwich and A. G. Hopwood (eds), *Essays in British Accounting Research* (London: Pitman, 1981) ch. 10, 229–78.

Committee on Concepts and Standards–Management Planning and Control, *Managerial Accounting Literature Abstracts* (Sarasota, Florida: American Accounting Association, 1976).

J. S. Demski and D. M. Kreps, 'Models in Managerial Accounting', *Journal of Accounting Research*, XX (1982) supplement entitled *Studies on Current Research Methodologies in Accounting: A Critical Evaluation*, 117–60.

E. Dörner and J. Kloock, 'A survey of Management Accounting Research from a German View', in A. G. Hopwood and H. Schreuder (eds), *European Contributions to Accounting Research: The Achievements of the Last Decade* (Amsterdam: Free University Press, 1984) ch. 5, 83–102.

H. Hart, 'A Review of Some Recent Major Developments in the Management Accounting Field', *Accounting and Business Research*, XI 42 (Spring 1981) 99–115.

R. E. Jensen, 'Some Thoughts on, and a Partial Bibliography of, Quantitative Models – Applications in Selected Managerial Accounting Topics', *The Accounting Journal*, (Winter 1977–8) 244–76.

R. S. Kaplan, 'Application of Quantitative Models in Managerial Accounting: A State of the Art Survey', *The Accounting Journal*, (Winter 1977–8) 218–42.

R. S. Kaplan, 'The Evolution of Management Accounting', *Accounting Review*, LIX 3 (July 1984) 390–418.

C. F. Klemstine and M. W. Maher, *Management Accounting Research: 1926–1983* (Sarasota, Florida: Management Accounting Section, American Accounting Association, 1984).

J. Kriens, J. T. van Lieshout, J. Roemen and P. Verheyen, 'Management Accounting and Operational Research', *European Journal of Operational Research* XIII 4 (August 1982) 339–52.

R. W. Scapens, 'Management Accounting – A Survey Paper', in R. W. Scapens, D. T. Otley and R. J. Lister (eds), *Management Accounting, Organizational Theory and Capital Budgeting: Three Surveys* (London: Macmillan/ESRC, 1984) 15–95.

Suppliers of Software Packages

Package	Supplier
OPTIMIZER	Supersoft 51/53 The Pantiles Tunbridge Wells Kent TN2 5TE England
MINITAB	Cle. Com Ltd Kings Court 92 High Street Kings Heath Birmingham B14 7JZ England
TK!SOLVER 86	Digital Equipment Co. Ltd Jays Close Basingstoke RG21 4BS England

Index